W9-CEI-750

VOYAGES
TO THE
SOUTH SEAS

In Search of Terres Australes

DANIELLE CLODE

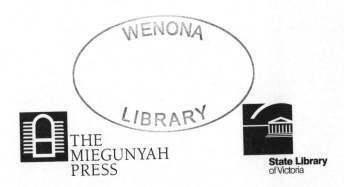

THE
MIEGUNYAH
PRESS

State Library
of Victoria

Initial research for this book was undertaken as a
State Library of Victoria Creative Fellowship.

THE MIEGUNYAH PRESS
An imprint of Melbourne University Publishing Limited
187 Grattan Street, Carlton, Victoria 3053, Australia
mup-info@unimelb.edu.au
www.mup.com.au

First published 2007
This edition published 2008
Text © Danielle Clode 2007
Design and typography © Melbourne University Publishing Ltd 2007

Edited by Clare Coney
Cover designed by Pfisterer + Freeman
Text design by Ellie Exarchos
Typeset in Stempel Garamond by TypeSkill
Printed in China by Imago

National Library of Australia Cataloguing-in-Publication entry:

Clode, Danielle.
Voyages to the South Seas.

Bibliography.

ISBN 978 0 522 85542 5.
ISBN 0 522 85542 3.

1. Australia - Discovery and exploration - French.
I. Title.

919.4042

THE MIEGUNYAH PRESS

The general series of the
Miegunyah Volumes
was made possible by the
Miegunyah Fund
established by bequests
under the wills of
Sir Russell and Lady Grimwade.

'Miegunyah' was the home of
Mab and Russell Grimwade
from 1911 to 1955.

CONTENTS

List of Illustrations

Acknowledgements

This project began as a Creative Fellowship generously supported by the State Library of Victoria. Without the impetus of the Fellowship program and access to Library's excellent collections on the French expeditions to Australia, this project would never have materialised. I would particularly like to thank Shane Carmody and Dianne Reilly at the State Library for their support and encouragement. I would also like to acknowledge the assistance of my fellow fellows, Carolyn Rasmussen and Paul Fox, for their insightful observations on research, natural history and many other topics besides.

I have been most fortunate to have shared this project with my good friend Dr Carol Harrison, University of South Carolina. It has taken us many years to devise a project that incorporates both French history and zoology, but I think the outcome has been worth the wait. It has been a joy to have someone to share the minutiae and obsessive fascination of research, and I have gained immeasurably from Carol's historical and linguistic expertise.

As always, my colleagues at the Department of Zoology, University of Melbourne, have been supportive of my strange discursions into other fields. I would particularly like to thank David Young for his expertise on the history of evolutionary theory. I would also like to thank Jenny Lee from the Department of English, University of Melbourne, for both the opportunity to teach writing in the Publishing and Communications course and for replacing me so that I could complete this book.

A project of this nature is always dependent upon the support of numerous libraries and their staff. Des Cowley and Peter Mappin at the State Library of Victoria provided invaluable assistance in accessing expedition accounts and reproducing images. The Baillieu Library, University of Melbourne, and the interlibrary loans department have made access to interstate and overseas material so easy. Thank you also to the staff at the National Library of Australia for generously providing copies of manuscripts and for taking the time to read sections over the phone from French journals that could not be loaned. It is a great privilege to have so many primary materials brought to my door, particularly when I could not have afforded to travel to see them myself.

For the same reason, I am indebted to all those who have worked so hard to bring primary sources to a broader audience, particularly through the online provision of texts and manuscripts by Lamarck, Cuvier, Buffon, Darwin and others. On the same issue of accessibility, I would like to thank all those, past and present, who have taken the time and care to translate French works into English and to publish previously unpublished manuscripts, such as those by Baudin and Dumont d'Urville. A work like this could never have been even considered without a large body of previous research on people, places and events and I am indebted to the generations of scholars and writers who have studied and published on French scientists and explorers.

For numerous discussions, advice and help, I would also like to thank Sandra Gulland, Paul Corcoran, Klaus Toft, Jean Fornasiero and John West-Sooby. Everyone has been most generous with their time and offers of assistance. Identification of the modern names of species was greatly assisted by Gary Poore, Patsy McLaughlin, Steven Haddock, Phil Pugh, Martin Gomon, Ken Walker and Catriona McPhee.

As always, I would like to thank Jenny Darling and Donica Bettanin for their encouragement. It has been a pure delight to work with Tracy O'Shaughnessy and Cinzia Cavallaro at Melbourne University Publishing. Most importantly, I must thank my family—Mike, Lauren and Rachel—for their understanding and support during this project, even when it got pretty boring. My mother is responsible for the French ancestry which sparked my interest in this subject, while my father's life-long Anglophobia fuelled my pursuit of French explorers. This book may not be as anti–Captain Cook as you would have liked, Dad, but I hope you'll agree that in this case the facts don't get in the way of a good story.

Prologue

I grew up in a small South Australian town perched on the end of Eyre Peninsula, overlooking Spencer Gulf on one side and buffeted by the Southern Ocean sweeping in across the Great Australian Bight on the other. Port Lincoln boasts a harbour three and a half times the size of Sydney Harbour and the second largest wheat silos in the Southern Hemisphere. Across the bay, on top of Stamford Hill, is a white cairn dedicated to the eight men who lost their lives here while exploring the area under the command of Port Lincoln's official discoverer, Matthew Flinders in the *Investigator*.

But Port Lincoln has a shadow-history. In this alternative world of what-might-have-been, it is the port of Champagny (named after Napoléon's Minister of the Interior) that looks east across the twin gulfs of Bonaparte and Joséphine. The Sir Joseph Banks group of islands, named after England's foremost scientific authority on Australia, becomes Îles de Léoben. The Investigator Strait becomes Détroit de Lacépède, after France's foremost authority on fish and reptiles. French explorers spent several days in

Champagny, charting and exploring the area. The official account of the Baudin expedition concluded that the port is 'one of the finest and safest harbours of all New Holland' with 'so many superior advantages' that 'we may without hesitation assert, that of all the points of this land, this is the most proper for the establishment of a European colony'.

Despite the tantalising prospect of a French Australia, neither Baudin's expedition nor any of the other French explorations of Australia had any serious intentions to colonise New Holland. They were driven not so much by a desire to possess territory or claim commercial gain, but by a passion for discovery and knowledge. Their claim on Australia was an intellectual claim of knowing this land, her people, her plants and her animals far better than the British who claimed to own them. The French expeditions were, above all else, expeditions of scientific discovery.

Unknowing the present

I'm told there are two ways of studying the history of science. The external perspective is the view of the historian seeking to understand scientists within their social and political milieux. The internal perspective is that of scientists looking at the history of their own discipline from within. The external perspective, with its focus on broader social and political factors, sometimes neglects the internal—the intellectual fervour and the personal motivations. The internal perspective, on the other hand, often focuses entirely on the ideas. Scientists naturally write intellectual histories because that is their dominant mode of communication with each other. Scientific articles are intellectual maps, locating each discovery—each claim to knowledge—within a landscape of prior research liberally sprinkled with signposts acknowledging the contributions of others.

When I first tried to write about the French exploration of Australia, as a scientist I particularly wanted to write from the inside, from the point of view of the scientists who came and the people who sent them here. I wanted to explain the driving force behind the desire for knowledge and for discovery and how that alone was enough to justify a century of expensive and costly expeditions, without recourse to failed colonial ambitions or unsuccessful searches for commercial exploitation. But a retrospective account of eighteenth-century science is fraught with difficulties. In these historical activities I seemed to be constantly searching for some kind of relevance for modern science. The pitfall of writing an 'extrapolation of the present towards the past', where the science of the past becomes the past of today's science, seemed unavoidable. But in the end, I realised that what matters is not how important the discoveries of these French explorers and naturalists are for modern science or modern Australians, but how important they were for the people doing them at the time, for their own country and within their own culture.

There seemed to be no alternative but to take a deep breath and try to step back into the past, into a totally different world and different culture. For this reason, I decided to write this book from a contemporary viewpoint, from the perspective of the people at the time. However, this is not a work of historical fiction. Although I can't be certain that people thought the things I say they thought when and where I've said they thought them, I can be fairly certain they did think those things, and they were in the places I've said they were. There is very little difference between what I have written and what might be written in an academic book—the primary difference is that I've used an active voice instead of a passive one. Other than that, there is about the same level of speculation and, I hope, the same level of academic rigour.

In an effort to present these stories from the perspectives of the participants, I have written each chapter from the point of view of a different narrator. In many cases these narrators have written accounts of their voyages themselves (Labillardière, d'Entrecasteaux, Péron, Baudin, Rose de Freycinet and Dumont d'Urville) or have left an extensive archive of their own writing on various topics (Banks, Geoffroy Saint-Hilaire and Cuvier). Some accounts—such as those of Labillardière and d'Entrecasteaux—are measured and carefully edited for public consumption, revealing little of the men behind the words. Other narrators are even more hidden, leaving little written material of their own, just a collection of attributed sayings (as in the cases of Louis XVI and Joséphine), but to compensate they attracted a wealth of contemporary descriptions of their lives and actions. In other accounts—such as Baudin's long-unpublished journal—the writing provides a vivid, uncompromising evocation of the man himself. Many accounts contradict one other, most notably in the case of Baudin and Péron, whose versions of the same events are often diametrically opposed or are supplemented by divergent views from other observers and participants at the time. In all cases, my efforts have been supported by the extensive, at times overwhelming, body of literature written about both the people, places and times described.

In pursuing this somewhat unusual approach, I've taken great comfort from Greg Dening's advice on historical research:

> The webs of significance of any event, place or person are fine-lined and faint. It takes a lot of looking to see them. And the answers to any question that we have of them are never obvious, because the questions we ask of them are not the questions the people of the past were asking of themselves . . . The most unhistorical thing we can do is to imagine that the past is us in funny clothes. Our imagination has to allow us to experience what we share with the past and see difference at the same time . . . When we empower the past by returning it to itself, we empower our imagination to see ourselves. Our certainties are our greatest enemy when we approach the past. Hindsight is always blinding. We know from our living experience that our present moment—this moment—has all the possibilities of the future still in it. None of us prescribes the reality we live in. None of us controls the consequences of our actions. None of us can predict with

absolute certainty anybody else's reaction to the simplest gesture, the clearest sign, the most definite word. But we have to cope with these ambivalences, interpreting these never-ending possibilities. Hindsight, on the other hand, reduces all possibilities in the past to one. Hindsight leaches out not all our uncertainties, but all the past's uncertainties. Hindsight closes down our imagination. In hindsight we do not see the past as it actually was, only as it would have been if all of its uncertainties were taken away. Hindsight freezes the frame of every picture of the past. Hindsight removes all the processes of living. Makes the past our puppet.

The process of 'unknowing' required for this kind of history is particularly difficult for the scientist trained in the cumulative acquisition of knowledge. It is particularly difficult for the biologist whose path into the past is blocked by the mountainous legacy of Darwin and whose science is dominated by the paradigm overarching all modern biological science, that of evolution by natural selection. All roads lead to Darwin—or do they?

There is a good reason why Theodore Dobzhansky proclaimed that 'nothing in biology makes sense without evolution'. Natural selection pervades every thought I have in my science, my whole world view. To imagine a world without natural selection, without even evolution, is to imagine a world without foundation, without a past, a world in which life is one great amorphous substance; undistinguished, undivided, unnamed and unclassified.

Imagining the Past

We must step back to a time before Buffon had noted the consistent geographical differences between species on different continents, before Jussieu and Linnaeus had developed systems of classification and nomenclature, before Lamarck had developed his evolutionary theory and before Cuvier had established the 'fact' of extinction. We have to go back to a time where there was no established concept of species, no clear hierarchy of lineages, no points of connection and difference between families, no variation, no continuity. A sheep was just a sheep and a barnacle goose was just a barnacle goose—except when it was being a tree. This is a time when the world stretched barely past Europe and back in time no further than human history, when great expanses of the world were unknown, when large stretches of ocean were unmapped, when whole pasts were unexplored, when whole continents remained 'undiscovered'. It is in the context of this past that the men and women I'm writing about lived and it is with this heritage that some of them began to practise what we call science and apply themselves systematically and rigorously to unlocking the secrets of the natural world.

We begin at a critical turning point for both France's political history and her history of exploration. By 1793, France had not only lost her king, but also the first of her government-sponsored expedition leaders, Lapérouse. The next fifty years would see a tumultuous period of political change and upheaval, through the revolutionary Terror to Napoléon's imperial ambitions, to the Bourbon Restoration of Louis XVIII and Charles X and finally to the constitutional monarchy of the July Revolution and Louis-Philippe. Yet despite this political turmoil, despite wars and financial chaos, France remained committed to sending expensive, well-equipped professional scientific expeditions to the Pacific and to Australia—d'Entrecasteaux, Baudin, de Freycinet, Duperrey, Hyacinthe de Bougainville and finally the voyages of Dumont d'Urville.

Their tasks were neither political nor mercantile (despite requests to take these considerations into account in the course of their voyages). It was primarily because of France's commitment to science and through the efforts of her scientists that these expeditions were undertaken. Without understanding the role these factors played in the expeditions, the purpose and ideals of the voyages remain obscure in the politically expedient phrasing of the official instructions. These were voyages of discovery—to find what was new (the lands of the southern and Pacific regions and all that they contained) and to find what was lost (Lapérouse). D'Entrecasteaux was sent to rescue Lapérouse, Baudin to map the south coast of Australia. De Freycinet was driven by an ambition to complete what he had been unable to complete on the Baudin expedition, while Hyacinthe de Bougainville, despite heading an expedition of political expediency, retained his personal goal of following in his famous father's first French footsteps across the Pacific. Both Duperrey and Dumont d'Urville were inspired to reclaim those glory days and, for Dumont d'Urville, to doggedly exceed and surpass them.

During these forty-seven years, 1793–1840, Australia and the Pacific remained symbolic of the great unknown for the French, a region where reputations could be wrought and dreams fulfilled. In the French imagination the lost expedition of Lapérouse was a tragedy of lost opportunities, a heroic epic and a romantic fantasy. For years, far-fetched stories of Lapérouse's imagined fate filled theatres, music halls and books. In these fictions we can see the power of the Pacific fantasy over ordinary French men and women. And still today, it is Lapérouse whose name resonates, even for those who've never heard of French exploration in Australia.

The final conclusive discovery, in 1828, of Lapérouse's fate closed a chapter in French exploration in the Pacific region. But there remained one last great challenge to meet, the challenge set by the naturalist Buffon a century earlier, a challenge that even the legendary Cook had left unfulfilled—the discovery of the Antarctic continent. With claims to discovery hotly contested by the Americans and the British, it was the French who first indisputably discovered land beyond the southern ice and snow and fog. With the incontestable proof of a handful of rocks in 1840, Dumont d'Urville completed the task assigned to so many of his predecessors, and claimed discovery of the last great southern continent, Antarctica.

For all these men and women who searched for and explored Australia, whether in reality or—as in the case of Louis XVI, Joséphine Bonaparte and the scientists at the Muséum d'Histoire Naturelle—in imagination, Australia was a blank canvas upon which to project their own ambitions. These expeditions travelled in search of elusive, indefinable goals, as much a part of national glory and pride as of personal ambition and desire. The defining motif of all the narrators of this book is their quest. They are all searching for something that they hope this unknown land can provide. For the British, Australia soon became Port Jackson, but for the French it remained a vast unexplored continent—still a part of the great unknown.

ENCOUNTERING THE 'OTHER'

My own interest in the French in Australia was enhanced by the fact that my maternal great-grandfather, Frank Jaunay, emigrated from France (after selling his champagne mark to his brother-in-law, Paul Krug) and brought his young family to the burgeoning wine regions of southern Australia to ply his trade in the *méthode champenoise*. Certainly my interest in writing about the motivations of the scientists who came to Australia was prompted by my training as a biologist. There are significant differences (as well as great similarities) between the scientific and humanities disciplines and it seemed to me that the history of science written only by humanities scholars would always be missing some essential element of the 'internal'—what makes someone want to be a scientist, what drives them and motivates them.

Of course, the scientists of the early nineteenth century faced considerably different challenges from those facing scientists today. In seeking to understand something of their experiences, I have been assisted by some facets of my past. At the age of twelve, I left Port Lincoln to sail around the Australian coast with my parents on a gaff-rigged yawl, so much of my own exploration of my country has been from the sea. I do not know what it is like to live on a small smelly ship crammed with men, eating rotten food and drinking putrid water with the ever-present threat of death from disease or starvation, but I do know what it is like to be sick as a dog in a Bass Strait gale, what it is like to find refuge in a calm, safe, untouched harbour, and to visit places inaccessible by land and by everyday travel. I've never been shipwrecked or faced abandonment, but I do know what it is like to be obsessed with the weather, to lie awake listening to the pull of the anchor, knowing that attending to such things can make the difference between survival and disaster. I know the adrenalin rush of urgent action, of seemingly impossible physical feats performed without a thought in the heat of the moment. I remember the contrasts of sailing's unceasing demands and long stretches of tedious inactivity. I don't have any experience of naval discipline but I do understand the inherent discipline required for maritime life and the absolute necessity of a single line of command. I know how your feet toughen against the cutting ropes of the ratlines, how your muscles condition to the rhythmic hauling of halyards. Thanks to my father's interest in traditional boat-building and an early acquaintance with one of the last sailing-ship builders, Axel Stenross, I have a passing familiarity with sewing sails from cotton duck, the smell of Stockholm tar in the rigging, building timber spars, dead-eyes and lanyards and many other features of a craft and a life long past.

My first voyage overseas was also by boat, to the small coastal villages of Papua New Guinea, where we traded fresh fruit and vegetables for fish-hooks with villagers on outriggers, just as countless generations of sailors must have done before. Surprisingly often our charts were based on those of Bougainville—many areas had not been charted since. It was in Papua New Guinea that I first discovered what it is to be the 'other'—an object of curiosity, attraction and dislike. It was here that I tripped over the absence of my own familiar societal rules of property, possession and privacy. In Australia's closest neighbour I felt more alien than I have ever done anywhere else in the world. Time and again, in the accounts of French voyages, I've been struck by that same sense of miscomprehension, on both sides of the cultural encounter. The relief felt by the French at encountering even their traditional enemies, the English, on the other side of the globe is comical, but understandable.

Being neither anthropologist nor historian, I can't hope to do justice to the cultural encounter between the French and indigenous people. This book is based on nineteenth-century French descriptions of that encounter, from the point of view of scientists for whom the very study of humans, the science of anthropology, had just been invented. The description is neither politically correct, nor culturally sensitive. This is how these men and women saw the world and how they saw these 'others'. I will leave it to anthropologists to describe how the indigenous people saw these intruders themselves.

This book is a story about the exploration of Australia, about the French in the Pacific, about discovery and knowledge and Enlightenment ideals. It is about the birth of a science and the role of Australian fauna and flora in the development of that science. It is about men and women whose passion and thirst for knowledge and discovery drove them to achieve remarkable things. Australia may never have been at much risk of being a French colony, but for many, many years she was the intellectual property not of the Britain that best exploited her, but of France, who understood her.

Looking for Lapérouse:

d'Entrecasteaux

(1791–1794)

D'Entrecasteaux's ship the Espérance
in a storm off the Western
Australian coast.

Louis XVI

Île de la Cité, Paris

21 January 1793

Louis XVI was born on 23 August 1754, grandson of Louis XV. He married Marie-Antoinette, an archduchess of Austria, at sixteen and he was crowned at twenty. He was a robust, healthy young man, popular with the people at first but prone to depression and indecision. Serious and sensitive, he lacked social skills. He disapproved of his grandfather's excesses but remained devoted to his wife, despite her frivolities. He was fascinated by geography and watch-making but seemed ill-suited to statesmanship. He found in Lapérouse's voyage a way of escaping the complexities of royal life while still achieving glory for France, and himself. Despite the efforts of his advisors, Louis was unable to implement taxes on nobles to relieve France's financial woes. In 1789 the Estates-General met for the first time since 1614. The national assembly was formed, primarily from the third estate of commoners or merchants. In 1792, Louis was arrested for treason and on 20 January 1793 he was sentenced to death and executed the following day. Marie-Antoinette was executed in October of the same year. Their son, the Dauphin, died in prison.

He was far more calm and composed than a man on his way to certain death had any right to be. The carriage rumbled relentlessly through the Paris streets, the hooves of the surrounding horses and distant drumbeats drowning out any sounds from the gathering crowds. The king looked up momentarily from his book of prayers, his face impassive as he gazed distantly through his guards. The psalms offered some comfort to a man who had just last evening farewelled his tearful wife and children; fearful for their future though certain of his own. Louis's tired eyes betrayed a flicker of pain before the regal mask slipped back into place. He steered his thoughts firmly away from his family's distress.

'What news of Lapérouse?' he asked the English priest accompanying him.

The gendarmes shifted uncomfortably in their seats. They were not supposed to allow the king—the condemned—to speak. An awkward cough broke their silence.

Even in these turbulent times, the name Lapérouse was synonymous with valour. All of France bathed in his success against pirates off the Malabar coast, against the English in the American Revolution and in the tactical brilliance of his engagements in Canada. Yet if Lapérouse was venerated for his military and navigational skills, he was loved for his humanity. 'An enemy conquered should have nothing more to fear from a civilised foe; he then becomes a friend.' The captain led a charmed and romantic life, extricating himself effortlessly from the most difficult situations. For the last five years all of France had waited with bated breath for word of the great sea captain, who had not been sighted since sailing out of the fledgling English settlement at Botany Bay in January 1788. Surely news must soon come from d'Entrecasteaux of the fate of Lapérouse in the South Sea?

'No news, your highness,' murmured the priest, glancing anxiously at the guards.

Louis XVI—king of France and fifth monarch in the Bourbon lineage, which had ruled France for nearly two centuries—stared out of the window at the lightening sky, still grey and damp with the night's cool air. His fair hair was streaked white and his once plump features (more like a farm boy than a king, his brothers had teased) were ashen and drawn. How he envied Lapérouse—whatever his fate—far away in the Pacific. He imagined a distant South Sea island, a tiny outpost of France on a green jewel in the crystal sea. Were the commander and his men, as the National Assembly had feared, 'confined to some beach, their eyes wandering over the far distances of the sea, to discover there the lucky sail which might return them to France, to their families, to their friends'?

The king had held such great expectations for Lapérouse. This expedition was to be his great legacy to the nation, his lasting monument, just as Charles de Brosses had forecast in his history of navigation to *terres Australe* published fifty years earlier.

Amongst all the Sovereigns of these latter ages, is there one whose name can be put on a level with that of Columbus? Or where is the Potentate that can assure himself that his name will live as long as Amerigo Vespucci? ... Geographical researches are the best and surest foundation for any Prince to build a lasting fame upon, and that most celebrated potentate, of modern times, will be he who shall give his name to the great Southern Continent.

Louis agreed that 'the discovery of *Terres australes* is perhaps the most noble and the most useful enterprise that any sovereign can aggrandize his name by'—but his grandfather had not. Not even Gonneville's long-lost account of discovering the great southern land in 1504 (a Frenchman before the Portuguese!) had excited him. Even the influential naturalist Georges Buffon could not sway the old king. Aside from the distractions of court, wars in Poland and Austria were more than enough to occupy Louis XV. He had little interest in following France's earlier piratical activities in the Pacific with more legitimate endeavours. 'Glory is generally the first passion of kings, but, unfortunately they commonly pursue this favourite object in war; that is, in the mutual misfortune of their neighbours and subjects.' De Brosses knew his superiors only too well.

It had been the king's mistress, Madame de Pompadour, who eventually took up the challenge. Charmed by the enthusiastic Louis-Antoine de Bougainville, she had persuaded the king to support the soldier's plan for a scientific journey of discovery around the world. It was, Louis recalled morosely, one of her more constructive indulgences.

When Bougainville returned in 1769 he brought with him the elegant, self-possessed Tahitian, Ahu-toru, who seemed to many the very epitome of Rousseau's 'noble savage'. The Tahitian became a popular guest at Versailles, being seen in all the fashionable salons, at the opera and often walking the streets of Paris. Despite his own preoccupation with his impending wedding, Louis recalled the buzz of excitement that surrounded Bougainville's return. The plant and animal collections had delighted Buffon, the director of the Jardin du Roi. There had been numerous species new to science and horticulture—spectacular South American bougainvilleas, huge nodding hydrangeas and luscious over-sized strawberries, not to mention the strangely disturbing coco-de-mer, which had excited so many men of science.

Bougainville's successful return sparked as many questions as it answered. The lure of a great southern continent, not found by Bougainville, remained powerful in the French imagination. Where was the sophisticated—and rich—society Gonneville had described? In New Holland, or perhaps New Zealand, or even further afield, on an as yet unknown Antarctic continent? And if such a continent existed (as almost all were sure it did), was it confined to the icy latitudes of the freezing southern oceans, or did it extend up into warmer climes amenable to exploitation by man?

A flurry of mostly privately funded expeditions headed off from France to the Pacific. Surville's Pacific voyage redis-covered New Zealand, not seen by European eyes since Tasman 130 years earlier. Marion du Fresne sailed through the frigid southern oceans, past tiny specks of land clad in birds, seals and sea-mist to reach Van Diemen's Land. His crew were the first Europeans to befriend the shy, primitive people there, through the novel approach of sending two officers ashore naked.

But the French were not the only men inspired by Brosses' books. Just two years after Bougainville's departure, the English hastily launched their own Pacific expedition, headed by a most unlikely commander who turned out to be a *navigateur par excellence*. A humble man (and certainly no *littérateur*), James Cook had the determination to carry through his instructions and the skill to avoid disaster, returning with painstakingly detailed charts and records of his travels.

Like Bougainville, Cook had come within sight of New Holland's east coast. Like Bougainville, he decided to head north to the familiar waters of south-east Asia. But whereas Bougainville had been kept offshore by the terrible teeth of the Great Barrier Reef, Cook had started from further south, below the reef, and had fortuitously unlocked the hidden treasures of an eastern coastline pocketed with sheltered harbours, tree-clad mountains and fresh flowing rivers. In his youth Louis had devoured Cook's published *Voyages*, tracing every description, every event on the maps, identifying what had been left undiscovered—what remained for France.

Finally spurred into action by Cook's great celebrity, his grandfather Louis XV mounted his own exploratory expedition—this time paid for by the Court. The well-bred and well-connected Kerguelen, with impressive naval credentials, had promptly delighted them all on his return in the *Fortune* with his promising accounts of the great Antarctic continent he had discovered—a southern France with soil and climate promising grain, crops and timbers, perfectly suited for settlement. It was precisely what they had all wanted to hear, despite the loss of one of Kerguelen's ships, the *Gros Ventre*, abandoned in the Southern Ocean to an unknown fate. Only Buffon seemed unimpressed, demanding details, charts, specimens, artefacts. Kerguelen was dispatched on a second expedition—this time circumnavigating these high latitudes, using his supposedly rich Antarctic continent as the base for refuelling and restocking.

Rather unenthusiastically Kerguelen departed—and promptly returned to France having done little more than skirt once more the tip of his so-called continent, failing again to land on its shores. Tempers flared, accusations flew from senior officers. It had been Louis's misfortune, on ascending to the throne, to witness the sordid litany of deceit, corruption and misconduct that emerged from Kerguelen's trial. Perhaps most damning of all was the return of the *Gros Ventre*, the ship Kerguelen had abandoned.

Following the mysterious disappearance of his commander, the *Gros Ventre*'s captain, Saint-Allouarn, had simply followed his instructions. He landed, claimed possession of the fog-bound land, noting that the intense cold and bad weather made it unsuitable for settlement. He then sailed along the coast, observing it to disappear still further into the freezing south. Sailing on to the west coast of New Holland, Saint-Allouarn established beyond doubt the absence of any substantial land mass north of the 50th parallel. The mythical Antarctic continent, Terre Australe, if it existed at all, existed in the snow and ice of the high latitudes further south.

Of New Holland itself, Saint-Allouarn reported a dry, burnt landmass, with bays of treacherous shallow shoals, which he duly charted and claimed on behalf of his king, before setting sail for home. His death in Timor and Kerguelen's theatrics overshadowed these achievements and little interest was taken in the barren and unproductive tract of wasteland claimed for France on the opposite side of the globe. It was clear now that whatever land Gonneville had visited, it was not New Holland. Nor did it seem likely that the fabled great southern continent, mirroring the Eurasian land mass and stretching across the Pacific down to the South Pole itself, existed at all. Cook had proven once and for all that New Zealand was not the northern coast of a mythical Terre Australe. Saint-Allouarn had ruled out the existence of a second great land mass north of the 50th parallel. If a great continent did exist near the South Pole it was shrouded in ice and fog, isolated by the furious storms of the Southern Ocean. But despite this disappointment, there remained much to discover, both in New Holland and elsewhere in the Pacific.

The shadow of a smile lightened Louis's pinched face as he recalled happier times planning for his great South Sea voyage of discovery. His passion for geography was shared by his Minister of Marine, Comte de Fleurieu, a man with unparalleled knowledge of all matters maritime. As France's foremost authority on the Pacific region, Fleurieu had published several books and his technical understanding of marine charts was exceptional. Louis could still recall with fond admiration the exquisitely intricate workings of the marine chronometer Fleurieu had created. How he longed to lose track of time again inside its predictable mechanics . . .

In Lapérouse and Fleurieu, Louis had found kindred spirits and, with the aid of the latest charts of the region, the three men shared their extensive knowledge and passionate enthusiasms, in the quest for discovery. The resulting one hundred or so pages of instructions for Lapérouse were admittedly exhaustive. In their outline the king included every voyage, every exploration he had ever wanted. No corner of the region was to go unvisited, no island left uncharted. This expedition would be the defining monument to his reign, his triumph and glory. All other failings, all other weaknesses, would be swept aside if he could be remembered for this one great achievement. Just this once, the royal robes of kingship fitted comfortably, his regal responsibilities in rare exquisite coincidence with his own passion.

His majesty had commanded Lapérouse to sail with two ships, the *Boussole* and the *Astrolabe*, from Brest in August 1785, as soon as preparations were complete. The expedition was to sail south past Africa to South Georgia before rounding the tip of South America. Easter Island and a comprehensive tour through the Pacific Islands were to be followed by a detailed circumnavigation of New Holland, from New

Guinea around the west and south coasts to Van Diemen's Land (thus canvassing that greater part of the continent left unexplored by Cook). From New Zealand (in about March 1787), Lapérouse was to cross back through the Pacific to the north-west American coast, charting all that area through Alaska, Russia down to China and Japan before arriving back in the south-east Asian spice islands and heading back across the Indian Ocean to France's base in that quarter of the globe, the Île de France, formerly the Dutch colony of Mauritius. From here the expedition could return around Africa, perhaps endeavouring on the way to ascertain the precise situations of the islands of Gough, Alvarez, Tristan d'Acunha, Saxemburg and dos Picos. There had seemed little reason to doubt that the expedition would arrive in Brest some time in July or August 1789, after a voyage of three years. Weather and circumstances permitting, of course.

Nor were Lapérouse's instructions restricted to the details of his route. Political diplomacy was obviously vital for the success of a voyage negotiating so many foreign countries and powers, some of whom were or might be at war with France. For all the recent treaty with Britain granted immunity from military action for scientific expeditions, misunderstandings could easily arise and a commander needed also to be a skilled diplomat. Detailed geographic and historical notes to keep Lapérouse fully informed consequently occupied as much space as the instructions themselves.

Diplomacy was also required towards foreigners of a less powerful kind. As an advanced nation, France eschewed some of the more brutal, conquistidorial activities of the past. Lapérouse had expressed strong views on how ridiculous it was for men to assert their authority over countries occupied by others for countless generations, simply on the basis of firearms and bayonets. Surely, Lapérouse had exclaimed, 'religion could no longer be used as a pretext for violence and rapine?'

Louis's inherently compassionate nature was stirred by the passion of Lapérouse's arguments. He commanded that 'on all occasions the sieur de la Peyrouse will behave with great gentleness and humanity to the different people he may visit' and 'enjoin every one of the crew to live amicably with the natives, to endeavour to conciliate their friendship by civility and good behaviour', although obviously some element of self-protection must be allowed in extreme circumstances.

The king frowned. Philosophical debates on the rights and duties of man and sovereign brought him uncomfortably close to his present circumstances. The carriage had made slow progress at walking pace along the bank of the Seine. From the window Louis could see the classically Italianate lines of the Louvre, restored to some of its former glory by his grandfather and used to display the royal collection of masterpieces. Here too, the Royal Academy of Science met twice a week—fifty-six of France's, indeed Europe's, finest *savants* devoted to the advancement of both the physical and mathematical sciences.

The Academicians had naturally contributed detailed instructions of their own to Lapérouse for scientific investigations in geometry, astronomy, mechanics, natural philosophy, chemistry, anatomy, zoology, mineralogy and botany. The Academicians had also set the *savants* on board the task of answering, if they could, a series of specific questions relating to the inhabitants of foreign lands. These included fourteen on the topic of anatomy, six on hygiene, six on diseases, eleven relating to medicine and six specifically surgical enquiries. Some of the sceptical *philosophes* might scoff at the extent of such a research program, but the Academy included men such as Bougainville whose practical experience aided them greatly in developing achievable goals. Ten specific experiments were to be conducted on board, while the instructions provided to the gardener were both detailed and exhaustive.

Nothing had been spared in the planning of this expedition. As with the previous French expeditions, specialist scientific staff were commissioned to record astronomical data and make collections of plants and animals. The ships were laden with all manner of equipment—astronomical quadrants and clocks, telescopes and theodolites, compasses and magnets. From England, Joseph Banks from the Board of Longitude had graciously loaned two dipping needles as used by Cook. The superiority of recent English innovations (verified and confirmed by Cook) in solving the vexatious problem of longitude was well recognised and the French expedition could do no better than to travel equipped with an English chronometer, reflecting sextants and variation compasses.

For the chemists, an assortment of barometers, thermometers, eudiometers, hydrometers, aerometers and hygrometers were aboard. Microscopes, with both single and compound lenses, an electrical machine, pneumatic apparatus, reverbatory furnace, hydrostatical balance, air pump and a 26-foot-high linen balloon lined with papier-joseph were all indispensable for the experiments to be conducted. A one-foot concave burning mirror capable of setting fire to a small building at a distance of several feet with the power of the sun alone was also aboard, re-created by the talented Buffon from Greek descriptions of the ancient weapon.

The tools of the naturalists were rather simpler—copious reams of paper for drawing and drying, numerous boxes of paints and pencils, and assorted nets and boxes for catching insects. A large assortment of shrubs, plants and seeds was also loaded according to the instructions of André Thouin, head gardener at the Jardin du Roi, in order to introduce useful food crops to the new lands for the benefit of natives and future travellers alike.

The libraries aboard the two vessels ('for the use of the officers and men of science') were vast. Published accounts of every major voyage of discovery to the Pacific region were provided, including Cook's *Voyages* in both French and English. The latest publications on astronomy and navigation lay alongside key texts on natural philosophy and chemistry. The naturalists made up for their lack of sophisticated equipment with an impressive array of books, not least of which included all eleven volumes to date of *Histoire naturelle* by Buffon. The great man shared shelf space with his Swedish one-time nemesis, Carolus Linnaeus, whose works on the classification of plants and animals were now compulsory reading for any natural historian.

No expense had been spared in equipping the ships with the most skilled *savants* and sailors. France would not stint on the acquisition and dissemination of knowledge. Competition had been fierce among botanists, gardeners, astronomers and geologists—and also among naval officers with an enthusiasm for science—for a place on Lapérouse's ships. The opportunity to be part of such a great voyage of discovery was not to be missed and many a young naturalist and midshipman dreamed of seeing strange and foreign lands for himself.

In truth, the expedition was more than any commander could ever hope to achieve in a single voyage. Lapérouse carried with him not just the ambitions of a nation, but also the hopes and aspirations of her king. But if any man could succeed, if any man could be France's answer to Cook, it would be Lapérouse.

Initial reports were most promising. They had lost no men and had completed large components of their instructions before disaster struck, nearly a year after their departure from Brest, with the loss of twenty-one men in the fierce currents off the Alaskan coast. Lapérouse was devastated by the loss. One of the young men had been his own nephew.

With no letters or news from home, the men on the expedition must have felt abandoned, unaware of the *Résolution* and the *Subtile* gallantly battling the full force of the north-east monsoon to rendezvous with them in Macao. Their captain, d'Entrecasteaux, had fearlessly driven his ships east of the Philippines and New Guinea through shoal-riven uncharted waters. His dedication opened up a new safe shipping lane in the region but he missed Lapérouse by days at Macao. With dogged determination, d'Entrecasteaux sent the faster *Subtile* with letters and additional men to catch up with the expedition, both of which Lapérouse gratefully received after his losses in America.

Since the expedition's departure, the king had learnt of an English attempt to establish a penal colony on the east coast of New Holland, at Botany Bay. Fleurieu had immediately sent dispatches instructing Lapérouse to amend his instructions to include a visit to the new colony as soon as might be convenient. Lapérouse obviously took these instructions to heart, for his final report was sent from Botany Bay.

Despite his eagerness to visit the new colony, Lapérouse had taken the time to undertake some of his exploratory commitments among the Pacific Islands. Bougainville had found the Navigator Islands to be a reliable source of water, food and timber, populated by a statuesque and handsome race of people, their womenfolk as exquisite and mild as their menfolk were fierce and deceitful.

And yet, as Marion du Fresne had discovered before them, the friendship of native people was not to be trusted. Barely recognising any rule of law even among themselves, the islanders showed scant respect for the foreigners.

Diplomatically skirting numerous infringements of property and decorum, Lapérouse had been in the process of congratulating himself for 'having attached no importance to the small vexations we had suffered' when news came of a terrible massacre. A thousand islanders had converged on a party of sailors collecting water. Twelve Frenchmen, including the captain of the *Astrolabe*, had been killed. More than just their colleagues and friends had died in this massacre. With them too, died the noble savage of the *philosophe*'s dreams. Who could blame these islanders for being no better than they should be—were not unrealistic expectations to blame? Lapérouse wrote, 'I am a thousand times more angry with the philosophers who praise the savages than with the savages themselves'.

After such confusion and difficulties, the expedition must have sighted the English fleet in Botany Bay with a relief that bordered on affection. Here at least were familiar foes with unambiguous rules of engagement established through generations of conflict. 'All Europeans are fellow countrymen when they meet so far from home,' mused Lapérouse as they made their slow approach to the anchorage. The English, however, were less enthusiastic about the arrival of their fellow Europeans at a most delicate stage in establishing a new colony. The selected site of Botany Bay was unsuitable for settlement and Governor Phillip had already left for a new destination which was, of course, to be kept secret from the French.

With all the brittle confidence of a dog on unfamiliar turf, the English officers politely offered assistance to their first and most unexpected guests—provided it did not mean sails, food, munitions or information on the new colony. Actually, they could extend little more than goodwill. The official constipation of command, however, did not extend to the English crews, who happily divulged the location of Port Jackson, a safe deep harbour a few miles north. Nor did the French remain isolated from the activities of the new colony, with Lapérouse's last entry in his journal complaining that 'we had afterwards but too frequent opportunities of hearing news of the English settlement, the deserters from which gave us a great deal of trouble and embarrassment'.

Louis wondered what that trouble had been and what Lapérouse had thought of the English colony at Port Jackson. Was it true the English had set out to establish a new colony with not a single botanist, nor even a gardener, who might have some horticultural knowledge to assist them in developing their crops? King George might be laughingly known as Farmer George, but few of his interests seemed to be put into practice. George, however, exerted far less control over English expeditions than Louis had wielded over the Lapérouse expedition—probably because he did not pay so much of the bill. Even the wealthy entrepreneur Joseph Banks had financed more of Cook's voyage than the Crown. Louis XVI had been prepared to bear the full cost of the Lapérouse expedition—in return for all the glory.

But it was Lapérouse's habit to compose his reports after leaving a destination, thus each report from a location concerned the previous, not the current section of the voyage. After a month at Botany Bay spent refitting his ships and restoring his men to health, Lapérouse had set out for further explorations of the South Pacific, never to be seen or heard from again. Nor was there word yet from the capable d'Entrecasteaux, sent again into distant waters to search for his missing colleague.

Louis had dreamed of these strange and foreign places lately, in the long lonely months of imprisonment in the tower of the Temple. It consoled him to regale his son, the young Dauphin, with imagined tales of Lapérouse's voyage as they pored together over the little books on the history of exploration in the South Seas that he had had published particularly for his son's education. After so many years, though, it did not now seem likely that Lapérouse would return in triumph bearing maps emblazoned with French names and leaving a trail of plaques across the Pacific claiming French sovereignty. The king's lasting fame, it seemed, was not to rest with the discovery of the great southern continent. His legacy seemed destined to offer little prospect for the happiness of his people, much less the glory of his own and France's name.

The sounds of distant oceans receded from the king's mind, replaced by frenzied drumming. The carriage slowed amid a sea of sullen, silent onlookers. This was no time for recriminations or regrets. This was no time for futile dreams of glories lost. He could do no more as his country's king than die like one.

'We are arrived, if I mistake not,' said Louis XVI quietly, stepping out of the carriage to meet his destiny.

> Citizens, the tyrant is no more. For a long time the cries of the victims, whom war and domestic dissensions have spread over France and Europe, loudly protested his existence. He has paid his penalty, and only acclamations for the Republic and for liberty have been heard from the people . . .
>
> Now, above all, we need peace in the interior of the Republic, and the most active surveillance of the domestic enemies of liberty. Never did circumstances more urgently require of all citizens the sacrifice of their passions and their personal opinions concerning the act of national justice which has just been effected. Today the French people can have no other passion than that for liberty.
>
> Proclamation of the Death of the King,
> 23 January 1793

Jacques-Julien Labillardière

Rue des Fossés Saint-Bernard, Paris

21 January 1791

Jacques-Julien Houtou de Labillardière *was born in Alençon, Normandy, on 28 October 1755. From an upwardly mobile bourgeois family, he pursued his studies at the medical school in Montpellier before turning to botany in Paris. Labillardière seems to have been a solid, well-built man with thick, dark hair who favoured the casual, unkempt republican look over the immaculately coiffed aristocratic fashion. He had a surly, stubborn and unsociable disposition. He made several voyages (including to England where he met Joseph Banks), before embarking on the d'Entrecasteaux expedition, upon which he hoped to make his name with a great collection to rival that of Banks. Labillardière was imprisoned temporarily by the Dutch in Java after the expedition's disintegration. His collection was seized by the British on its way back to France but was eventually returned through the intervention of Joseph Banks. After participating in Napoléon's cultural 'collecting' in Italy, Labillardière pursued a successful if reclusive career in botany, being elected a full member of the Institut National in 1800. He rapidly became disenchanted with Napoléon's imperial ambitions, remained a staunch republican and became increasingly morose and withdrawn in his old age. He married in 1799 but separated in about 1810. Labillardière died at the age of seventy-nine in 1834.*

Just two years earlier and Paris had seemed so full of promise to the ambitious young naturalist now preparing to embark on d'Entrecasteaux's rescue mission. The old shackles imprisoning much of France's potential had been broken. The Declaration of the Rights of Man and Citizen had enunciated the principles of *liberté*, *égalité* and *fraternité*. All men were born free with equal rights—to be ruled under the same laws regardless of social distinction. A peaceful transition to a constitutional monarchy had seemed assured.

The good city was brimming with opportunity, thought Jacques-Julien Houtou de Labillardière as he stepped out of his lodgings on rue des Fossés Saint-Bernard. Shucking his shabby coat back up onto his shoulders, Labillardière surveyed the busy Left Bank street with its characteristic bustle of people coming and going in bookshops and cafés. His bulky figure filled the narrow doorway as he stepped confidently into the flow of foot traffic, passers-by stepping aside to make way for him.

Striding purposefully towards the gardens, Labillardière seemed absorbed in his own thoughts, his disapproving expression not inviting intimacy. Yet his sharp eyes kept watch at each familiar door or passage from where one of his many colleagues might emerge. This was a popular neighbourhood for *philosophes* and *savants*, being so convenient for the Jardin des Plantes, yet with rents so reasonable. He had no time for chatter and smalltalk but he enjoyed the opportunity to discuss his studies with colleagues during the short walk to work. But no one stepped out to join him today and, unperturbed, Labillardière walked on alone.

Thanks to the National Guards, the city was very quiet at present, albeit with an undercurrent of tension that rarely seemed to abate these days. Some of the priests, it is true, continued to rail against the demand that they sign an oath of loyalty to the new French nation. These disloyal dissenters had recently been barred from performing their public ministry, reportedly causing some discontent in the rural areas. Marat continued to rant against the excess powers of the king and promote a model of limited monarchy. One could not help but admire the energy of this man—once a successful doctor and chemist. Marat's vitriol for the king, however, was unsparing. A momentary disquiet passed over Labillardière as he recalled Marat's bitterness at being rejected from the Royal Academy—Marat did not seem the type either to forgive or forget such an insult.

Many of his colleagues found the political ferment distracted them from their studies, but Labillardière allowed nothing to intrude on his work. His passion for botany had brooked no rivals since he had first become enamoured of her charms as a medical student in Montpellier. It was for the sake of this infant but entrancing science that he had gravitated to Paris, with its prestigious university and the royal gardens. His enthralment had led him on many voyages since then— to England, to the Alps, to Asia Minor and to the island of Crete. Each time he returned to France with a bigger haul of botanical treasures for his collections.

Collections alone, however, would not be enough to secure his place among the ranks of France's premier *savants.*

The collections must be described and illustrated, new species named and old names corrected. With the discovery of species previously unknown to science came botanical immortality. The first volume of his *Plants of Syria* already featured several new species annotated with the authority 'Labillardière 1790' appended to them. His book had been acclaimed at the Royal Academy. He had even been nominated for a hotly contested associate membership. His good friend L'Héritier had beaten him to it but Labillardière was undeterred. He could wait. His next project would assure him of membership. Having steadily built up his experience and credentials collecting in and around Europe, Labillardière was ready for his next challenge—a great voyage rivalling that of Bougainville, to amass collections rivalling those of Joseph Banks—a voyage to the South Sea.

The long wall enclosing the gardens gave way at last to an ornate iron grille and Labillardière passed from the busy bustle of the Paris streets into the cool serenity of the Jardin des Plantes. No matter how often he came here, he could not help but be impressed. It was not just the quiet grandeur of the trees, but who and what these trees represented. Bernard de Jussieu had carried the mighty cedar of Lebanon in his hat as a sapling from England. The black pine was a more recent addition by Bernard's nephew Antoine-Laurent. The robinia was old even when it was transplanted here, three hundred years ago, from the gardens at the Paris Medical School. The maples, like so many of the yews and oaks, were planted under the direction of the late Comte de Buffon, whose spirit and intellectual legacy still lingered, as if he were part of the atmosphere itself. These trees were living testimony to the generations of *savants* who had created, lived, studied and died here, and in whose lineage Labillardière sought to take his place. These gardens were the embodiment of Lamarck's *Flore française*. Here were the collections of plants and animals that formed the basis of Buffon's voluminous *Histoire naturelle*, to which Daubenton and now Lacépède had also devoted many years.

The Jardin des Plantes had been established in 1640 by the king's physician as a research and educational garden. Unlike Versailles, it was not a princely garden designed to impress dignitaries with the breadth and vision of the French empire, but a practical garden intended to improve health, knowledge and education. Here was a place where scientific investigations into botany, chemistry and anatomy could be carried out uninterrupted by the petty disturbances of minor nobles at the Court. Here was a place where the foremost wisdom of the time could be had by anyone willing to turn up to the free public lectures provided by the resident *savants*. Under Buffon's careful cultivation, the Jardin had expanded dramatically and its finances had been secured. And almost singlehandedly, Buffon had made natural history fashionable.

The enormous popular success of Buffon's *Histoire naturelle: générale et particulière* had all of Paris collecting eggs, butterflies, beetles and seashells. These voluminous and well-crafted volumes vastly outsold those of Rousseau or even Voltaire. Buffon had shamelessly courted his public and they loved him in return. The well-to-do now collected nature as they had once collected books and works of art. Nor was this passion restricted to the wealthy—even men of trade and business could show their erudition through a thoughtfully displayed collection of moths or birds' nests. The urban masses herborised on their days off, engaging in the kind of healthful activity for mind and body so recommended by Rousseau. They attended the free public lectures in the gardens by their hundreds. It was the golden age for natural history in France, but how long it would last, no one could tell.

Labillardière counted himself as fortunate indeed to be a citizen of France, one of the only countries in the world civilised enough to employ men of science to pursue knowledge for the greater good of all. Science could not be left as a pastime for idle aristocrats. Only in France, with a centralised and unified approach to study, was the world just beginning to unfold before them. The Jardin des Plantes, thanks to Buffon's careful cultivation, offered a number of modestly salaried positions (although more than one wealthy courtier responsible for the Jardin's finances had advised that the scientific mind might best be cultivated in an environment of abstinence undistracted by material luxuries). Other *savants* were not so fortunate. Most Academy members had to supplement their scientific interests with either private means or some other occupation. Lavoisier was a tax collector as well as a chemist, while Lamarck traded in duplicates of the seashells he studied and lived meagrely off the royalties of his publications. Labillardière's merchant family could support his interests for the moment. But surely in time, Academy membership would bring entitlement to a state pension, at least?

The gravel crunched loudly underfoot as Labillardière made his way through the gardens. In the distance, Buffon's ornate summerhouse stood on the hill, overlooking the gardens he had ruled for so long. Buffon had certainly strengthened the institution in which so many young *savants* prospered, but a considerable number regarded his influence on French natural history as oppressive. His colleagues accused him of an attachment to style over substance—'*Le style est l'homme même*'—and of too willingly extrapolating in generalities rather than confining himself to the proven details. Buffon straddled the divide between *savant* and *philosophe*. Not content with merely observing and documenting the world around him, he sought to explain its broader patterns in lucid and elegant terms, as evident in the subtitle of his magnum opus—*Histoire naturelle: générale et particulière*.

For his part, Labillardière was content with the particulars of natural history. Generalities left the author open to attack from the young and vitriolic. Many a young man's career was founded on the ruins of an older (perhaps braver) man's edifice. Yet with age, and authority, perhaps every *savant* might succumb to the lure of the grand theory in the end?

The world had changed so much even during Buffon's lifetime. No longer were plants and animals imbued with some kind of life essence, enabling barnacle geese to grow from trees or Tartary lambs to have the quality of both plants and animals. Species were now distinct from one another, discrete and identifiable. The binomial classification system of Swedish botanist Carolus Linnaeus, with its hierarchy of orders and genera, had swept across Europe and been adopted with enthusiasm. But where Linnaeus saw God-given absolutes, the secular Buffon saw continuity, variation and change. He had nothing but contempt for the simplistic Linnaean classications based only on the reproductive system of flowers. It was unnatural to classify species on the basis of a single trait, he argued, and vastly inferior to the natural systems developed by the Jardin's own botanists such as André Thouin. Especially when applied to animals, Linnaean logic was full of holes—what advantage was there to put sloths and scaly lizards in a group with men? To put hippopotamuses with shrews? The classifiers might variously regard a mongoose as a badger or a weasel or an otter or a rat, but to Buffon, it would always be a mongoose.

The two giants of natural science, Buffon and Linnaeus, both riding on the waves of their mass popularity, faced off, unrepentant and unforgiving. Labillardière was not interested in hippopotamuses, scaly lizards or mongooses. He was a botanist and his plants stayed still—remained the same. Apparent variation could always be accounted for by finer gradations in classification. What might appear as one species to the untrained eye, might actually be two, or three. If Linnaean classification worked for plants, it worked for

Labillardière. Its very simplicity was its strength (even suitable for women, Linnaeus had boasted).

Whatever system he used, the classifier's efforts to divide
the world into different kingdoms were revolutionary. No
longer would enthusiasts collect together objects simply
because of a similarity in shape. Egg collections had once
included not only birds' eggs of all descriptions, but also
dragons' eggs of fossilised rock and eggs fabulously engraved
and encrusted with jewels. But now the world was divided
into the living and the non-living, the plant and the animal,
the vertebrate and, as Lamarck termed it, the invertebrate. As
Buffon had noted, through the study of nature the observer
could not help but 'form a general idea of animated matter, he
will distinguish it from non-animated matter ... naturally
he will arrive at the first great division, Animal, Vegetable
or Mineral'.

Buffon may have held back the tide of Linnaean systematics during his lifetime, but upon his death even this last
French bastion of resistance had been swept away.
Labillardière had been in Crete at the time, but he'd heard all
about the funeral on his return. Twenty thousand people
lined the streets to mourn the passing of Buffon's coffin,
pulled through the streets of Paris by fourteen horses adorned
in black and silver and accompanied by a crier, six bailiffs,
nineteen matching servants, thirty-six choirboys, sixty cler-
gymen, a detachment of the Paris Guard and an assortment of
schoolchildren. Some of his colleagues, however, had treated
Buffon's death with less dignity. Young Georges Cuvier had

shouted gleefully, 'The naturalists have finally lost their leader. This time, the Comte de Buffon is dead and buried!'

Labillardière was not so foolish as to allow any such unwary comments pass his lips. Buffon had made an immense contribution to French science and whatever Labillardière's personal views on his work, he kept them to himself. But as he passed beneath the new statue of Linnaeus erected in the garden, a sly grin flickered across Labillardière's features. What would the mighty Buffon have thought of an effigy of his old adversary in the very heart of his own empire?

When Labillardière arrived back in Paris from his expedition to Crete he enthusiastically joined his friends every Friday evening to read papers in Latin in their defiantly named 'Société Linnéenne'. It was they who were responsible for this fine statue of Linnaeus. Such youthful disrespect was tolerated for a while, but it was soon known that prospects for election to the Academy would not be aided by such bravado and the society was re-formed under a new name. Labillardière confided to a friend, 'We have at present a *Société d'histoire naturelle*, or rather the old society, of which I was a member, has regenerated itself'. So long as the society itself continued, Labillardière did not particularly care what it was called.

The fiery young radicals who made up the bulk of the society's membership (or at least contributed most vocally to its conversations) were not alone. Daubenton himself (Buffon's once-loyal assistant) was not above recommending Linnaean systematics should they prove appropriate to the circumstances. Jean-Baptiste Lamarck deigned to edit the journal in which the fledgling society published its correspondence. The young Cuvier, like Labillardière, was a protégé of Lamarck and his papers on wood lice had been read with interest at the newly formed Société d'Histoire Naturelle. The young naturalist showed great promise. He had illustrated Lamarck's articles on molluscs most beautifully and showed a fine appreciation for anatomical detail.

A slight figure hurried across the gardens towards the laboratories. His coat was flung open, careless of the cool morning air. The heavy cravat enveloping his neck was not to protect against the wind, Labillardière knew, but to conceal the unsightly scars on his neck that had ended his military career. At forty-three, Lamarck should have been one of the premier *savants* at the Jardin des Plantes, despite his late conversion to a scientific vocation. He had made an impressive start all those years ago when, as a student, he had boasted of being able to produce a vastly superior system of identifying France's plants than any currently in existence. Readily accepting a challenge to prove his words, he astonished his colleagues by producing *Flore française*, a simple guide that used the novel approach of a dichotomous key to help even the amateur enthusiast accurately identify plants. Buffon had been most impressed, paying for the book to be printed and allowing Lamarck to keep the royalties.

The other botanists at the Jardin were less enthusiastic. Lamarck's work certainly had merit, but his failure to adequately acknowledge their work rankled. But if his fellow botanists were cool, it was nothing compared to the Arctic blast that met Lamarck when he attempted to similarly bring new light to the disciplines of meteorology, chemistry and physics. His naïve efforts had been mercilessly rejected and had done little to improve his career prospects at either the Jardin or the Academy.

Labillardière cared little for these criticisms of Lamarck. Not everyone found Lamarck easy to deal with. He was like a mimosa plant, with its intriguing sensitivity to touch. Prickly and well-armed, yet wilting dramatically at the slightest touch, only to recover—unaffected—moments later. His physical frailty and the hardship of his personal life lent itself to sympathy. Yet Lamarck's fragile exterior concealed a spirit single-mindedly dedicated to his work and neither mockery, poverty nor even the threat of death would turn him from his self-appointed task. Labillardière understood Lamarck's dedication, although he himself was far more politically savvy. Labillardière was well aware that to survive in science, one had to be thick-skinned and doggedly determined. It was not an easy career to forge.

The tranquillity of the Jardin seemed an inviolable sanctuary from the turmoil outside, but even this peace could be misleading. Labillardière paid little attention to his senior colleagues' concerns for the garden's future; he was not interested in the solemn conversations and anxious debates about all their prospects. But an air of worried anxiety underlay the Jardin's workshops nowadays. Many were anxious to distance the Jardin from its royal patronym—the Jardin des

Plantes was also commonly known as the Jardin du Roi. Perhaps a new name, a new focus, would be appropriate, better reflecting the modern goals and ideals of an enlightened society? Would the name *Musaeum*, redolent of the scholarly antiquities of Alexandria, better reflect the purpose of the gardens, combined with the Cabinet of Natural History and the public lectures?

But Labillardière's thoughts of the future lay in a different direction altogether, in a different world, in a different hemisphere. Just a few weeks ago, the once-powerful Fleurieu had arrived cap in hand, to ask the assistance of the Société d'Histoire Naturelle. Fleurieu, as confidant and advisor to the king, had once held the power to dispense favours and grant funds to the *savants*. Well aware of his declining authority, Fleurieu now sought to enlist the enthusiasm of the young and upcoming and their influence with the Convention to send a search party for the missing Lapérouse. And the young and enthusiastic gentlemen had responded promptly.

Gentlemen:

We call to your attention the Citizens who have braved great dangers on little-known seas for the progress of Natural History and Navigation, who have put their lives at risk to serve their fatherland and all Peoples—M. la Peyrouse and his unfortunate companions.

Legislators whose wise decrees proclaim their love of their fellow man cannot but be interested in the fate of Navigators who have distinguished themselves by their dedication.

France has waited for the return of M. la Peyrouse for two years in vain, and those people who are interested in him or in his discoveries know nothing of his fate. Alas! The fate they imagine is perhaps even more terrible than that which he is actually experiencing; perhaps he escaped death only to be subject to the continual torment of revived—yet always disappointed—hope. Perhaps he has landed on one of the Islands of the Southern Sea and waits there, stretching his arms out toward his fatherland from whence he awaits a Liberator.

This hope, which we feel revive on his behalf, will not be disappointed. It was not for frivolous objects, for his personal advantage that M. la Peyrouse braved all sorts of dangers; the generous Nation that will harvest the fruit of his glorious effort owes him its aid.

We have already learned of the loss of several of his companions who succumbed

*to the waves or were massacred by savages:
let us encourage the hope that remains—to
rescue those of our brothers who escaped the
furor of the sea or the rage of the
Cannibals. May they return to our
shores, even if they die of happiness as
they embrace this free earth.*

Signé Lermina, *Président*; Brogniard, *Secrétaire*; Pelletier,
Louis Bosc, Fourcroy, Aubri, Louis Millin, Macquart,
Besson, Bergaret, de Rousseau, Bernard, Labillardière,
Ventenaze, Lezeruses, Lelièvre, RC Geoffroy, Groteste,
Desfontaines, Iberti, Richard, Jacob Forster, et autres.

And their call had been answered. In the midst of all the
turmoil and upheaval, the National Assembly nonetheless
found time to promptly order Fleurieu to arrange a rescue
expedition which, should the search prove fruitless, would
also be fully armed with botanists and gardeners, artists and
meteorologists, to extend the scientific and cartographic
advances so hoped for from the missing ships. The
d'Entrecasteaux expedition of two ships had been launched
to find the missing sea captain—and to return with whatever
scientific bounty their officers could muster.

Labillardière hoped to make an immense collection
during this historic voyage. An immense collection that
would seal his professional career irrespective of political
issues. The prospect of years at sea in uncharted waters held

no fears for Labillardière—he was, after all, a seasoned sailor who had spent three months navigating in the Mediterranean. He had no way of knowing where he would be on a fateful day for France in two years' time, no way of knowing that the little ship on which he launched himself would carry on it a microcosm of France, with all her turmoils and travails, an offshoot of society developing on its own separate course while France herself sped towards her own bloody destiny.

In the meantime, however, there was still much work to be completed. Following Lamarck, Labillardière entered the Hôtel de Magny and immersed himself among the rustling papers wafting with camphor and dried foliage.

Antoine-Raymond-Joseph Bruni d'Entrecasteaux

Recherche Bay, Van Diemen's Land

20 April 1792

The sharp salt spray smacked his face, shocking the air from his lungs. Water swept him bodily from the deck, pain shooting through his injured ribs, even as his hands gripped the rail to save himself. Ignoring the pain, the general steadied himself against the sliding deck and wiped the water from his eyes. He peered through shafts of foam and spray to the foredeck, instinctively accounting for each man present.

'Reef that foresail,' he roared over the southerly gale in a voice long accustomed to authority.

His order echoed down the chain of command. Men clung precariously to ratlines and bollards as the waves washed over them. In the brief lull as the ship righted herself, they scurried with frantic activity to control the bulging sail, spilling the wind that drove the ship at breakneck speed. The ship heaved to starboard again and the men clung to her instinctively as wind and wave tried to tear them away. The world turned furious white then green—sinking into the waters' momentary seductive silence—until the ship ripped free and they emerged once more into the deafening roar of the storm.

D'Entrecasteaux squinted northward into the dull gloom of the pre-dawn horizon. The ship tipped slowly onto the crest of the wave. Shielding his eyes from the wind, the general peered anxiously across the foaming ocean. Nothing.

'Ship ahoy!' shrilled the young lookout. 'The *Espérance* off the starboard bow.'

The ship's descent gathered speed, flinging them down into the valley between the mountainous swells.

Antoine-Raymond-Joseph Bruni d'Entre-casteaux *was born 8 November 1737 in Aix en Provence. The son of a local magistrate, he entered the navy in 1754 and was promoted to captain in 1779. D'Entrecasteaux had a strong sense of Christian duty and obligation and, despite his distinguished appearance, was agreeable and good-natured. He was pious without being intolerant, and candid but also willing to listen. He sought to resign from the navy over a family scandal involving a nephew murdering his wife; however, his resignation was not accepted and he was appointed Director of Ports and Arsenals where he assisted Fleurieu to arrange the Lapérouse expedition. In 1785 d'Entrecasteaux negotiated trade relations with China and rendezvoused with the Lapérouse expedition. He was Commandant of the French India Naval Station and Governor of the Mascarene Islands (Île de France and Île Bourbon) in 1787–89. He was given command of the expedition to search for Lapérouse in 1791, a responsibility that he no doubt took very personally given his previous involvement with the Lapérouse expedition. He died in August 1793, probably from the combined effects of scurvy, dysentery, and possibly injury, and was buried at sea.*

D'Entrecasteaux waited, his eyes fixed where the lookout had pointed. He felt the ship change altitude, rising imperceptibly up the mountain. There! A glimpse of masts just disappearing between the waves. The *Espérance* was still with them.

As the strain left d'Entrecasteaux's shoulders he became aware of another silent tension on the poopdeck. Catching the captain's eye, he saw d'Auribeau motioning below, managing to convey in an almost imperceptible bow and tight smile his overwhelming concern for his injured commander. D'Entrecasteaux stiffened but graciously surrendered the deck and control of the ship to the captain, retiring below decks.

D'Entrecasteaux's promotion to Rear Admiral upon their departure from Brest had been a welcome one, although he was still not quite accustomed to relinquishing the role of captain to another. Being relieved of some of the more onerous duties of captain certainly gave him more time to devote to the administrative duties of expedition leader (tasks that, in all honesty, he preferred), but it also placed him in an awkward position. As commander of the expedition, he retained ultimate responsibility for the ships and their crews, but he had to relinquish control of their daily operations. D'Entrecasteaux was only too aware that, just as deficits in the first lieutenant reflected poorly on the captain, any weakness in his captains reflected poorly on himself. Not that the captains of the two ships under his command were ill-equipped for their task. He thought highly of both men. Huon de Kermadec, captain of the *Espérance*, had served

under him before and d'Entrecasteaux found in him a friend
and confidant. D'Hesmivy d'Auribeau, who captained his
flagship, the *Recherche*, had also come highly recommended.
But neither enjoyed the best of health. The small, vapourish
d'Auribeau was worryingly dependent upon the opiates of
the surgeon while d'Entrecasteaux's dear friend Kermadec,
already frail before embarking, was worryingly vulnerable to
the ailments of shipboard life.

In skills, the two captains were as different as salt and
pepper. Huon was more like d'Entrecasteaux; his skills lay in
the art of negotiation and management. D'Auribeau was
a highly talented navigator but his high-handed, autocratic
approach to command did not make for a comfortable climate. Declining to countermand his captain or undermine his
authority in any way, d'Entrecasteaux had broad shoulders to
bear the barely concealed critiques of junior officers. It was
all too easy for less experienced men to underestimate the
burden of command. More sensitive to d'Auribeau's needs
than d'Auribeau himself would have been, d'Entrecasteaux
stayed in his cabin as much as possible, emerging only when
his presence was required, when his duty overrode the need
for diplomacy.

Gingerly easing himself into his chair, d'Entrecasteaux
gripped the edge of the writing desk responsible for his pain.
Two weeks ago, a violent squall had hit the ship with such
force it seemed they had struck rock mid-ocean. A monu-
mental wave had flooded the deck cabins and filled the men
with terror. The naturalist Labillardière had been swept from

his bed, convinced that his unending *mal-de-mer* was to be finally cured only by drowning. The general himself had been flung across his cabin, breaking his fall on the desk. The surgeon could find no obvious injury, but the pain, particularly when he sneezed, assured the general that injury was both present and severe. The fury of the Southern Ocean was not to be trifled with, and although d'Entrecasteaux had managed to bring most of his men through thus far unscathed, he himself had paid a heavy penalty.

For six weeks the Southern Ocean had pummelled the two small ships with gale after gale. The frenzied waters had blazed with great balls of fire, while the eerie halo of Saint Elmo's fire fizzled its electric charge around the ship's masts. For the *savant*s on board, the combination of phosphorus, electrical discharge and low barometric pressure created much animated discussion—broken only by the demands of heaving stomachs. The crew were more superstitious and the prolonged ill winds, combined with these ominous meterological events, tested their spirits sorely. Their last sight of land had been the tiny crag of Amsterdam Island mid-ocean three weeks earlier and even that sighting had been tinged with unpropitious omens. As they sailed past, the island had mysteriously caught fire, ablaze along its entire length.

Even with just the foresail and mizzen jib, the ship was speeding eastward, peaking at a record-breaking ten knots. But strong currents also drove her northward, closer and closer to the invisible shores of Van Diemen's Land.

'Lay the ship to and tack to starboard.'

D'Entrecasteaux's order was relayed down through the ranks. The men responded instantly, but the general could feel their disappointment as the ship turned southward, away from the land they all knew to be nearby. The sky was still dark in all but the east, and they could not afford to make landfall too early.

It was half past nine before land was finally sighted and, recalled to the deck, d'Entrecasteaux recognised with some satisfaction the characteristic crag of the Mewstone with its two smaller outcrops to the west, just as Tasman had described it in 1642. After tracking across some ten thousand miles of open ocean, they had arrived exactly where their chronometers had predicted they would, approaching the safe harbour of Adventure Bay, first charted by Tasman and more recently visited by Marion du Fresne.

The day passed in excited anticipation as the officers busied themselves with precise astronomical calculations based on the position of South Cape. Every officer, and even the occasional seaman, sought to distinguish himself as a man of learning and talent. The white pages of sketchbooks festooned the deck in an early snowstorm as the young enthusiasts sought to outdo one another in the fervour with which they documented the coastline. Artistic ability notwithstanding, every angle, every manifestation of the distant shore was noted, reported, described, hatched and cross-hatched. As the coastline rose from the horizon, they began to make out steep mountain forests and precipitous cliffs. The massive swells began to drop away behind the shelter of the southern capes and although the wind howled just as viciously, the breaking seas seemed more merciful with the prospect of relief in sight.

D'Entrecasteaux scanned the coast anxiously, trying to make out the entrance to Adventure Bay. Something was awry. Disquiet tempered the earlier euphoria among the officers. Annoyed at having his navigational expertise questioned, the general called for the log book. He snapped it shut in irritation. An incorrect bearing had been entered—west instead of east—throwing all subsequent calculations off. Cutting short spluttered justifications and ignoring the accusatory glares between those responsible, the general returned to his cabin. The choice was clear—continue in the hope of finding Adventure Bay or risk seeking shelter in uncharted waters. By afternoon he had to agree with his officers that the ships should head into the open mouth of an unknown bay, hoping to find refuge by nightfall. Tacking painstakingly across the bay, the two ships inched their way into the entrance.

'No bottom,' cried the bowsman, pulling the leadline from the water and throwing it far ahead of the ship again.

'Twenty-five fathoms and fine sand,' came the next cry.

'Eighteen fathoms and sand.'

'Fifteen fathoms. Sand.'

The yawl was dispatched to survey ahead of the larger ships and continued to find good soundings and ground. In the head of the bay, d'Entrecasteaux ordered the two ships to anchor and after months of constant noise and motion, the world finally stilled in this strange, quiet land on the other side of the globe.

2 May 1792

The ship swung gently on its cable, a slight breeze all that reached them of the wind outside. D'Entrecasteaux felt the reassuring tug of the anchor as the ship pulled her cable taut before relaxing back to her original position. Their first fort-night here had revealed that the anchorage was good and could accommodate many ships with safety. D'Entrecasteaux glanced at the panorama that rolled past his cabin windows before turning back to his journal.

> It will be difficult to describe my feelings at the sight of this solitary harbour situated at the extremities of the world, so perfectly enclosed that one feels separated from the rest of the universe. Everything is influenced by the wilderness of the ragged landscape. With each step, one encounters the beauties of unspoilt nature, with signs of decrepitude; trees reaching a very great height, and of a corresponding diameter, are devoid of branches along the trunk, but crowned with an everlasting foliage. Some of these trees seem as ancient as the world, and are so tightly interlaced that they are impenetrable. They support other trees of equal measurement which fall from old age, and nourish the soil with their decaying

fragments. Nature, in all its vigour, and at the same time in decline, offers to the imagination something more imposing and picturesque than the sight of this same nature embellished by civilised man's industry. In wishing to conserve only its beauty, man has managed to destroy its charm, and ruin its exclusive character—the one of always being old, and always new.

The general's reverie was broken by singing from the foredeck. A joyful shout followed the dull thud and flapping of another fish on the deck. The men's spirits had recovered miraculously. Dry clothes and good sleep had refreshed the tired grey faces of the past month. Fresh water had washed the salt and weariness from their bodies. The men went about their work with renewed enthusiasm, weighting the frigate to port so as to caulk her leaking seams, making repairs to the sails and spars, exploring and charting the surrounding lands and bays.

As soon as they had laid anchor, d'Entrecasteaux had ordered an additional ration of brandy, ignoring the glances exchanged by the lieutenants. It was all too easy for these pampered noble sons to feel the men needed less indulgence. But maintaining authority on a ship, indeed as in France herself, was not simply a matter of brute strength. The commander's word might be law at sea, but in a world where even the divine right of kings was being challenged, 'law' had more to do with diplomacy, tact and negotiation than it did with brute strength.

D'Entrecasteaux knew that the line between a beloved leader and a hated one was narrow indeed. A less personable man might not have been able to impose the strict regime of cleanliness and hygiene d'Entrecasteaux inflicted on his men. His insistence on daily washing in salt or fresh water probably kept them cleaner than they kept themselves at home, and their accommodation, while spartan, was kept relatively free of vermin by an unrelenting cycle of cleaning and airing. While physical ailments and the ever-present threat of scurvy overshadowed every long expedition, the activity engendered by d'Entrecasteaux's efforts to prevent illness was even more important for keeping the men busy. Idle hands make devil's work and in the close confines of a small ship a clash of personalities could be just as dangerous as wind and weather.

And in this ship, the clash of personalities carried with it the clash of politics. When the *Recherche* sailed, she carried more than the seeds of watercress and apple trees. She also carried the seeds of dissension and revolution. Men of all persuasions were crowded into this microcosm of France on the far side of the world, with no contact, no word on what was happening in their homeland. If the world of d'Entrecasteaux's expedition was anything to go by, the constitutional monarchy they left behind would be safe, with wise and pragmatic rulers acknowledging the need for increased democracy and rights for all men. But d'Entrecasteaux knew at first hand the difficulties of keeping control over widely divergent views. Even in his small kingdom it was hard to appease the warring parties—how well had Louis XVI trodden that narrow path?

The revolution at home had exacerbated the normal tensions on board ship. It had given him officers unusually firm in their traditional beliefs. The navy was still a common career path for young provincial nobles, despite the abolition of the privileges of the aristocratic *officiers rouge* over the common *officiers bleu* by the National Assembly. Noble connections were a liability in France at the moment, and many a young royalist officer had sought a tactical absence from his homeland for a few years in the hope that prospects might have improved upon his return. These were the men who now served d'Entrecasteaux.

But the same Enlightenment principles driving the revolutionary fervour that gave him these officers also granted him ten civilian *savants*—all of whom held strongly democratic views. Conflict between the *savants* and the officers was inevitable. How could the *savants* help but feel outsiders in a tightly run military ship where everyone else knew their place? D'Entrecasteaux had heard the *savants* complain of favouritism towards the officers, but for all he supported the conduct of science, the running of the ship must come first.

D'Entrecasteaux despaired as he watched irritations grow into chafing antipathies. No doubt the very characters that made these young men such promising *savants*—their enquiring and questioning minds, their independence and unwillingness to accept the everyday and obvious—made them the worst of passengers on board a naval vessel. Their endless disputes seemed to infect the crew with dissatisfaction, while the lack of hierarchy caused each to scramble for dominance based not on any pre-assigned rank but on the basis of intellectual strength. Theirs seemed such a gentle, even temperate pastime—collecting plants, painting jellyfish, drying butterflies—to be associated with such passionate distemper.

Raised voices in the companionway reflected d'Entrecasteaux's thoughts. In the new France every man was a *savant*. However, it could hardly be said that Fleurieu's fond hopes had been realised; that 'each one, co-operating with the same zeal for the success of your voyage, will forget himself, so as to contribute to the glory of the nation and the increase in human knowledge'. Fleurieu had recognised the potential for disquiet among these non-naval expedition members and the Minister of Marine had drafted a special letter clarifying the respective functions of the *savants* so as to 'leave no one in doubt concerning the functions to be accomplished by those persons embarked extraordinarily under your orders'. The draftsmen were to take their directions from the naturalists. The gardener, Félix Lahaye, was not to be regarded as a naturalist and indeed did not dine with the officers like the other *savants*. Lahaye, who had risen through the ranks of the Jardin des Plantes from a position as gardener's boy, seemed to accept his relegation with resigned disappointment.

Unfortunately, these clarifications had not extended to the ship's medical officers. Several of the *savants* had already threatened to leave the expedition at the Cape of Good Hope over claims by the surgeon to be a naturalist just like them.

The naturalists battled constantly with the surgeon for control of the zoological specimens, over incursion into their territory. The surgeon responded with his own arsenal of professional weapons. He might lose specimens to the naturalists, but the naturalists risked losing their supper by way of a judiciously administered purgative. Ships' surgeons held an unusual position of confidence and they were not to be crossed lightly, either by the naturalists or the injured expedition commander and his ailing captains.

In any case, d'Entrecasteaux didn't particularly want to curb the enquiring interests of any member of his expedition. The general encouraged all men on the voyage to be involved in the spirit of discovery and learning. He himself instructed the younger men on navigation while the astronomers taught mathematics. All were encouraged, right down to the cabin boy. On this point d'Entrecasteaux perhaps showed more *égalité* than some of his *savants*, still anxiously clutching their newly acquired professional status around them.

Since their arrival here, Labillardière had constantly complained that he was not allowed a boat, or men to assist him in his work. He seemed to believe that his botanical work was of more significance than any other requirements on the expedition and the fact that the boats were fully engaged in hydrographical surveys and collecting water did not sway him. The very notion of allowing the naturalists command of their own vessel, no matter how small, was, of course, absurd. They had so little common sense in all matters maritime they would undoubtedly lose both the boat and probably their own lives if left to their own devices. Even putting them ashore carried risks the general was anxious to minimise. Few of the *savants* had any concept of time, tide or changing weather. Anxious to be ashore at the first sight of land, they rarely returned on time and frequently delayed the ship's departure and jeopardised its safety when bad weather threatened.

Just yesterday the naturalists had failed to return before nightfall. Heavy rain and winds made it difficult to keep the small boats out and many on board felt the naturalists should be left to spend the night ashore. A small party of officers was ordered to wait for them, however, and having finally accounted for all the stray *savants*, they were relieved to be able to return to the ship, leaving the naturalists in the rain to await a second trip. D'Entrecasteaux had then ordered the boatswain and crew to eat supper before returning for the naturalists. If the naturalists chose to miss their appointed rendezvous then they would have to wait until the ship's timetable provided another opportunity for them to be collected. The wind was blustery, making the trip heavy-going and uncomfortable but when the boat's crew finally struggled back to shore, the unrepentant Labillardière sourly reprimanded them for 'taking their time'.

D'Entrecasteaux lost his patience. 'You are in no way allowed to disturb the supper of the crew,' he had bellowed at Labillardière, 'or offer them reproach!'

He cut short Labillardière's protests. 'It is by the supreme power with which I have been invested that I am

'Melaleuca myrtifolia'
Scented Paperbark
(Melaleuca squarrosa)

'Dasyure maugé'
Eastern Quoll
(*Dasyurus viverrinus*)

'Scinque jaune et noir'
Southern Blue-tongued Skink
(*Tiliqua nigrolutea*)

'Arra-Maïda'
Tasmanian Mother and Child

permitted to do everything for the best or everything for the worst,' summarily dismissing the naturalist.

D'Entrecasteaux did not regret his fierce dressing down of the naturalist. In truth, it was long overdue. Labillardière may have been momentarily taken aback by the reproach, but the general suspected his confidence would not remain daunted for long. And indeed, within days, Labillardière was back in his cabin objecting that d'Auribeau had shifted their plant press out of the great cabin they shared with the officers, into the rain. His own cabin was already overflowing, he complained, the weather did not allow him to dry his specimens outside or on the beach and the press needed to be somewhere warm and dry where its valuable paper could be protected from theft. Somewhat against his better judgement, d'Entrecasteaux intervened to overrule the captain and the press was returned indoors.

For all the difficulties they engendered, the enthusiasm and energy of the naturalists in pursuit of their appointed tasks was much to be admired. Their strangely bedecked figures would plunge immediately into the dense undergrowth. They cut an inelegant swathe through the wilderness in their baggy jackets, leather gaiters and broad-brimmed hats, festooned with hammers and forceps, knives and guns, bags, pins and wads of linen. The habitually dishevelled air of the naturalists was exacerbated by their endeavours ashore and their appearance was a further source of amusement for some of the more manicured officers.

Already the naturalists had identified several new species, including the now familiar glistening silver and white gulls with smart red feet and bills. Gaudily plumaged parrots wheeled at speed in great flocks overhead, flashing green and carmine with the tinkling of a thousand tiny bells. The unfettered shrieks of sulphur-crested cockatoos, so silent and enigmatic in the portraits of Dutch merchants, found their natural place in this antediluvian amphitheatre. The wailing cries of unseen predators in the woods at night were more disturbing. The naturalists feared a leopard, although Marion du Fresne had reported nothing more disturbing than a little cat and they themselves had seen only a black and white creature the size of a dog. But who knew what great beasts lurked in the impenetrable undergrowth of the great unkempt eucalypts, weeping jewels of ruby-red gum?

Ample evidence of kangaroos was deposited along the grassy foreshores but only one large animal had been seen. Labillardière had already, on his first day ashore, been fortunate to have shot a smaller kangaroo with thick, flecked fur, turning reddish on its underbelly, and with palatable flesh. Another pretty creature of a smaller variety had been captured while seeking retreat in its burrow, releasing a pungent odour in complaint at its incarceration.

There were fish and shellfish in abundance, eaten or salted almost as quickly as they could be drawn or described by the naturalists. Many of these bore a superficial resemblance to catches at home—mackerel, mullet, perch, salmon, wrasse, sharks, rays and sole—but on closer inspection were very different. What seemed to be a skate turned out to have the body of a shark, or the head of a shark might be attached to the body of a mullet. Many of the plants, too, seemed familiar but little edible fruit or vegetable had been discovered—a few wild brambles, some wild celery and a species of plantago which made for a passable salad. Other species were of value for their beauty alone: tiny exquisite orchids of the most unusual shapes were found, while others were remarkable for their sheer abhorrence. Labillardière had already named the vile-smelling crimson starfish fungi *Aseroe rubra*—disgusting and red.

If there had been natives in the area, the foreigners might have sought advice on more palatable foods, but they had seen no one—just the tell-tale signs of north-facing shelters burnt out at the bases of the largest trees. Keen as they all were to meet these shy, puzzling people described by Marion du Fresne, d'Entrecasteaux knew they could not wait long in this southern refuge. Certainly no one was anxious to exchange these sheltered shores with their abundant safe anchorages, dense forests and fertile waters for the unknown hazards of the open ocean and coral seas. But their main task still lay ahead of them—to chart the uncharted southern coast of Australia, discover any as yet undiscovered Pacific isles and above all, find Lapérouse.

D'Entrecasteaux's brow furrowed as he thought of Lapérouse. The careers of the two men had run very much in parallel, and d'Entrecasteaux bore no grudge that the accomplished Lapérouse had taken his first command a good six years before himself, despite being three years his junior. Both men had recognised in each other a fundamental character to which spite and vitriol were foreign. D'Entrecasteaux, as the newly appointed Director of Ports and Arsenals, had taken great pleasure in assisting Fleurieu to organise Lapérouse's expedition. And he had greatly regretted having missed Lapérouse by just a few days in China, despite having been able to send on fresh orders and men in his faster sister ship.

Lapérouse's words about the disaster at Port des Français still haunted d'Entrecasteaux. 'On that melancholy occasion I lost the only relation I had in the many, a young man, who of all those who accompanied me in my voyage, appeared to possess talents the most happily adapted to his profession. He held in my affections the place of a son; nor has any event in my life so deeply affected me.' D'Entrecasteaux knew the pain of failing in a duty of care. He too had had a nephew once. His nephew had fallen not into death, but into a disgrace for which d'Entrecasteaux felt at least partly responsible. If he had only taken more care with the boy, if he had only offered more guidance, if only he had been there . . .

The general stretched at his desk, wincing slightly. At fifty-seven, he was too old to be doing battle with the wrath of the Southern Ocean. He wondered if Lapérouse was feeling his age too and rather hoped he was, for that at least would offer some thin hope that he was still alive. In his heart, the general knew that the odds of survival were not great for any of them—least of all Lapérouse.

He spread the large-scale chart of the Pacific Ocean across the desk, retracing with his finger Lapérouse's last-known movements. The final despatch from Botany Bay had outlined his intention to return to the Friendly Islands, New Caledonia and Santa Cruz before seeking an alternative route between New Guinea and New Holland. He had departed in July 1788. D'Entrecasteaux frowned. That was late in the season and the south-easterly trade winds would have been squally. Surely Lapérouse would have beaten south as long as possible before allowing the trade winds to drive him north. D'Entrecasteaux tracked an imaginary path east across the Pacific. But if the trade winds had been fierce, Lapérouse would have been driven north no matter what. The general spread his fingers north as if to encompass all possible trajectories of the ill-fated expedition. A thousand islands lay scattered in his path, littering a million square miles of ocean. Even assuming the ships had not been sunk mid-ocean by foul weather—even assuming they had landed and left some trace of their passing—the probability of finding them in this coral labyrinth was slim indeed. Slimmer still was the chance of finding any survivors.

Elisabeth-Paul-Edouard de Rossel

Santa Cruz Islands, South Pacific

19 May 1793

Lieutenant Rossel had the deck. They had been searching the Santa Cruz archipelago for some days now, tacking back and forth through the myriad small islands. He raised his eyeglass, scrunching his face tightly with his mouth slightly ajar, to focus on the closest island. The humid wind teased his already thinning hair and brushed against his sweating skin like a mocking slattern.

The island presented an inscrutable uniformity; impenetrable green blanketed it from shore to rocky shore. Fragile thatched huts perched on the very edge of the forest with small pirogues pulled up alongside as if ready for a hasty departure. The brisk breeze drove waves foaming against the outer reef, preventing the ship from approaching too closely. The island yielded no secrets.

Rossel turned his attention to the cluster of pirogues chasing gamely in their wake, their triangular sails peaked like devil's horns. The islanders in these parts were neither treacherous nor friendly, neither timorous nor aggressive. However, his commander, d'Entrecasteaux, took no chances and was ready to demonstrate the destructive force of French cannon fire. He had no wish to suffer the fate of Marion du Fresne, Cook or de Langle.

Yet an impressive show of force must be balanced against the need for food, water and information. It did not help to scare the locals witless as they had in the Admiralty Islands. The general's first rocket there had been met by a stunned silence, then the sudden eruption of sparks overhead caused mass panic as the flotilla of islanders fled for the safety of

Elisabeth-Paul-Edouard de Rossel was born into a noble family on 11 September 1765. He was described by fellow officers as a short, round, ugly man, but good-natured enough to accept his colleagues' teasing. He began the d'Entrecasteaux expedition as lieutenant, taking command of the Recherche after the death of Huon de Kermadec, and then command of the expedition after the deaths of d'Entrecasteaux and d'Auribeau. After a brief imprisonment on Java, he attempted to return to France with the expedition's papers and collections on a Dutch merchant ship but was captured by the English and imprisoned for seven years. Staunchly royalist and loyal to France, Rossel seems to have lacked confidence in his own ability to command but found a comfortable career in naval administration. For Rossel, the expedition was probably a necessary hurdle in his naval career, one he was pleased to survive unscathed. Rossel completed the official narrative of the voyage from the journals of d'Entrecasteaux and other officers. He became a Rear Admiral and Director of the Hydrographic Office. He was a member of the Academy of Sciences and the Bureau of Longitude. He died unexpectedly in 1829 while attempting to muster support for Dumont d'Urville's recently returned expedition.

the shore. In an effort to appease, the general then gently drifted a small raft with a paper lantern towards the terrified villagers. In the calm weather, the candle stayed alight for two hours while the unfortunate souls lit fires along the shore and chanted angrily to repel the malevolent apparition. D'Entrecasteaux had been most disgruntled by his lack of success but had been unable to contain the hilarity of his crew.

The natives of Santa Cruz were made of sterner stuff. The first salvo was greeted with applause and whoops of delight so a second was provided for their pleasure. An amicable, if wary, trade for trinkets and weaponry soon followed—arrows with one ship (tips removed) and bows with the other. But there was no trace of French artefacts, no evidence that a French ship had passed this way, no sign of the missing expedition.

Rossel lowered his eyeglass and pursed his mouth in habitual disapproval. The savages here struck him as sombre and ugly. They had none of the grace or flirtatious beauty (which Rossel admired from afar) of the Otaheetian women. The women here dressed with decorum, with skirts to the knee and their heads and bodies covered with cloths. The men never smiled, never laughed. Rossel could not trust them and was anxious to be gone. Their sullen aspect was all the more repellent for its contrast with the open good-natured disposition of the people of Van Diemen's Land, in whose company they had so recently passed several weeks.

Naturally they first suspected the natives of Van Diemen's Land of foul acts of cannibalism, but closer acquaintance revealed a gentle, intelligent people interested only in their visitors for themselves. Their curiosity was untainted by any desire for acquisition. They had little interest in retaining the trinkets offered to them, accepting only those implements whose immediate use could be demonstrated. They mastered the axe, saw and fish-hooks rapidly and with skill, and enthusiastically lit fires with the magnifying glass.

Contrary to the licentious habits of many savages, the Van Diemenians showed no signs of sharing wives, each man being quite clear as to the children and woman for whom he took responsibility. Their affection for each other was manifest. Fathers played tenderly with their children, reprimanding them firmly but lovingly and drying their tears with caresses. The young women were both shy and modest despite their nakedness, thus forestalling the indiscretions that gave rise to animosity between sailors and natives in other parts.

As Rossel conscientiously noted the behaviour and habits of these primitives he couldn't help but notice their amused expressions as they observed him. They hid their smiles behind their hands and stifled their laughter, but could not disguise the merriment in their eyes. Their perceptive wit discomfited Rossel, for all he was accustomed to being the subject of jest among his own kind. The natives teased all the sailors for their collections of rocks and shells, marvelled at their smooth skins and youthfulness, and insistently delved into their privacy, astonished as they discovered not a single woman among them. They watched, fascinated, as the sailors carefully braided and decorated each other's hair with ribbons. Their men laughed when the Frenchmen asked why they allowed their womenfolk to do all the work, diving for shellfish even in the freezing waters. The native men sat back and ate, watching the Frenchmen do all the 'women's work' themselves.

With more discretion, the natives might have seen a Frenchwoman. The commander's steward had been keen to meet these alien people, but on hearing of their boldness, suddenly changed heart. The officers raised their eyebrows and smirked, but kept their insinuations to themselves. As long as the steward did 'his' work, the commander condoned no further enquiries into this 'Louis' Girardin's past. Besides, the steward had already fought one duel with a sailor who accused him of being a woman and no one wanted to be challenged to another.

Rossel did not approve of such blatant disregard for regulations. Absent-mindedly smoothing the crumpled lapels of his once-smart red uniform, Rossel drew himself as tall as his lack of stature would allow and stalked portentously across the poop. At twenty-seven he had occupied his position of *lieutenant de vaisseau* for just three years. This expedition afforded excellent opportunities for advancement. As third in charge, he was often in a position of authority, particularly when the captain was indisposed. Even General d'Entrecasteaux had recognised his talents, asking him to assume responsibility for the astronomical surveys.

The expedition's astronomer had disembarked at Cape Town and it had been no great loss: Rossel had taken over his duties with conscientious satisfaction. Pity that some of the other *savants* had not followed through with their threats to leave at the same time. Some of these civilians acted as though the expedition was purely for their personal benefit, that their collections were their own. The rumour that the naturalist Labillardière intended to publish his own journal of the voyage on their return to France had greatly displeased d'Entrecasteaux. He reminded the *savants* that this was not a private collecting expedition. All collections and all journals were to be handed to the commander at the end of the journey, to be sent to the Minister of Marine, as His Majesty the King's representative. Like Lapérouse's voyage, this was a royal expedition, sent out under royal decree. It would be the general's task to edit the official narrative of the journey and oversee the compilation of the accompanying atlases of scientific work—ecological, botanical and cartographic. At Cape Town the remaining *savants* seethed, but stayed.

But today even Rossel found his enthusiasm for the tasks at hand waning. They had passed this way before as they criss-crossed the islands of the Pacific in their vain search for Lapérouse. What little hope they had of finding any trace seemed to disappear after their visit to Santa Cruz. Few items of European origin were seen and there seemed no reason to suspect that Lapérouse had been this way before them. After so many months at sea, illness and injury were beginning to take their toll on the crew. The dreaded scurvy had finally appeared, with several men stricken in the last few weeks. Fresh water was short, the wine was soured, the flour over-heated and their provisions were all but exhausted. They were all on half rations, even the commander at his age and in his poor health. Rossel admired his self-sacrifice but doubted his wisdom. Without d'Entrecasteaux, the expedition would be left like children without a father. They were still reeling from the death not two weeks ago of Huon de Kermadec, which had left him, Rossel, in charge of the *Recherche*. The uncom-promising and often sickly d'Auribeau was hardly the man to unite a disparate and divided expedition. Rossel shuddered to think what would happen if they lost d'Entrecasteaux. For all their sakes, it was imperative that they make Java soon.

Rossel turned his back on the receding islands, frowning anxiously at the newly shouldered responsibilities of com-mand, as the distant peaks of the newly named, but unex-plored, Recherche Island disappeared over the horizon. There was nothing to be found here.

Unknown Sailor

Recherche Island, Santa Cruz Group

19 May 1793

The sailor sitting on the shoreline on the far side of the island was unaware of this latest change to the name of his refuge. He had called this place many things in the years he had been here, few of them as pleasant as Recherche Island. The natives called it Vanikoro. It was his prison, his torment—his own Botany Bay, patrolled by waters writhing with black and yellow seasnakes.

The man's appearance gave little indication of who he was or what he had been, the shredded remnants of his clothes might equally have belonged to an aristocratic officer or to the commonest of peasant sailors. Nothing remained of his role in the Lapérouse expedition. He had long since lost or discarded any pretence of rank or status. A relic now, he sat on the shore, aimlessly throwing pebbles into the water. His thin legs folded in front of him, he soon lost enthusiasm for his half-hearted sport and sank his emaciated cheeks onto his bony knees.

He gazed hopelessly at the horizon. How long had they been here, wrecked on this abandoned isle? Two years? Three years? Four? The days passed without change. Each evening the sun abandoned its fierce task with sudden negligence, plunging him helplessly into darkness. No gentle evening extended its grey light to indicate the approaching night. No soft dawn whispered her tender greeting to wake him from his slumbers. There was only light and dark. The brilliance of the white sands and crystal waters blinded those who hopefully, helplessly scanned the horizon. The endless dark

Most of the sailors on the Lapérouse expedition were from coastal towns in Bretagne. Descended from generations of sailors, pirates and fishermen, these Celtic Bretons retained their own distinctive language, culture and traditions. Nearly all were in their twenties, but even the youngest would have had more sea-going experience than their junior officers. Although food and conditions on board were poor, French sailors did better than their English counterparts with corporal punishment being rare. Sea-life was a potent mix of fear, excitement and boredom. Sickness, shipwreck and savages were common causes of deaths, yet veterans were proud of their Pacific experiences, absorbing local words and displaying their tattoos. Song, dance and decoration were important parts of daily ritual. They spent hours plaiting each other's hair, decorating their clothes and carving trinkets and mementos. Of those who survived the shipwreck on Vanikoro in 1788, some were killed by natives. The remainder left several months later on a boat they had built. Some sources claim that two Frenchmen remained on the island and so it is possible that one might have been present when the d'Entrecasteaux expedition sailed past in 1793.

'Indigofera australis'
Austral Indigo
(Indigofera australis)

'Potoroo White'
Long-nosed Potoroo
(*Potorous tridactylus*)

1. 'Sillago ponctué' King George Whiting (*Sillaginodes punctata*)

2. 'Sillago de Bass' School Whiting (*Sillago bassensis*)

3. 'Ambasse de Dussumier' Malabar Glassfish (*Ambassis dussumieri*)

4. 'Apogon orbiculaire' Orbiculate Cardinalfish (*Sphaeramia orbicularis*)

5. 'Apogon à nageoires roses' Ring-tailed Cardinalfish (*Apogon aureus*)

'Pirogue des Îles de Vanikoro à la Voile'
Vanikoran Outriggers

verdure of the omnipotent forests rejected them mercilessly, pushing them to the shore, to the edge of the world. No seasons—no spring, summer, autumn or winter. There was only rain and more rain. Feeding the forest as they fed the insects it harboured. Feeding the fevers that had claimed so many of them since their arrival here.

He could barely remember the terror of the wreck, the storm that had descended on them with sudden, savage fury. Water, air, water, air, wreckage, screams, coral, sand. Nothing. Memories drifted back to him of his slow recovery, sheltered in a makeshift hut on the edge of the bay, while those who were stronger retrieved wreckage from their ships and repaired the yawl that had washed up on the beach. The healthiest had left in the yawl to find help, to send back a rescue party for the remainder, the last survivors of the once-great expedition of Lapérouse. For a little while, a cheerful hope had imbued the survivors, despite their quiet solitude.

But they were not alone on this wretched island. The natives visited, furtively at first, then with increasing confidence as the weakness of the intruders became apparent. A small supply of ammunition and weapons kept them from brazen attack. Sometimes the natives came as friends, sometimes as foes, offended by some unknown transgression of laws the sailors could not begin to comprehend. Murder was soon added to the tally of deaths from disease and hunger. Perhaps death was a mercy. Only his longing for France, for his homeland, for his wife and family kept him from seeking its solicitude.

A white flash on the horizon caught the sailor's attention. He struggled to rekindle the ember of hope that flickered erratically in his heart. Maybe this day, maybe this hour, a French ship lay just over the horizon, on its way to rescue them. The ember glowed faintly, but the familiar fantasy had lost its potency. Helpless even to control his own imaginings, the ship receded in the sailor's mind, sailing off into the distance, unknowing and unaware. Despair washed over the castaway like great waves from the endless ocean that imprisoned him.

Alone, alone, all all alone,
Alone on the wide wide Sea;
And Christ would take no pity on
My soul in agony.

The many men so beautiful,
And they all dead did lie!
And a million million slimy things
Liv'd on—and so did I.

Joseph Banks

Soho Square, London

4 August 1796

Joseph Banks was born into a wealthy family in 1743 near London and inherited his fortune at an early age. With the confidence and self-assurance of the seriously rich, Banks attended Oxford before pursuing botanical interests in Newfoundland and Labrador. He was made a Fellow of the Royal Society in 1766 before undertaking the traditional 'gentleman's tour' in the grand form of a voyage around the world with James Cook (1768–71). His sexual exploits in the Pacific were widely lampooned, but he remained an impressive, yet approachable, figure in international science. He travelled around Iceland in 1772. Banks married in 1779 and lived with his wife and eccentric sister Sarah. Banks became a patron of the sciences, particularly interested in both Australia and botany. He was President of the Royal Society from 1778 to 1820 and helped found the Kew Botanic Gardens. He maintained an extensive network of scientific colleagues and was a great supporter of French science. He was granted a baronetcy in 1781, a KCB in 1795 and became a Privy Counsellor in 1797. His weight and gout caused him great discomfort with advancing age and he became paralysed in 1806; he died in 1820.

The cheerful buzz of conversation receded down the corridor as the last of his morning guests departed, replete with coffee, rolls and the latest volume from the French Academy—or *Institut National*, as it was now known. At last Banks could turn his attention to the delicate correspondence 'to the French naturalist Labillardière' with which he had been occupied for the last few months. The whole situation placed him in a very awkward position. There was no doubt about what had to be done, but how to achieve it was testing his powers of diplomacy to their limits.

Soho Square
9 June 1796

Sir,
    I have spoken to different members of our administration on the subject of restoring the Collections made by you & your Companions in your late voyage, & have had the pleasure of Finding them much inclind to acquiesce in my opinion of the Propriety of doing so. I was Promisd to be made acquainted with the Determination of the Cabinet on the subject last Sunday, but owing to the pressure of other business it has not yet been taken into Consideration.

I am confident I should before this time have been empowerd to Restore them had not an application been made for them in the name of the Brother of the Late king of France. I have combated this claim with all diligence, and I hope not without success.

Whatever the event may be, & I entertain Good hopes that it will be Ultimately favorable, rest assurd of my unwearied Diligence. That the science of two Nations may be at Peace while their Politics are at war is an axiom we have Learned from your Protection to Capt. Cook, & surely nothing is so likely to Abate the unjustifiable Rancour that Politicians frequently entertain against Each other as to See Harmony and good will Prevail Among their Brethren who cultivate Science.

Believe me, Sir
with Real Esteem and Regard,
Your Faithful Hble Servant,
Jos: Banks

Banks shifted his weight in his chair, his arms shaking slightly from the effort. His swollen, gout-ridden legs gave him no relief, no matter how comfortable his surroundings. The warm light of the midsummer air streamed in through the large south-facing windows, brightening the room despite its walls being crowded with books and portraits. Large desks took advantage of the light under the windows, piled with neat stacks of papers and books indicative of a multitude of well-organised projects. A plethora of knick-knacks and ornaments adorned the window ledge and mantelpiece, evidence of a life well travelled and a sister who shared his enthusiasm for collections. A small fire crackled cheerfully in the fireplace, despite the warmth of the season. The room generally had a well-kept and well-lived-in air. Like its inhabitant, the room's undeniably grand and impressive proportions were softened by an aura of warmth and welcome.

And indeed, this room had welcomed a great many people and still more found comfort and succour in the vast library and museum surrounding his inner sanctum. The outer rooms were opened each morning to whomsoever felt need of their resources. Fires were lit in every room and tea and coffee provided to sustain the intellectual pursuits of his visitors. Whether the sons of princes or sons of farmhands, they were all received as equals here. A meeting of minds transcended all barriers of politics, class and language—it was the only way in which progress could be made in the fledging sciences, and cultivation of these earnest young souls who arrived on his doorstep was a pleasure as much as a duty for Banks. Some came from the provinces and some from abroad, some seeking support, others simply the society of like-minded individuals with a passion for natural history. And who better to provide that support and society than the President of the Royal Society himself, Sir Joseph Banks?

It was in just such a manner that Banks had become first acquainted with the young French naturalist Labillardière, whose future now rested in Banks's hands. The young man had arrived at his house, like so many others, to view Banks's legendary library and herbarium. He had impressed Banks with his dedication and enthusiasm. Even at his young age, Labillardière had amassed a sizeable collection of plants, had travelled extensively and produced work of considerable merit. But then, such dedication was to be expected from one trained at the Jardin des Plantes, whose systematic approach to both research and education were the envy of naturalists across the Western world. How fortunate that the Jardin, unlike so many other scholarly institutions, had survived recent events in France, with little more than a change of name and a reorganisation. The *savants* at the Jardin had not only managed to keep their heads, but had emerged from the turmoil of the revolution with more funding, better resources and even greater respect than before, as founding members of the new Muséum d'Histoire Naturelle. Perhaps it was because, unlike the Academy that Marat had vindictively abolished, the Jardin had not been dominated by noblemen—

most of its staff, in fact, were ordinary men from a great diversity of backgrounds.

Banks had heard a great deal of first-hand information about events in France. Many visitors fleeing events there had almost taken up residence in his library. The quiet, solid calm of his house in Soho Square seemed far removed from the upheaval and passions of Paris. The Channel, and the stoic good sense of the English people, seemed to offer protection from the madness infecting France, but still all the events of the past few years had been bathed in the crimson light of the French Revolution.

The storming of the Bastille in July 1789 had seemed just a storm in a teacup, of no great significance in itself, but it opened a floodgate of pent-up rage and passion. Poverty and hunger could drive men to strange things. Louis XVI had neither the support nor the personal will to oppose the mob and had given in to their demands. But it had not been enough to save him. Who could believe ordinary men and women would rise up against the monarchy itself? Louis's attempt to flee France with his family in 1791 had enraged the people still further, and even war with Austria did not deflect them from the terrible wounds the French people seemed determined to inflict upon themselves. The palace at the Tuileries had been invaded, the King arrested and put on trial, the monarchy abolished, and finally—to the astonished disbelief of English observers—the king had been executed.

Despite all this, Britain had tried to remain neutral to the events in Paris, waiting for order to restore itself. Some, like the Irishman Burke, believed that contagion of revolution would spread to England. Banks had more faith in English men and women than that. The French seemed almost to take pleasure in anarchy and confusion. Instead of taking heed of the benefits that tradition and history offered, they imbibed to excess the opinions of their atheist and democrat *philosophes*. And now, like the starving dog in Aesop's fable, they dropped one piece of meat to snap at the shadow of another. Banks was confident that the fever, ultimately, would burn itself out, although he could see no way in which a cure might be affected without the medicinal necessity of copious blood-letting.

And recent events seemed to have proved him right. Forty thousand had met their deaths at the hands of the mob and from the caress of Madame Guillotine. The French nation had not only declared war on Britain but also on Holland and Spain—like a madwoman she fought not only herself but all those who dared come near her, even those with the most peaceful intentions. But with Robespierre's execution in 1794, the reign of prompt, severe, inflexible justice seemed over. The growing power of the army, and a young general by the name of Napoléon, might make France's warring neighbours uncomfortable, but it at least seemed to have stabilised matters within France itself. In recent months, Banks had been able to resume his friendly communications with fellow naturalists across the Channel. Monarchy and religion may have been unfortunate casualties, but even during the height of the Terror, French respect for science had never abated.

During war and upheaval, the French accorded priority to science, which is perhaps one reason why the French would always be superior in natural history, for all they seemed destined to remain inferior to their English cousins in matters military. What other nation in the midst of war and revolution would have sent out a fully equipped, state-financed scientific expedition to rescue an explorer? Banks had not hesitated to offer his every assistance to the d'Entrecasteaux expedition, entrusting the young French naturalist Labillardière to pass on a set of Cook's own compass needles to the commander. He had no doubt that they would make great discoveries of benefit to all nations. Nor would he fail to support the remnants of d'Entrecasteaux's shattered company on their return.

Like so many expeditions, the French sailors had lost their commander. D'Entrecasteaux had died before they arrived in Java. The expedition had left Europe at peace with all nations, under an oath of loyalty to the king and with the path to constitutional monarchy assured. When they arrived in Dutch Surabaya, they found themselves without a king, without a leader, uncertain of even their own government and at war with almost every other country in Europe. Small wonder the expedition fell apart after its arrival in Java.

Banks had initially taken a rather dim view of his former protégé Labillardière. Surely Captain d'Auribeau would not have handed Labillardière, along with twenty-two other *savants* and officers, over to the Dutch authorities for imprisonment without good reason? He had heard that they had refused to swear allegiance to the new King, the young Dauphin—although Labillardière staunchly denied that this was the case—and were kept prisoner by the Dutch for a year. The ships and their cargoes were sold to pay for their increasing debts to the Dutch and, after d'Auribeau also died, the ranking senior officer, Rossel, attempted to fulfil his duty by returning with the remaining collections to France aboard a Dutch merchant ship.

But the expedition's misfortunes were not to end there. The Dutch were now at war with Britain and the Dutch ships, along with Rossel and the collections, were soon captured off St Helena. All the French charts and journals had been sent to the Admiralty, where they could be stripped of anything new and useful for the British Navy. The collections had been offered to the exiled King Louis XVIII, brother of the executed king, who promptly offered them to Queen Charlotte. The Queen had sent them to Banks to recommend what among the thirty-seven cases might tantalise her interest in botany.

Banks had opened the cases greedily—guiltily—feeling like a pirate revelling in ill-gotten treasures. The delicate papers opened to reveal unimaginable delights. The scents of alien forests, of eucalyptus and tea-tree, swept him on a wave of nostalgia to the expedition of his youth. He smiled as his hand cupped the curvaceous cheek of a smooth brown coco-de-mer. The unmistakable pungence of coconut oil transported him back between sable thighs and recalled to him those blissful nights rocking harmoniously in a royal vessel, with naked skins coated only by the warm tropical air.

Banks could not help but wonder if Labillardière had had any time for such pleasures, for he had certainly been exceedingly productive in his collections. Specimen after specimen had been duly preserved and annotated, diligently pressed and dried, washed and pickled, gutted and tanned. So many new species! So many new localities! How fabulously this material would augment his magnum opus, his long-awaited *Florilegium*.

Even as the thought entered his mind, Banks checked his enthusiasm. Every fibre of this collection, the careful placement of every object, spoke of a man dedicated to his science. Even before Banks had received the first letter from Labillardière, assuring him that he had not been a mutineer and begging for his assistance, Banks knew he could not keep these specimens. Whatever the political legality, no matter how much he envied and coveted them, morally they belonged to their collector. Only Labillardière could do them full justice and judging from his previous work there was no doubt that, reunited with his collections, he would produce some very fine work indeed.

Banks had not forgotten, unlike most of his countrymen, what a debt he owed to the French nation. Were it not for the inspiration of de Brosses and Bougainville's voyages, the

English might never have looked beyond their mercantile prowess to voyages of discovery. Were it not for the works of the French astronomers there would have been no reason to send Cook to Hawaii to chart the transit of Venus from the other side of the world. The *Endeavour* had travelled armed only with a passport of free passage from France. For the French, the cause of science was the cause of all nations— *causa scientiarum causa populorum*. Now Banks had an opportunity to repay that favour granted by the French nation and he was determined to make sure his political superiors agreed.

It was two months since he had written to Labillardière assuring him that he would soon be able to restore his collections, and still there had been no approval. Banks rang for his servant—he had reached the limits of his powers of written persuasion, it was time to beard the lion in his den.

William Wyndham Grenville, Secretary of State for Foreign Affairs, was clearly even less happy than usual. Lord Grenville's habitually anxious expression, accentuated by a receding hairline, large nose and small chin, had given way to an almost morbid air of despair. French politics were unpleasant enough at the best of times and whenever he could avoid them, he did. Politicians had done their best to keep Britain neutral over the Revolution, adopting a wait and see policy, but recent events had forced their hand. In the midst of a war against France, Grenville now had to accommodate the President of the Royal Society suggesting—nay, insisting— they should be returning some rightfully seized scientific collection to France. He shuddered to think how this would be interpreted by those supporting the French émigrés' counter-revolution. But for all his native antipathy to the French, Grenville recognised an unstoppable force in the righteous zeal with which Banks was prepared to pursue his campaign. His arguments were, after all, most persuasive.

Banks pushed the documents across the table towards Grenville, and delicately played to Grenville's sensitivities.

'Monseiur de la Billardière is Director of the Botanical Garden at Paris, at the head of his department of science, and in a country where, however humanity may have been outraged by popular leaders, science is held in immeasurable esteem.' Banks paused—the strict truth was sometimes a necessary victim in politics—'He will have it in his power to appeal to Europe if in this case justice is refused.'

Grenville glanced at the papers. France was advancing on three fronts in Europe and Britain needed all the allies she could gather into coalition. There must be no pretext offered for anyone in Europe to take up the French cause against Britain. He frowned despondently.

Banks took this as an encouraging sign. 'I fear Europe is more likely to take part with the complainant than with a nation which refuses such a reasonable indulgence to science.'

Grenville pressed his fingers against the bridge of his nose. After months of unrelenting pressure, he could see it would be far easier to acquiesce to Banks. But how could he explain snatching a personal gift from the French King to their own Queen, to return it to some French nobody of dubious reputation?

'I would be honoured, of course, to write to Major Price on the subject of this Collection of Curiosities,' interjected Banks smoothly. Grenville visibly brightened at the mention of the Queen's Secretary. If anyone could smooth things over with the Queen, Banks and Price could. He had other, more pressing matters to attend to.

Banks returned to Soho Square feeling more optimistic than he had in several months. It was fortunate that Lord Grenville was not particularly familiar with the intricacy of French expeditions or French science. It had been relatively easy to persuade him that the collections themselves belonged to the collector, Labillardière, rather than to the French Crown, given that most English collections were private rather than state-sponsored. Convenient then that this particular expedition had originated in the heat of the Revolution itself, when it was less obvious who had ordered what, and what belonged to whom.

As he eased himself into his chair Banks felt as if a weight had been lifted from his shoulders. At last he could begin to draft the letter he had wanted to write for so long. All that remained was to pray that heaven sent peace at last and there would be no more unwelcome intrusions of politics upon the free interchange of materials and ideas across the Channel.

LA NOUVELLE - HOLLANDE MIEUX CONNUE   VÉGÉTAUX UTILES NATURALISÉS EN FRANCE

LES CORVETTES LE GÉOGRAPHE, LE NATURALISTE
ET LA GOËLETTE LE CASUARINA.

M.DCCC.   M.DCCCIV.

Picking up shells and catching butterflies

BAUDIN

(1801–1804)

*A view of Joséphine's idyllic garden
at Malmaison, featuring some of the
Australian plants and animals
that returned to France from the
Baudin expedition.*

Joséphine Bonaparte

Malmaison, Paris
10 Germinal, Année 8
(31 March 1800)

Joséphine Bonaparte was born Marie-Joséphe Rose Tascher de la Pagerie in 1763 on the island of Martinique in the West Indies. She returned to France when she was sixteen and married Alexandre de Beauharnais in 1779; they had two children, Hortense and Eugène. Left a widow by the Revolution, Joséphine married the aspiring general Napoléon in 1796. She purchased Malmaison as her personal retreat in 1799, where-after it became famous for its fabulous gardens and hothouses. She became Empress of France in 1804. Joséphine was renowned for both her natural beauty and her intelligence. She had enormous popular appeal and inspired devotion in many who knew her. Passionate and outspoken, she nonetheless rose to the position of Empress with dignity and elegance. She indulged her passion for gardening, clothes and interior decoration with extravagance, but also generosity. Unable to have further children, Joséphine was divorced by Napoléon in 1809 and retired to Malmaison until her death in 1814. Malmaison and its gardens were both Joséphine's escape from the pressures of being Napoléon's wife, and her monument to her beloved husband's achievements.

Distant laughter trickled in the calm afternoon air across the still waters of the lake. The remnants of a meal lay strewn across the white tablecloths in the middle of the lawn, mingling with the artful abandonment of wildflowers decorating the table. Napoléon lay back on the grass contemplating the ladies' efforts to propel the punt across the water. His companions were similarly in post-prandial contentment. Only Bernard Lacépède, the professor of zoology, was engaged in a vigorous discussion about Captain Nicolas Baudin and his recently approved South Sea expedition.

Joséphine kept one ear on the conversation, while still managing to give the appearance of undivided attention to her companion as they strolled around the garden. Her diaphanous white muslin gown had a most pleasing glow in the afternoon light. Everything about her, from her unadorned chestnut hair to her embroidered slippers and shawl, was simple, elegant and pastoral. Hers was a natural beauty that could only be acquired through the most studious of application, particularly given her age. But today she was not overly attending to her appearance. Instead, she listened carefully to the debate—she had a special interest in this expedition.

The general focus of the discussion did not interest her greatly. Was the southern continent really as young as Buffon had suggested? Certainly from all accounts the Australian natives were simple and primitive and the landscape flat with few rivers, suggesting that it had only recently emerged from the sea, but its fauna was not so much degenerative forms of Old World animals (like America's) but rather totally new and different creations, just like its plants. Joséphine's wavering attention suddenly focused. New species—new specimens—this was her interest.

Napoléon sat in the midst of the group, always the centre of the discussion. Talk grew heated, voices raised. Napoléon belched loudly, and joined in the conversation. The *savants* proved to be exceptional guests for her husband. It was increasingly rare to find men willing and able to stand their ground with Napoléon in conversation. There were few in France prepared to risk the displeasure of the First Consul; neither general nor politician dared to disagree with him. But the *savants* were different, recognising only the superiority that comes from intellect, and Napoléon relished the opportunity to gain their respect.

In his leather boots and kid breeches, Napoléon could have been in some army encampment. Indeed, some of the men present had been part of Napoléon's Italian campaign, responsible for 'bringing Rome to Paris', as the news-sheets put it. Monge the mathematician, Berthollet the chemist and even the now-reclusive botanist Labillardière had turned their attentions from science to art. André Thouin, once a royal gardener, now a commissioner, had orchestrated a grand procession of the Italian treasures, beneath a banner bearing *Monument to the victories of the Army of Italy*. Such a procession, Thouin argued, would teach the French people 'a grand and sublime truth', that art and science were the ultimate realisation of victory and of liberty. Napoléon had not been displeased with such a rationalised justification for his military activities. 'True conquests,' Napoléon was fond of saying, 'the only ones which leave no regret behind them— are those which are made over ignorance. The most honour- able, as well as the most useful, occupation for nations is the contributing to the extension of human knowledge.'

Together with Napoléon, Joséphine had watched the wagons laden with the spoils of war make their way along the flag-festooned streets of Paris. Huge crowds had lined the streets to see the celebrated bronze horse of St Mark's, the paintings of Raphael and Titian and the ancient statues of Laocoön, Venus and Apollo. The procession had been fortuitously supplemented by Captain Baudin's recent col- lection of natural history from Trinidad. Luxuriant tree ferns, avocado and pawpaw trees, banana, coconut and cabbage-tree palms all added tropical verdure to the procession, elegantly decorated with pyramids in anticipation of Napoléon's exploits in Egypt.

Jussieu, the director of the Muséum d'Histoire Naturelle, was delighted by Baudin's zoological haul 'rich in madrepores, petrifications, insects, shells, molluscs, fish, and the skins and skeletons of birds and quadruped animals'. Lamarck was particularly impressed by Baudin's eye, not just for the bright and beautiful butterflies, but also for the obscure and nocturnal moths of the West Indies. But Joséphine had barely even noticed these desiccated remains. It was the living, breathing plants and animals that enraptured her. Here were the voluptuous, uninhibited tropical plants of her child- hood. Here were the fragrant, sensuous blossoms of her own island of flowers, Martinique. Here were the brash and bold birds of her homeland, so different from the subdued greys and browns of Europe. Baudin had miraculously resurrected her past—and delivered it to her door.

Baudin's unique talent for succouring these delicate organisms across miles of treacherous ocean, which all too often took the lives of sailors and naturalists alike, was widely appreciated at the Muséum:

> Never before has there been brought to Europe such a large collection of living plants, or one so well chosen. We are astonished that such a quantity should have been collected in such a short time, and also that it should have been possible to keep the plants alive in a single ship, during a long journey and despite the bad weather that was encountered ... The plants have been brought together in the largest of our hothouses which we have set aside for them, and which they completely fill.

Joséphine had admired the collection. In the Jardin's hothouse, she had closed her eyes and breathed in the warm humid oxygen exhaled by the plants. As she stroked the smooth ginger leaves, she could almost imagine herself freed from the structured stately world of consular obligations and returned to a youthful, carefree past. It had been a year since Napoléon had seized control of the flailing French state and brought order to chaos, reason to passion. When he had married her, she had been his entrée into noble society, the tragic widow of an executed aristocrat. But Napoléon now created his own destiny, dragging Joséphine with him, consolidating his power and authority over a people half-resentful, half-wistful for the absolute monarchy they had destroyed. As First Consul, Napoléon was the most powerful man in France. As the First Consul's wife, Joséphine's life was no longer her own.

Lost in her memories in the hothouses of the Jardin des Plantes, Joséphine's reverie was shattered by Napoléon, impatient to visit the elderly naturalist Daubenton. Dutifully—regretfully—she left the world of her past, determined to re-create it for herself. She wasted no time in importuning Jussieu for duplicates and seeds surplus to the museum's requirements for her garden here at Malmaison.

Malmaison was her sanctuary, her security against the foibles of an uncertain marriage and her retreat from the strictures and constraints of Napoléon's position. Here at Malmaison she could create her own world, inside and out. She could immerse herself in natural beauty—simple and elegant. Here she could realise her vision of the brilliant flowers, enamelled meadows, fresh shades, streams, woods and verdure that Rousseau had craved to purify his imagination. Like Rousseau, she sought only to wander nonchalantly from flower to flower, from plant to plant. 'There is in this idle occupation a charm which can only be felt when the passions are fully calmed, but which is enough then to make life happy and agreeable.' She understood what Rousseau meant when he wrote of the deep and sweet reverie [that] seizes your senses, and you lose yourself with a delicious drunkenness in the immensity of this beautiful system with which you identify yourself. Then all particular objects fall away; you see nothing and feel nothing except in the whole ... I never meditate or dream more delightfully than when I forget my self. I feel indescribable ecstasy, delirium in melting, as it were, into the system of beings, in identifying myself with the whole of nature.

It was only at Malmaison that Joséphine could be released from the burdens and strictures of Napoléon's increasingly complex life. Here she could lose herself in nature.

While the approach to Malmaison followed the formal geometric lines so beloved of French gardens, in the rest of the grounds Joséphine indulged her passion for the informal, naturally landscaped gardens the English had perfected. Around the house itself, perennial borders concealed a wealth of rarities from around the world. She had plants from every region of France, from the Americas, from her mother in the West Indies and, via her English contacts, from Botany Bay. More still had come from Jussieu and the Muséum d'Histoire Naturelle. She loved her tulips, phlox, camellias and roses of course, but it was the rarities that truly excited her. Few moments could compare with the first time tiny stars had winked from the pink buds of her boronia, wafting their unforgettable scent across the garden.

Like Joséphine, Baudin too had assiduously cultivated Jussieu and the other *savants* for his own purposes, sending them seeds, specimens and drawings and making erudite presentations to the Institut National (the latest manifestation of the Royal Academy) on the promises of the south-west corner of that great island, New Holland:

> Here all the sciences claim the care and attention of the traveller. Astronomy and geography still have many points to fix, coasts to outline, harbours to survey. History and political economy require comprehensive ideas on the races which inhabit these parts, on their population, their manners and customs, their form of government, and the kind of commercial relations which might be established with them. Agriculture has need of the cultivated products of these places ... Natural history, which has found nothing but new objects in the collections of animals and dried plants gathered on these shores, requires that the same objects be transported alive to people its gardens and menageries, and must hope as well that new researches will produce further new discoveries.

An expedition had been approved by the Directorate, but delayed indefinitely. Baudin appealed directly to Napoléon. The *savants* lent their weight to Baudin's appeals, requesting a meeting with the First Consul. Within days Fleurieu, Bougainville, Lacépède and Jussieu took Baudin to meet Napoléon, and soon found that they were all men of one mind. Within a week, the expedition had been approved by the Consul.

Napoléon was well pleased with the prospect of a voyage to explore the south-west coast of New Holland, where Europeans had not yet penetrated. As a youth he had once dreamt of joining Lapérouse's ill-fated expedition. Like many brilliant men, there were too many careers, too many paths he longed to have taken, too many areas upon which he could have directed his great insight and effort. Science and exploration was, perhaps, the path Napoléon most regretted not taking. There were so many things, so many plants, animals and places he wanted to see, like that strange furry duck-billed creature recently described as *Ornithorhynchus paradoxus*.

The *savants* too were pleased with the prospect of extending still further their knowledge of this distant continent, where every specimen was a novelty and collections were guaranteed to abound with oddities. They had their own theories about the *Ornithorhynchus*. If the creature was a mammal, how could it suckle with a beak? Given its similarity to the echidna, should both be considered Edentata along with the other anteaters, sloths and armadillos? Would New Holland be home to a great empire of Edentata, just as it was to marsupials? Only time, exploration and their own specimens to examine would tell.

But for her own part, Joséphine's heart raced at the prospect of a collection of beautiful birds and quadrupeds, flowers, trees, seeds, shells, insects, butterflies, precious stones

and wood suitable for fine marquetry. She glanced up towards
the magnificent hothouses with their great gleaming panes of
glass. She could see them already, filled with plants no one else
had seen, no one else could grow. She could see flowers forming and bursting forth in this cold world so far from their
southern sun—mimosas sprayed with fine golden blossoms
and melaleucas foaming honey-scented flowers. She could see
Rousseau's bust in the centre of the hothouse entwined in a
natural crown of glorious purple pea flowers, so worthy of the
author of *Emile*. She would fill her grounds with exotic creatures from far-off lands, a horticultural and zoological tribute
to her husband's achievements. But this would not be some
pale shadow of the former royal menagerie, any more than
Napoléon saw himself as a poor copy of the Bourbon kings.
Her garden would have depth and resonance, scientific meaning and significance in every plant. Like Napoléon himself—
the black sheep, the prodigal son—her royal emblems would
not be traditional white swans but inverted black ones from
an antipodean underworld.

And Baudin would be the man to bring them to her.

Nicolas Baudin

Sea Elephant Bay, King Island

23 Frimaire, Année 11

(14 December 1802)

1. 'Vanessa amelia' Lurcher (*Yoma algina*)
2. 'Eurybia Carolina' Metalmark (*Eurybia carolina*)
3. 'Satyrus Bazochii' Bushbrown (*Mycalesis bazochii*)
4. 'Nymphalis australis' Nymphalid (*Prothoe australis*)

'*Xeranthemum bracteatum*'
Everlasting Paper Daisy
(*Bracteantha bracteata*)

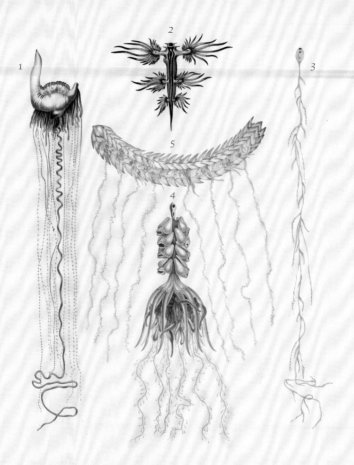

1. 'Physalia Megalista' (*Physalia physalia*)
2. 'Glaucus Eucharis' (*Glaucus atlanticus*)
3. 'Rizophysa Planestoma' (*Rhizophysa eysenhardti*)
4. 'Physsophora Muzonema' (*Physophora hydrostatica*)
5. 'Stephanomia Amphytridis' (*Stephanomia amphytridis*)

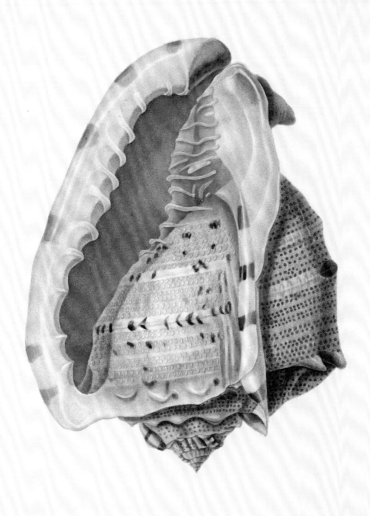

'Casque tricoté'
Helmet Shell
(*Cassis cornuta*)

Captain Nicolas Baudin stared morosely across the grey waters at the small English schooner anchored close inshore. The diminutive *Cumberland* swung gently at anchor in the calm waters. At 29 tons she was barely larger than the *Casuarina,* which he had had built at Port Jackson to undertake the coastal survey work for which neither his cumbersome *Géographe* nor the painfully slow *Naturaliste* were suitable. Baudin waited for the *Géographe* to steady herself from a sudden bout of yawing rolls before examining the English schooner in more detail through his eyeglass. The boy commanding her had made a poor choice of anchorage. The *Géographe* could have anchored in the calmer inshore waters too, if Baudin had more concern for convenience than safety. Despite the choppy seas that picked up on every flow of the tide, it was better to be offshore in case of a strengthening easterly or south-easterly. Indeed, the *Géographe* had already broken one anchor cable and been obliged to spend an uncomfortable night at sea. Rather surprisingly the *Cumberland* had ridden out the bad weather at anchor, which only proved her captain to be a fortunate rather than prudent man.

The *Géographe* lurched unexpectedly in the heavy swell, causing Baudin to stumble. King Island was proving to be an uncomfortable anchorage in more ways than one. The *Cumberland* had arrived just as he farewelled his sister-ship, the *Naturaliste,* on her way back home to France, with her precious cargo under the capable care of Captain Hamelin. He had sent detailed instructions with Captain Hamelin as to the

Thomas Nicolas Baudin was born in the small coastal town of St-Martin-de-Ré in 1754 to a large merchant family. He joined the Merchant Navy as an apprentice, transferring to the French Navy in 1774, being promoted in 1786 to sublieutenant. In 1786 and 1792 he travelled to India and China in the service of Archduke Franz-Joseph of Austria to collect specimens. He returned to France in 1795, but made another journey to the West Indies for the Austrian king in 1796–98. The more traditional, aristocratic elements of the French Navy regarded this uncompromisingly critical provincial merchant's son with suspicion and dislike. Baudin's expedition to Australia in 1800 was rife with turmoil and interpersonal strife. With his dry sardonic humour, teasing wit and idiosyncratic approach to discipline, Baudin seems to have been resented by aristocratic officers and republican savants alike. Baudin in turn made no secret of his distaste for the indolence and pretensions of his aristocratic officers and those who sought to befriend them. He died of tuberculosis on the way back to France, having succeeding in making an impressive collection, but ultimately failing to restore his reputation, which remained tarnished for decades by the accounts of his detractors.

care of the menagerie. While many could make a collection of
dead creatures, not everyone had the skills necessary to bring
living plants and animals across hundreds or thousands of
miles of sea. A plant that lost its leaves was not always dead—
indeed, it was better not to encourage excessive growth during
the voyage. Even weeds must be left, in case they should turn
out to be new species. Water must always be tasted in case
malicious souls substituted salt for fresh. It was best, in fact,
to keep people away from the plant collections despite their
popularity—excessive contact was always detrimental to the
plants. The animals, too, required fastidious care, a fact not
always appreciated by the officers whose cabins had been
seconded for the purpose of animal husbandry. The kangaroos, wombats and native dogs were fairly straightforward
inmates, but the emus were fussy. They needed lots of water
and sometimes refused to eat even the specially prepared rice,
raw wheat and corn porridge. Under these circumstances,
Baudin had found it necessary to roll their food into balls, and
force-feed them, like turkeys being fattened.

Every extra day spent at sea was a risk to the animals—
even more than it was for the sailors. Baudin was anxious to
get the animals back to Paris as soon as possible. At least he
could be certain that his plants and animals would be well
cared for on their arrival, for they were destined for a life of
luxury in the private menagerie and garden of Madame
Bonaparte herself. It was under her personal instruction that
this additional collection was being made. It was good to see
them finally on their way, just as it was good to see the worst,

the laziest and the most recalcitrant of his officers on their way too.

He would miss Hamelin though, for all he was pleased to see the back of Hamelin's officers, who did not even have the courtesy to dine with him on their last night. No matter. He had wryly thanked them all for their politeness and assured them he was happy to have no farewells to offer them. They were barely out of sight when the English schooner had arrived, hot on their heels from Port Jackson. This ship had clearly left in haste, for the crew were ill-prepared for the voyage. Ostensibly, they were on their way to found a colony in Van Diemen's Land. It was apparently pure coincidence that they had come across the French ships and were able to deliver a letter from Governor King to Baudin.

To the Commander of the Expedition etc.

You will no doubt be surprised to see a ship so close on your heels. You are acquainted with my intention to establish a settlement in the South; however it has been hastened by information communicated to me immediately after your departure. This information is to the effect that the French wish to set up an establishment in Storm Bay Passage or in the area known as Frederick Hendrik

Bay. It is also said that these are your orders from the French Republic. This is what Colonel Patterson told me after your departure, having himself been informed by a person from your ship.

You will easily imagine that had I had such information before you left, I would have asked you for an explanation of it, but I knew nothing about it. At present I do not even believe it and consider it to be idle gossip. However I have thought it right to inform you of it, should the Cumberland happen to meet you. The commander of this ship carries my orders and he is charged with communicating them to you.

My family and I wish you all that you could desire and shall long remember the pleasure that we had in your society. We ask to be remembered to all your officers and to Captain Hamelin.

(Signed) Governor King

Baudin's irritation at the letter was softened by his recollection of Governor Philip King's generosity. What a relief it had been to find a kindred spirit on their arrival in Port

Jackson. A civilised man who spoke French, was generous in his attention to the sick and who demonstrated a profound love for the progress of science. It had been such a delight to have someone his own age and experience to talk to. The loss of senior expedition members had left Baudin with a ship full of children—*savants*, junior officers and midshipmen—with hardly a grain of sense or experience among them. As commanders each of their own realms, King and Baudin shared a common bond in calming the turmoils that erupted among their juniors over who was or wasn't invited to dinner, whose flag had been sufficiently honoured or who was distributing rum in the colony.

Rest and recuperation at Port Jackson had allowed them to almost forget the hardships of a long and arduous journey. It had been a relief to get ashore and out of the close confines of the ship. From his lodgings near the Governor's house, Baudin had become a daily visitor. Dining at the Governor's house, conversing with his delightful wife and daughter, Baudin had almost been able to forget the quarrelsome belligerence of the young Frenchmen camped with their English counterparts from the *Investigator*.

They had met the *Investigator* and her young captain Matthew Flinders before, off the south coast of this vast unexplored continent. Surprised and delighted to meet a fellow European so far from home, Baudin had welcomed Flinders aboard, chatting openly about their discoveries and plans. He had done his best to put the stiff young man at his ease, waiving away his earnestly proffered passport from the French

Ministry of Marine and bypassing the translator, with heavily accented English. Flinders was initially very reserved, but with encouragement he unbuttoned a little to discuss their mutual interests and discoveries. He had already charted much of the south coast they had hoped to discover themselves. News of his discoveries soon rippled through the French ship, causing disquiet and resentment among those members of the crew who felt, like the English, that simply sailing past a cape and christening it after some self-important dignitary constituted an advancement of knowledge. Flinders barely seemed to notice the carefully tended plants and specimens crowding Baudin's cabin—he was obviously no man of science.

It had not been such a surprise to Baudin when, two months later, limping into Port Jackson, it had been the *Investigator* and her crew who had met them at the Heads. There was no doubt Flinders was a competent and highly skilled navigator, for all his youth and impetuosity might cause him difficulties in areas requiring diplomacy and tact. They had since met often at Governor King's house, where it was clear Flinders had earned the envious admiration of many of Baudin's officers.

They had been discussing the fate of Lapérouse— Governor King had been a lieutenant on the First Fleet and one of the last people to see him alive—when Flinders' attention was drawn to a heated conversation among the lieutenants further down the table.

'Captain,' said Henri de Freycinet, addressing himself to Flinders, 'if we had not been kept so long picking up shells and catching butterflies at Van Diemen's Land, you would not have discovered the South Coast before us!' He spoke half in jest, but Flinders looked pleased by the comment all the same.

Baudin did not bother to respond to his lieutenant's implied criticism, but occupied himself with mopping up the last of the gravy from his elegant blue china plate. Henri de Freycinet—a man far too young for his naval rank—was much occupied with hunting, eating and ensuring that he did not compromise his position in life by an excess of effort. His younger brother, Louis, shared his brother's faults but was a more amiable, less violent character. They were drones in the hive of shipboard activity, interested only in their own pleasures and promotions. Baudin knew these officers regarded him with contempt, as he did not belong in the French Navy—he had always been an outsider, a misfit. The de Freycinets might be aristocrats at a time of revolution, but they had always served France. Baudin, on the other hand, forced to make his own fortune wherever opportunity presented itself, had served the king of Austria—France's enemy. The fact that he actually served science, not the Austrian military, hardly mattered to such men.

Even worse than the officers, who all seemed convinced they were more fit to manage the ship than their commander, were the midshipmen who made up for their lack of experience with a surfeit of expectations. Recognising their shortcomings before he sailed, Baudin had explicitly requested that no midshipmen be sent with his expedition. He sailed with fifteen. The most expert at falling ill at the first sign of work was young Hyacinthe de Bougainville, inseparable from the troublesome de Freycinet brothers. For all he was the son of one of France's pioneering Pacific explorers, he would never make a good officer.

It had not been long after that dinner that Flinders had left Port Jackson. He had been anxious to head north, even though the monsoon season threatened. Baudin suspected the English were eager to investigate options for a north-west trading port and to pre-empt his own plans to chart the area. Where was Flinders now, Baudin wondered, as he watched a sudden flurry of activity on board the *Cumberland*. Had he completed his northern voyage without mishap and was he even now heading south again? Or perhaps west towards home? Keen to reciprocate the generosity with which the English had treated his own expedition, Baudin had offered Flinders a letter to the Administrator-General of the Île de France.

Governor King has given the whole of Europe the example of a benevolence which should be known, and which I take great pleasure in publishing ... After such treatment, which ought in future to serve as an example for all the nations, I consider it my duty, as much out of gratitude as by inclination to recommend particularly to you, Mr. —, Commander of HMS —

Flinders had declined his offer and confidently assured him he would not need to stop at the French outpost. Surprised by Flinders' confidence in his own plans, Baudin nonetheless left copies of the letter with Governor King, which might be used at his discretion by any English ship that might need it. He hoped Flinders would take one with him. Weather and circumstances could always change, forcing a visit to Île de France, and Baudin knew from personal experience that not even French ships were necessarily welcomed at the colony. It was only with difficulty that he had been able to convince the suspicious regional authorities in Île de France that his intentions were scientific, not political. Flinders, he was sure, would find that task even more difficult.

It was mildly amusing that the English constantly suspected his own expedition of having secret political motives when their own ostensibly 'scientific' expedition was so blatantly strategic. Even the good Governor King was not immune to the corrosive influence of rumour and suspicion. The idea that a ship as ill-prepared as the *Cumberland* was on its way to found a colony in Van Diemen's Land was as preposterous as the idea that he himself intended to found one.

Baudin raised his glass to his eye again, scanning the shoreline for the French camp. The ship was unusually calm and peaceful, with work proceeding smoothly and in an organised manner. This could surely only be attributed to the absence of some of his officers, who had been dispatched on the shallow-drafted *Casuarina* to complete survey work, a freedom they enjoyed probably as much as their commander did their absence. As an added bonus, he had been able to put all the naturalists ashore to camp here as well, and was rid of their presence too.

They had gone in the large dinghy, loaded with their knowledge and their baggage, for these gentlemen never moved without pomp and magnificence. Assured of making a great contribution to knowledge, their ability to contribute to the important task of collecting specimens was rather less tangible. Unlike the men he had recruited and recommended for the voyage, the *savants* selected and promoted by the Muséum enjoyed a preponderance of wit over work. Despite having no expertise on the topic at all, young François Péron, for example, delighted in shovelling up large quantities of broken shells, in the hope that among the debris someone might find something of value. As an 'observer of man'—the task for which he had managed to inveigle his way on board—Péron's temperament seemed to be remarkably ill-suited. But his enthusiasm remained undiminished. Baudin still chuckled at the memory of Péron and the surgeon Lharidon, both besplattered with blood and shark innards, engaged in an unseemly tussle for the creature's heart. Other incidents were less amusing. Péron constantly demonstrated his dedication by failing to return to the ship when required, or taking note of where he was or what time it was, even seeming to be unaware of the peril he placed himself and everyone else in by his actions. Next time Péron was late or lost, Baudin swore, he would leave him behind altogether.

The provincial Péron seemed an unlikely ally of the de Freycinet brothers. But they were united by their youthful ignorance and contempt for their commander. Even the weakly Péron styled himself as a war hero, having hastily abandoned his family and clerical profession for the Volunteer Corps of the nascent revolution at the first bar of *La Marseillaise*. Now, of course, he passionately supported his idol Napoléon. The man was a *girouette,* thought Baudin contemptuously—a weather vane whose opinions and interests shifted with every breeze.

Turning away from the gunwales, Baudin shrugged off the ineptitudes of his fellow expedition members. As long as the crew remained healthy, he needed only one or two officers of moderate competence to run the ships. And while there were many aboard (himself included) who did not qualify for the grand designation of *savant*, between them they were collecting, recording and drawing such a diversity of species and observations as to quite make up for the inadequacies of the naturalists themselves.

He missed his friends dearly. The expedition's head gardener, Anselme Riedlé, and the two zoologists, René Maugé and Stanislas Levillain—all dead now. He would make sure when they returned to France that due credit was given to those who had made the greatest contribution to science. They had only volunteered for another dangerous voyage out of affection for him and they had paid dearly for their friendship. Maugé's last words haunted his dreams: 'I am dying because I was too devoted to you and scorned my friends' advice. But at least remember me in return for the sacrifice that I have made for you.' As if he could ever forget.

A call from starboard heralded the arrival of Mr Robbins from the *Cumberland*. No doubt he had come to request more assistance for his ship. It amused Baudin that the *Cumberland* should have left Port Jackson so hastily that they must now beg and borrow supplies from the French ship that they were meant to be watching. Having agreed to Mr Robbins' request for four iron rings to be made for his anchor, Baudin watched the English captain go ashore. He was heading for the naturalists' camp. Baudin wondered what he would find there, and what strange interpretation the English might put upon the activities of the *savants*. It would be as well to check upon the naturalists himself. The weather was fine and work recovering the anchor lost earlier in the week was progressing well.

An angry woman's shriek emerged from his cabin, followed by a loud crash. Baudin winced. He was beginning to wish his good friend Governor King had not agreed to turn a blind eye to the pretty young convict stowaway. She had not proven quite so companionable a passenger as he had first imagined. The sounds of angry shouting grew louder. Baudin made up his mind—he would go ashore shortly and see how the *savants* had been occupying themselves these last few days.

Despite the calm, a low rolling swell still broke with some force against the shelly beach. Baudin rocked back in the dinghy with the regular strokes, instinctively timing the waves as they broke ahead of them. Catching a breaker, the dinghy drove itself into the sand as the rowers stowed their oars and leapt overboard to steady the boat in a single well-orchestrated motion. Baudin stepped ashore onto the firm sand, quickly moving out of reach of an incoming surge, and left the men to secure the dinghy beyond the water's reach.

The naturalists' camp was up ahead, sheltering in the thick scrubby tea-tree that dominated the coastline. Protected from the wind, the sun's rays reflected pleasantly from the sand, warming Baudin as he peered towards the haphazard collection of tents. Giant skeletons littered the foreshore, testimony to the industry of the resident sealers. From here the dense foliage of the tea-trees revealed itself to be hollow underneath, creating a low, sheltered cave nestled beneath the arching leaves and branches. On the soft moss beneath, the naturalists had piled the tools of their trade and their spoils of war. Fish dried in patches of sun, skins lay crucified across boards and jars of alcohol stood ready for pickling. More broken shells, sniffed Baudin.

A flash of red hanging from a post caught his eye. Washing perhaps? Hanging limp in the still air, it was hard to identify until he spotted the English soldier standing to attention beneath it. With growing astonishment, Baudin realised it was a flag. A dishevelled figure emerged from behind the tents, coming to meet him. It was Péron.

'What is this?' Baudin barked, gesturing towards the flag.

'They came about an hour ago,' replied Péron, shrugging his shoulders, 'and hoisted their English flag up a big tree. They fired several volleys of musketry, gave three cheers and read the Act of Possession of 1788.' He paused, looking at the flag with some bemusement. 'Mr Robbins is staying for dinner,' he added.

Baudin was astounded. He turned abruptly and strode up the hill above the camp, leaving Péron to resume whatever vital tasks he was about. Hands clasped tightly behind his back, he gave the appearance of a man surveying the lie of the land with studied intent, but his thoughts raced furiously ahead. Quite apart from the inappropriateness of such a territorial claim on an island the English had neither explored nor mapped, to raise the flag over a scientific camp was simply rude. Certainly, the English fishermen had discovered and frequented the island first—this was indisputable—but if possession of it belongs to whoever circumnavigated it first, then it was patently obvious that the island belonged to the French, should they have any interest in claiming possessions. Having interests entirely in science, he should not really care about such trivial ceremonies, but he knew how much they meant to the English. It was through these repeated public performances that the English had arrogated vast areas of land and sea for their own exclusive use and exploitation across the Pacific, with little attention to claims of prior discovery or to the native inhabitants. It was in just this manner that the English claimed half of the entire expanse of New Holland, from the north to the far south of Van Diemen's Land and including all the islands in between, on the basis of one small colony in the middle—and without having charted, explored or even seen the greater part of that area.

As Baudin returned to his ship, he mentally began composing his reply to Governor King.

Sir,

The arrival of the Cumberland would have surprised me by reason of the contents of the letter you did me the honour of writing me, if Mr Robbins, who commanded her, had not by his conduct made evident the real reason for despatching him so hurriedly; but perhaps he has come too late, as for several days before he hoisted his flag over our tents we had left in prominent parts of the island (which I still name after you) proofs of the period at which we visited it.

The story you have heard, and of which I suspect Mr. Kemp, captain in the New South Wales Corps, to be the author, is without foundation; nor do I believe that the officers and naturalists who are on board can have given cause for it by their conversation. But, in any case, you can rest well assured that if the French Government had ordered me to remain some days either in the north or south of Van Diemen's Land, discovered by Abel Tasman, I would have stopped there,

'Callocéphale Austral'
Gang-gang Cockatoo
(Callocephalon fimbriatum)

'Le Wombat: Île King'
Common Wombat
King Island subspecies
(*Vombatus ursinus ursinus*)

'Casoar de la N.elle Hollande: Île Decrès'
Dwarf Emu
Kangaroo Island subspecies
(*Dromaius novaehollandiae*)

'Kennedia monophylla'
Happy Wanderer
(Hardenbergia violacea)

without keeping my intention secret
from you ...

   J'ai l'honneur d'être, etc.,
   N. Baudin

But King was his friend too and he deserved a more honest
letter, not couched in the polite terms of the diplomat.

I now write to you as Mr King, my
friend, for whom I shall always have a
particular regard ... To my way of
thinking, I have never been able to
conceive that there was justice or even
fairness on the part of Europeans in
seizing, in the name of their governments,
a land seen for the first time, when it is
inhabited by men who have not always
deserved the title of savages or cannibals
... it would be infinitely more glorious for
your nation, as for mine, to mould for
society the inhabitants of its own country
over whom it has rights, rather than
wishing to occupy itself with the
improvement of those who are very far
removed from it by beginning with seizing
the soil which belongs to them and which
saw their birth. These remarks are no

doubt impolitic, but at least they are reasonable from the facts ... not only have you to reproach yourself with an injustice in having seized their land, but also in having transported on to a soil where the crimes and diseases of Europeans were unknown ...

Back on board, Baudin noticed the sky to the east looked threatening, despite the calmness of the sea. The light easterly winds were freshening and the clouds darkened. The signs were ominous. It was only to his colleague and friend Jussieu at the Muséum d'Histoire Naturelle that he could confide the truth, admitting to the full bitterness of his alienation. 'I have never made so painful a voyage,' he confessed. 'More than once my health has been impaired but if I can terminate the expedition conformably [sic] to the intentions of the Government and to the satisfaction of the French nation, there will remain little to desire, and my sufferings will soon be forgotten.' When he finally returned home, all of Paris would see with their own eyes the wonders he had brought back from the ends of the Earth. He would be fêted, he would be accepted back into the fold, no longer a stranger in his own land, but honoured as a son returning to his homeland.

As night fell, the easterly winds brought stronger squalls. Rain began to fall heavily in a steady, continuous downpour, sending the crew scurrying for shelter. Baudin remained on deck, watching the shoreline, anxiously calculating the time it would take to hoist sail should the anchor drag or break, before the winds would drive them ashore. As the rain soaked through to his skin, he optimistically hoped that the gale would pass and that fine weather would soon reach his troubled expedition.

Etienne Geoffroy Saint-Hilaire

Port of Lorient, Bretagne

8 April 1804

Etienne Geoffroy Saint-Hilaire struggled through the crowded streets towards the port. Men of all nations, released from the constraints of shipboard life, shouted with joyful relief. Exotic tattoos identified the swaggering veterans of Pacific expeditions. Hardened, wizened, sun-bronzed men with bright eyes and broken teeth effortlessly swung their heavy loads on one shoulder, not even noticing as they brushed aside the pale and paunchy zoologist. Geoffroy paused to wipe his balding head with a handkerchief and straighten his cravat before stepping into the fray once more.

'*Excusez-moi* . . . '*Scusez* . . .' he muttered pointlessly. He wasn't sure these men could even understand him. A patois of French, Spanish and Portuguese filled the air, mixed liberally with obscenities, languages he could not place and a rich sprinkling of incomprehensible maritime vernacular. But despite the crush and activity, there was no ill-will—the atmosphere was charged with an infectious enthusiasm. The morning air was crisp and salty. The rains of the last few days had passed, leaving the sun gleaming with the pale promise of an early spring. Geoffroy's hat was knocked to the ground, only to be smoothly scooped up and re-placed with a grin by an impossibly tall *nègre*.

'*Merci, merci*,' murmured Geoffroy, clutching his hat to his head. He could see the forest of masts ahead, but which belonged to the *Géographe*? The journey from Paris to the south coast of Bretagne had been long, but he could understand the captain's reluctance to hazard the Channel

Etienne Geoffroy Saint-Hilaire *was born on 15 April 1772 near Paris. He completed a law degree in 1790 before studying medicine and science. He was appointed professor of vertebrate zoology at the newly formed Muséum d'Histoire Naturelle at the age of twenty. Two years later he invited Georges Cuvier to work with him in Paris. Geoffroy accompanied Napoléon to Egypt (1798–1801), a journey that transformed his work but also left him afflicted with cyclothymia, causing periodic bouts of depression and euphoria. Prematurely balding, a poor speaker and often relying on intuition rather than fact, Geoffroy found it hard to rival the charismatic oratorical skills of Cuvier, whose precision and knowledge of detail were legendary. Geoffroy married Pauline Brière in 1804 and they had three children. In 1807 he was made a member of the Academy of Sciences. Geoffroy's relationship with Cuvier progressively deteriorated as their philosophical differences became more apparent, culminating in a public debate in 1830. Geoffroy's emotional instability was often his worst enemy, yet he was a likeable and loyal friend. He died on 19 June 1844 at the age of seventy-two.*

and return to the port of Le Havre, closer to Paris. The *Géographe*'s sister-ship, the *Naturaliste*, had been arrested by the English in the Channel on her return earlier last year and escorted to Portsmouth, despite her scientific passport to free passage. Yet again they were indebted to Joseph Banks for his intervention and the ship's release. The *Géographe*'s captain would not wish to have his precious cargo confiscated after all the hazards they had braved to collect it. And at such a cost, reflected Geoffroy sadly—so many good men dead!

From a total of 120 men who left France on the *Géographe*, twenty-two had been buried on foreign soil, among them Commander Baudin and his most experienced naturalists, Rene Maugé, Stanislas Levillain and the head gardener, Anselme Riedlé. It seemed like only yesterday that they had all raised their glasses in a toast to the expedition at the Société de l'Afrique Intérieure, and Baudin, sitting next to Louis de Bougainville, had cheerfully exclaimed, 'That I may once more, returning from my expedition, be in the same room with the same persons.'

They had all laughed and cheered with the optimism of the adventure ahead. But like so many other commanders before him, Baudin would return to France no more. His remains lay buried on Île de France, where his last moments were devoted to protecting the collection he had so assiduously cultivated. He had died of tuberculosis and fever, apparently unloved and unmourned by his crew and officers. The small but steady stream of disgruntled officers who had trickled back from various ports after leaving the expedition had been vocal in expressing grudges against their commander.

Even the *Naturaliste*'s captain, Emmanuel Hamelin, while loyal to Baudin, had hinted at the difficulties of the expedition, the potent clashes of personality—rumour, innuendo and gossip were rife. The only surviving naturalist aboard the *Géographe*, François Péron, had said nothing about Baudin when he called on Geoffroy in Paris a few days ago, but his dislike for his late commander was palpable.

Already, it seemed, the value of the expedition was being undermined by what it had not done, rather than by what it had. The English had beaten them to the south coast of New Holland. Flinders might be imprisoned on Île de France under the baleful ire of General Decaen, but they all knew he held the rights of discovery to much of the coast France had hoped to explore first. 'Baudin did well to die,' Napoléon was rumoured to have snapped, 'on his return I would have had him hanged.'

It was telling that there was no representative of the French government to greet the returning expedition, just a local official and himself, representing the Muséum d'Histoire Naturelle. As soon as Péron had advised him of the expedition's return he had set off for the port, to ensure that the collections were correctly transported to their final destination in Paris, particularly the live plants and animals, which would make such a fine addition to his new menagerie at the Jardin des Plantes. The distribution of collections at the end of an expedition was always a delicate operation, as so many developed a sudden unwillingness to be parted from their treasures.

Others had a stake in the collections too. Madame Bonaparte did not share her husband's disdain for the expedition—

letters were arriving from all quarters reminding everyone concerned of her 'interest' in the collection. She had already sent her bird-handler to take his pick of the menagerie for Malmaison. The thought of someone rifling through the precious material, creaming off the prize specimens, made Geoffroy nervous. He was anxious to be on the scene.

Geoffroy was well suited for the task. He was not by nature a difficult man to get along with. Unlike many of his colleagues, he did not exude a sense of effortless superiority. He seemed so harmless and good-natured that few could take offence at his well-intentioned suggestions. The seemingly bumbling and innocuous Geoffroy rarely elicited the naturally competitive streak so apparent in many of his companions. His appointment at the age of just twenty-one as professor of vertebrate zoology at the newly created Muséum had taken many by surprise, himself included. The position rightfully belonged to Lacépède, but the latter's noble connections had made it prudent for him to be absent from Paris for the time being. Even so, few begrudged Geoffroy his good fortune and Lacépède was soon accommodated within the growing staff at the Muséum on his return. The original twelve professors appointed in 1793 had now been joined by many others, including Geoffroy's friend, the enormously talented and tempestuous Georges Cuvier.

A sudden shriek of terror, followed by embarrassed laughter, drew Geoffroy's attention to a cluster of men on the docks. Something dashed through their legs, causing men to scatter, shouting, in confusion. Behind them lay a stack of newly constructed cages, with shadowy inhabitants pacing restlessly within. It could only be the *Géographe*'s cargo. Someone stepped forward from the crowd, barking orders to the men, before disappearing behind the boxes where the escaping creature had fled. The men fell quiet and then cheered as the young man emerged triumphant holding a small jackal aloft by the scruff of its neck. This must be Charles Lesueur, the expedition's artist, who had been left in charge of the collections while Péron had sought directions in Paris.

For all their enthusiasm, no one volunteered to assist Lesueur to secure the animal. Geoffroy hurried forward to hold the cage open as Lesueur struggled to insert the animal's flailing limbs into the small opening.

'No, no, here . . .' exclaimed Geoffroy, neatly taking the animal's scruff and pinning its forelegs back against its body. He expertly threaded it headfirst into the cage where the jackal fled with relief into the darkness and sat chattering with fright. Lesueur secured the cage and thanked Geoffroy, clearly relieved to see him.

There was much to be done here. Geoffroy prepared to set to work.

After four days, a full tally of the animals was complete. The living plants, almost three hundred in total, were to travel separately. Two of the four emus had survived the voyage,

along with an ostrich, a cassowary from the Moluccas, five
king parrots from Port Jackson, three coots, two ducks, two
pigeons and a falcon. Forty-five other birds had died en route
from Timor, many in the cold rain just off the French coast.
The jackal had been joined by four panthers, two lions, two
mongooses, a hyena and a civet cat. The smell was rank—
heaven knows what it must have been like on board ship. The
porcupines were not much easier to handle—at the slightest
provocation they turned their backs and shook their quills
threateningly. It had taken all of Geoffroy's diplomatic skills
to entice them into their temporary homes. More obliging
were the thirty-two tortoises, five lemurs, two kangaroos,
two axis deer, two monkeys, a gnu and a zebra. The loss of
so many Australian animals was disappointing—in addition
to the emus, six kangaroos and two wombats had been lost.
The survivors, however, were now all safely loaded onto their
nine carriages. Once in Paris, they would join their companions from the *Naturaliste*: an emu, a black swan and six other
birds, three wombats, two dingos, two Indian gazelles, a ram
with four horns and a long-necked tortoise.

Geoffroy heaved himself into the carriage at the rear of
this ungainly procession, ready for the slow journey back to
Paris. He would have ample time to prepare his report for the
director, Jussieu. It seemed such a shame, when so much had
been achieved by this voyage, that they would have to devote
so much effort simply to resurrecting its damaged reputation.
With Baudin's name already tarnished and out of favour with

Napoléon, it might be best to focus on the positives—draw attention to the survivors and their success rather than on what had been lost.

Napoléon was no longer the uncertain leader of a shaky coup d'etat dependent upon the support of influential and respectable *savants*. He was no longer the man Geoffroy had come to know so well at their camp in Egypt—a man whose enthusiasm for knowledge, attention to detail and under-standing of the minutiae, the tedium and the necessity of a life's dedication to the pursuit of science was legendary. Even then, as mere First Consul, Napoléon—the most important man in all of France—still regretted that he had not chosen instead a scientific career. 'The profession of arms became my occupa-tion,' Napoléon had explained, 'it was not my choice, and I found myself caught up by circumstances. When I was young I had taken it into my head to be a discoverer, a Newton.'

Gaspard Monge had laughed dryly. 'It seems you don't know the saying of Lagrange,' he said. 'No one will achieve the glory of Newton for there was only one world to discover.'

Napoléon had snorted and responded heatedly, 'There is nothing at all exact in your saying of Lagrange! The world of details is still to be investigated. So there is that other world, the one that is most important of all, that I had flat-tered myself I would discover.' He paused—his face was pen-sive, almost wistful, Geoffroy thought—then continued, 'Thinking of it always fills me with regret; thinking of it sickens my soul.'

But Napoléon was a self-proclaimed Emperor now, powerful enough to crown himself, answering to no one. His irritation at the apparent failure of the Baudin expedition, coming as it did on the back of so many other failures, rippled across the empire, causing the *savants* to cling slightly more tightly to their fragile posts and glance anxiously at one another.

Geoffroy pondered the fate of the remaining collections from Baudin's expedition in the face of such antipathy. At least one of the naturalists had survived. Young Péron must be supported and praised if any funding for the important work of classifying and cataloguing the enormous collections was to be forthcoming. Péron had already indicated his willingness to undertake the official narrative of the voyage, in addition to the scientific material, which would naturally be so important. Apparently a lieutenant, Louis de Freycinet, had been one of the primary cartographic authors. Between the two, and drawing on the collected journals of Baudin, the officers and crew, a reasonable account of the expedition and its value to the French nation might be drawn.

The scientific value would be considerable. Geoffroy estimated there might be as many as 200 000 specimens— there must be hundreds, maybe thousands, of new species to be described. Péron himself had declared:

> Apart from a multitude of cases of minerals, dried plants, shells, fishes, reptiles, and zoophytes preserved in alcohol, of quadrupeds, and birds stuffed or dissected, we still had seventy great cases full of plants in their natural

state, comprising nearly 200 different species of useful plants, approximately six hundred types of seeds contained in several thousand small bags and finally, about a hundred living organisms, rare or absolutely new.

Combined with the earlier material sent back with Hamelin, these collections would probably double the current holdings of the Muséum. It was hard to imagine. Who knew what treasures he would find there?

One treasure he already knew about, and longed to see for himself, was the specimen of a 'watermole'. After all the debate about the creature, he wanted to see its anatomy for himself, to see how two such creatures so radically different in form as the echidna and the watermole could really be related. It was here that Lesueur's artistic talents were invaluable. His pictures provided the living detail of soft tissue and flesh that was lost in dried skins and skeletons. He had drawn the animal in its natural habitat, but more importantly, had also provided detailed sketches of the skull, jaw and masticatory plates, and the female genitalia.

It was the underside of the female, not the creature's strange beak and webbed feet, that provided the mystery of the watermole. It was the absence of any obvious nipples or mammary glands and the presence of just a single urinary, genital and intestinal opening—a cloaca—that presented such a puzzle in a creature that otherwise appeared to be a mammal. Could a mammal be a mammal without mammaries? Were not milk production and live young the defining feature of the mammalian class? The hard and fast lines of the classifiers blurred and wavered as they scurried to shore up their categories. And yet, to Geoffroy, it seemed that they were hoist by their own petard. If physiology must dictate behaviour (as Cuvier insisted), then a cloaca must indicate egg-laying. All other species with a cloaca laid eggs. Were these anomalies from New Holland egg-laying mammals? Surely that stretched the definition too far. Geoffroy called them monotremes, meaning 'one hole'. Lamarck thought they might be a transitional form between mammals and birds and placed them in their own class. Cuvier snorted his displeasure at such speculations and insisted that the facts would eventually reveal all.

As the procession slowly set off down the road, Geoffroy hung anxiously out of the window, watching the progress of his charges up ahead. The female axis deer bobbed her head gently up and down above her cage, calmly surveying the scenery as it opened out from the crowded town into the countryside. On the next carriage, another deer stuck its head out. But no, wait, that couldn't be. The deer were both on the same carriage. Geoffroy looked again. The second deer was down low, but as it turned its head towards him before withdrawing, he realised his mistake. It was greyer than the deer, its snout less recursive and its ears more central. But the resemblance of the two heads was striking nonetheless. How could two animals so fundamentally different as an Asian deer and an Australian kangaroo look so remarkably alike? He remembered now how Cook had first mistaken the kangaroo for deer in the long grass. In his mind he imagined the deer rearing up, its front legs shrinking and curving, its back legs squatting into a powerful spring and its tail extending out as a counterbalance, until it had transformed into a kangaroo. He had no doubt the same basic structure underlay both creatures, the same bones would lie in the same configuration, albeit modified with differences in size and structure. But why? What did this apparent unity of form mean?

Geoffroy leaned back in the carriage and closed his eyes. The skeletal kangaroo morphed again, straightening its backbone into an elongated horizontal line, tailbones fused for (sideways movement) propulsion, legs shrinking, snout elongating, eyes shifting dorsally—a gravid with classically crocodilian lines. The bones moved again, legs retracting, disappearing, the tail shortening, ribs broadening and flattening, regressing into a fish. The skeleton split and replicated into four, reverting back to their original fully fleshed forms—deer, kangaroo, crocodile and fish. For a moment Geoffroy contemplated their similarities before the transformations began again.

This time each species regressed through its own life, back into its own youth, childhood, infancy and neonate. As they regressed the forms became more and more alike, their differences disappearing until they all floated in Geoffroy's imagination as blind, pink, coiled embryos—indistinguishable and unidentifiable. How could such basic raw material give rise to such diversity? Could the same basic material give rise to diversity? Surely if one intervened early enough, might not the developmental plan be disrupted and an alternative path be taken? Might not a bird's egg, with the right intervention, give rise to a reptile? Might not whales retain the legs and teeth they had as embryos but lost as adults? Perhaps Lamarck was right after all, perhaps species could transform one into the other. There was a system here, there had to be— he just needed the key to unlock it.

'Science should be founded on facts, in spite of systems!' Cuvier's fierce voice rose unbidden and unwelcome in Geoffroy's mind, as intrusive and overbearing in imagination as the man was in life. Geoffroy frowned. Cuvier had no time for Lamarck's ponderings, no time for Geoffroy's philosophical musings. With his Germanic training and Lutheran commitments, Cuvier was almost a mirror opposite of Geoffroy, with his passionate speculative enthusiasms and black depressions. Cuvier progressed through science, as he did in his career, steadily, indomitably, inevitably, in regular incremental steps. He dealt in facts, in the known and the obvious. But where Cuvier saw discrete unchanging, unalterable species, Geoffroy saw connections, variation and continuity.

Unlike Cuvier, Geoffroy could cope with not knowing, with not being in control. He was content to ponder and wonder and not always know the answers, at least not yet. He didn't know what it all meant, but there had to be some reason, some explanation, underlying these patterns. There must be a reason why species shared such basic structural similarities even when their forms were so very different.

Geoffroy glanced out of the window again. The kangaroo had her head in the air again, placidly chewing on some forage provided as it watched the unfamiliar landscape move past. Perhaps he would find the answer somewhere among the myriad strange and wonderful creatures from a distant continent on the far side of the world? Perhaps, provided Cuvier didn't cream off the best specimens for himself and lock them in his laboratory, perhaps this time he might even be able to prove it.

François Péron

Malmaison, Paris

March 1807

François Péron was born on 22 August 1775 in Provence and was a classic rising talent from the working class. He displayed early academic skill and was supported by his grandfather to attend college. Unable to finance further education, Péron served in the army, then as a clerk before taking up a position as a 'salaried' student at the Paris School of Medicine. Jussieu and Cuvier secured him a last-minute position as assistant zoologist on Baudin's expedition. Enthusiastic, fervent and filled with the conceit of youth, Péron regarded Baudin's sardonic humour as cruel persecution. On his return, Péron and Louis de Freycinet compiled the official narrative of the voyage, feeling quite justified in adjusting Baudin's charts and accounts to suit their own ambitions. Péron's energy drove a frail body beyond its capabilities, earning a devotion from his friends that disguised the disingenuousness of some of his actions. Péron died on 14 December 1810 of tuberculosis, without having completed either the second volume of his voyages or the zoological work. Volume II was completed by Louis de Freycinet.

It was early in the season but, despite the inclement weather, Péron could not deny the Empress a brief tour around her garden. The sun had glowed weakly behind grey clouds all day but the air stayed damp and frosty. Péron pulled his fur-lined coat together and tugged his *casquette* down over his ears. He coughed guardedly into his kerchief. It had been months since his last visit and so much had changed, matured and developed. Plump buds swelled on the bare branches awaiting the arrival of spring. The first crocuses poked their delicate heads through the hard earth. There was no doubt the garden would soon be looking magnificent and the Empress was justly proud of it.

It was not just the cold weather and ill-health that had kept Péron from Malmaison recently—the Empress was often kind enough to send her own carriage to collect him, especially now that she had appointed him an honorary 'Reader to the Empress'. But ever since funding had been approved for the publication of his *Voyage of Discovery to the Southern Hemisphere*, he had been anxiously hovering over printers and plates and text, instructing and supervising every step of the process. Now, at last, Volume One was complete. Malte-Brun, the geographer, had written a glowing review of the book in *Le Moniteur*, which would ensure sales and perhaps enable an English, or even German, translation. It had been such a long battle, to obtain a small state pension to fund his research, to secure financial support for the publication, to revive the shattered reputation of their expedition. At last they had made it to the top of the first mountain and

Péron felt he could catch his breath for a moment before beginning the next ascent—Volume Two of the *Voyage*. Only then would he be able to turn his attention to the most important work of all—the zoological atlas.

Sharp air caught in the back of his throat. Thrusting a handkerchief to his mouth, Péron tried to suppress a painful coughing fit under the guise of closely examining a plant in the garden bed. But his deception did not escape the attention of the Empress. Turning from the tree she had been discussing, Joséphine called one of the men to assist him. Earnestly grasping her hand, Péron struggled to express the depth of gratitude he felt for her kindness, but she just smiled sweetly and hastened them all on their way.

Péron followed the Empress down the winding path that flowed past the open woodlands towards the *orangerie*. This was her favourite part of the garden, she explained in her mellifluous voice, away from the formal demarcations of the grand entrance. The wide beds nearest to the house were clustered with an artfully natural mix of herbaceous perennials. The contrasting foliage of the different plants provided almost as much interest as the flowers, which appeared on different plants throughout the year. It was all very *à l'anglaise*, despite the war.

The Empress's grip on the naturalist's arm tightened as she began her familiar recitation of plants, their scientific names and habits. She was always delighted by an attentive listener with whom to discuss her beloved plants. None were too small or insignificant for her attention. She had a botanist's eye for plants—a collector's passion—not that of a flower-arranger. She pointed out unusual anatomical features, marvelled at the peculiar, and was clearly obsessed with the new—not unnatural cultivars or horticultural creations—but newly discovered wild species in all their untrammelled, unrefined rambling confusion. She had an impeccable memory for names, allowing her to move effortlessly through a labyrinth of botanical detail.

Péron gazed transfixed. He always forgot this—her strange ability to direct a conversation, so rare in a woman, especially on matters in which he was clearly more knowledgeable. Even at her age, the Empress was a striking woman, but it was not her physical beauty that disturbed Péron. It was something else—something about her eyes perhaps, or maybe her low voice, some sense of authority unexpected in a woman. Perhaps it was *noblesse*? Peron dismissed the unfashionable thought almost as quickly as it had risen unbidden in his mind.

He noticed, as he had found before listening and attending to her questions, that he instinctively responded as if to an equal, almost as if he were talking to a colleague. And yet she was not like a colleague—there was no sense of criticism, no competition, no lurking fear of error, no need for bravado. He trusted her—wise and knowledgeable like a teacher yet kind and tolerant like a mother, sweet and tender like his sisters yet somehow sad and vulnerable. A small part of his heart that he thought had died with his mother sent out a new shoot, fragile and delicate, into a new world.

Of course, she was also the Empress. Rich, powerful and influential. Without her support—without her gentle words in Napoléon's ear—all his efforts might have been in vain. It paid to cultivate powerful friends and there was no one more powerful in France than Napoléon. Péron recalled the Romanesque coronation procession he had witnessed two years ago, which had brought to an end the uncertainties of democracy and revolution. Row after row, the regiments of hussars, cuirassiers, dragoons, carbineers and mamelukes had marched past. The sixteen carriages were filled with various princesses and dignitaries, each carriage outdoing earlier ones in the procession in splendour and magnificence. The Pope's carriage was drawn by eight white horses, sporting spectacular plumes. But even the Emperor of Rome was overshadowed by the extravagance of the final carriage. Surrounded by thirty pages, it was accompanied by France's most eminent field marshals on horses covered in gold cloth and with reins of silk. The carriage itself was drawn by eight pale horses bedecked with enormous pom-poms as high as a first-floor apartment. It had no less than ten glass windows, providing an unparalleled view of the great Bonaparte and his wife Joséphine.

As a *savant*, of course, Péron appreciated that such displays were mere bread and circuses for the people. But it did not hurt to acknowledge the achievements of the successful and the powerful. His late commander had often failed, alas— as he had in so many, many things—to seize such opportunities. It never hurt to provide one's seniors with information they wanted to hear. What he had said about Flinders to Decaen was true—his expedition was not scientific, it was entirely strategic in purpose. Flinders' detention had nothing to do with him. What harm could it possibly do to tell the authorities all he could of the English colonies, and where their weaknesses lay? Why should he protect English interests or refrain from benefiting from the information their hospitality had provided?

And what possible harm could come from gracing a distant peninsula with the name of this minister or that of his wife? Of course the name Napoléon must be immortalised in their discoveries. If he had corrected these oversights of his commander in editing the narrative of their voyage, it was only to give due credit to those who deserved it. Certainly he would not be giving any credit to those who did not deserve it—it was fitting that Baudin's name should only be mentioned once in the narrative of the voyage, and then in connection with his death. We all get what we deserve in the end, thought Péron, still smarting from Baudin's jokes at his expense, the dismissive sneers, the belittling comments. Even from beyond the grave, Baudin's sarcasm hit its target. Just as well it would be Péron's account that would be published—Baudin's own journal would languish in the depths of the Paris archives, unrecognised for all eternity.

Perhaps not everyone would agree with his compliance—but that was their loss, not his. The reclusive Labillardière, for example, had cut his contacts with Napoléon after his journey to Italy, declaring that Napoléon had betrayed the ideals of the

Republic by crowning himself Emperor. But neither the Emperor nor the Empress would have to suffer from Labillardière's absence. Péron was more than willing to fill the recalcitrant botanist's shoes. Péron, after all, was not merely a botanist, but had a broader interest in natural history, and the study of man and animals in particular. His knowledge of the fauna of New Holland, as the only surviving zoologist aboard the recent expedition, was unparalleled.

Had he not overseen the distribution of the plants and animals at the Muséum on his return? Had he not personally gifted to the Empress the black swans that now graced her central lake, the kangaroos grazing peaceably on her lawns? Had it not been through his efforts that the expedition had made its way home after the death of her commander in Île de France, defying the efforts of General Decaen to detain them there? Who could deny that he had provided the scientific leadership so sadly lacking from their late commander? No one would deny these things—Baudin was dead and Milius and Hamelin were busy fighting wars. Only his friends Charles Lesueur and Louis de Freycinet remained interested in the outcomes of the expedition—and they supported him. Even Baron Cuvier had been fulsome in his praise of Péron's work as he had delivered his report at the Imperial Institute last June.

After noting that of the original twenty-three scientists who had embarked on the expedition only three had returned, Cuvier congratulated Péron on his 'increased zeal and devotion to duty in assuming the responsibilities of leadership'.

He enumerated the astonishing size of the collection, extolled Péron for the breadth of species he covered, lauded his detailed and precise descriptions, and admired Péron's innovative studies of behaviour, both animal and human. Of course, Lesueur's paintings also drew acclaim, but what impressed the scientists above all was the manner in which the collections had been returned to France.

> All that was physically possible to keep was brought back. In alcohol, stuffed, dried, or in diluted sodium muriate. No means of expanding the collection has been neglected. When, as in the case of seals and sharks, the size of the animals has prevented their intact transportation, representative parts such as skin, jaws, teeth or hair have been returned. The collection of living animals has involved an equal sacrifice, some of them even being acquired by M. Péron at his own expense.

No one cared that most of the live collections had actually returned with Hamelin. So far as the public, the *savants*, the Empress were concerned, it was Péron who embodied the expedition—it was his triumph. Any lingering doubts vanquished, Péron stood slightly straighter on the Empress's arm as they approached the greenhouses.

The vast, heated greenhouses were home to the Empress's most treasured acquisitions. Inside Péron could see two men deep in discussion, one English and viewed with great mistrust by Napoléon, the other French with an unparalleled knowledge of exotic species. A wave of sultry warmth swept away the cool evening air as Félix Lahaye hurriedly opened the glass door for them.

Péron nodded a curt acknowledgement to the gardener, suddenly uncertain in the presence of a rival. Of course they knew each other. Lahaye had worked for Labillardière on the expedition to Australia where so many of the Empress's plants had originated. It had been Labillardière who had first described many of these plants, but it had been Lahaye, the lowly gardener, who had collected the seeds, germinated, propagated, understood, succoured and reared them to maturity on this foreign soil. It had been Joséphine's task to beg, borrow and buy seeds and plants from wherever she could. Many had been purchased from London, from Botany Bay and Port Jackson. Some had come from French expeditions. Joséphine had given them all a home and gardeners who understood their needs. Lahaye had completed the garden renovations at Versailles and was now commandeered on a regular basis for Malmaison. Lahaye caught Joséphine's eye as she passed. These particular plants were his triumph as much as hers.

The sharp intake of breath from the naturalist confirmed their success. Péron could no longer contain his admiration. The *orangerie* opened out before him in all its splendour, a profusion of smells and sights he recognised but had never seen before. Seeming to defy the Parisian winter itself, antipodean plants flourished and rushed themselves to an early spring. Young tea-tree saplings already several metres high towered overhead. He gently pressed their prickly leaves between his finger and thumb, releasing their pungent, familiar scent. The rustling buds of paper daisies still sheathed their golden petals beneath a silver sheen. Tiny buds of pea flower scattered in profusion over a scraggly bush he had only seen bare and dry, their yellow swollen tips ripe to burst at any moment. The gorgeous flame pea was already opening, revealing shades of pink and crimson shot through with yellow. A wonga wonga vine clambered over the nearby wall, cascading creamy bells in all directions against the papery bark of the honey myrtles. He was delighted to finally see the inauspicious scrambling leaves of the coral pea complemented with great wreaths of purple flowers.

Even the tasty sea parsley they had eaten in Van Diemen's Land grew in profusion here, brought safely back to France by Captain Hamelin on the *Naturaliste*. Nearby were other survivors from the voyage—the yellow-flowering hibiscus, not yet in bud, and the delicate herb named for the Empress herself, *Josephinia imperatricis*. From the *Géographe* was the brilliantly flowering *Callistachys lanceolata*, its yellow flowers shot with maroon, while the more subtle conchiums showed only the early signs of their delicate flowers among their needle-like foliage.

A small myrtle sported its first ungainly flowerhead, the pale buds adorned with curious red bristles. An elegant arch of feathery mimosa hung overhead, the heady scent from its bright golden flowerpuffs momentarily overwhelming his senses. It was an antipodean Garden of Eden, perhaps the finest living collection of Australian plants in Europe.

Péron smiled, the warm, moist air seeming to fill his lungs fully for the first time in months. He would finish the second volume of the narrative and start work on the zoology as soon as he could. He would dedicate it to the Empress, of course. He would be fêted, not just by his fellow academics, but by the fashionable and well-to-do. The humble tailor's son from Cerilly had arrived at the very apex of Parisian, indeed European, society. His place in history was assured.

The irritating cough that had plagued him all winter shook his chest again. As he pulled his handkerchief from his mouth, a smattering of red caught his attention. A cold hand wrapped itself around his heart, squeezing the warmth from his bones. He could see Baudin lying on one elbow, wiping the spittle from his chin. His sallow skin stretched over hollow cheekbones, his long, hooked nose shadowing the thin lips twisted in a sardonic grin. Baudin held up the jar he kept beside his bed, filled with clotted clumps of blood and flesh.

'Are the lungs essential to life?' the vision rasped, laughing at Péron's horrified expression. 'You see I no longer have any. Yet I still exist!'

Péron closed his eyes against the pain, against the vision in his mind. We all get what we deserve in the end.

Jean-Baptiste Lamarck

Muséum d'Histoire Naturelle, Paris

25 December 1810

Jean-Baptiste Pierre Antoine de Monet Lamarck was born in 1744. His strong, determined character marked him out early in his army career, but physical frailty and injury cut a promising career short. He worked as a clerk before turning to natural history, where he achieved surprising success with Flore française, *using a novel dichotomous key to identify species. During the Revolution, Lamarck defended his position of 'keeper of the herbaria' at the Jardin des Plantes and contributed to proposals for the Muséum d'Histoire Naturelle. He was an eccentric character, sensitive to criticism yet insensitive to others, arrogant yet seeking approval, reclusive and withdrawn but begrudgingly recognised as brilliant. Lamarck was allocated one of the newly created professorships at the Muséum d'Histoire Naturelle, in the least popular area of insects and worms. This change to zoology led Lamarck to develop his transmutationist theory of evolution, despite criticism from many colleagues, particularly Cuvier. Lamarck married three times and had eight children. He was blind for the last eleven years of his life and died in 1829 under the care of his daughter Rosaline.*

The small, frail figure sat hunched over the bench, peering myopically at the array of shells before him. A cravat rose high around his neck, exacerbating the boniness of his skull gleaming through wispy grey hair. Only his occasional mutters and muffled exclamations broke the silence of the room. Any sounds intruding from the outside would have been deadened by the heavy wooden door. But the Muséum was silent. Everyone else was at home with their families celebrating Christmas.

It did not even occur to Lamarck that he should be at home with his own family. They were accustomed to his absence. He sat alone, as he always did, amid the piles of boxes, drawers and cabinets lining every wall, stacked in every corner and occupying every inch of space in the room. Only the desk was relatively clear, along with a narrow path leading to the door. Otherwise the room was an image of organised disorder, a lifetime of facts, theories and bemusement all carefully placed within arm's reach of their creator.

A thin shaft of light stretched down from the high window, illuminating the bench at which Lamarck was perched. He barely registered the existence of the room, let alone anything beyond. The light from the window was only a bright blur, the walls and surrounding cabinets merely dark shapes providing a landmark for his occasional forays away from the bench to refer to some filed paper, book or object.

Lamarck's deteriorating sight had literally reduced his world to the cerebral space he had always regarded as his natural home. He could no longer see across the gardens he

walked in every day. He could no longer recognise his colleagues as they approached him. He could no longer judge
their expressions as they sat across the table from him at the
occasional meetings he still attended. But his vision of the
world he most cared about remained undimmed. His mind's
eye wandered undiminished across time and space, specu-
lating, seeking patterns and explanations. He remained the
naturaliste-philosophe. Lamarck's thin fingers grasped one of
the cockle-like shells on the bench, bringing it up close to
examine the intricate detail of its structure. He might not be
able to see more than a metre in front of him, but in the
microscopic world of detail his vision seemed enhanced, able
to focus on things overlooked by those who operated on a
broader optical scale.

Licking one finger, Lamarck rubbed the opalescent
centre of the shell, revealing the luminescent swirls of purple
and green nacre inside. He had handled these shells a hundred
times before, but he would never have guessed that, in life,
they could have been so beautiful. He rubbed his finger
across the flanged edge, where the broken valve would once
have been attached to its partner. The split teeth of the hinge
were unmistakeable—unique to the family Bruguière had
described as *Trigonie* after its species' three-cornered shape.
But Bruguière only had a fossil to describe, with silt filling the
shell and obscuring the hinge. From his specimens it was
impossible even to see where one shell joined another. There
were several species of fossil *trigonie,* their triangular shapes
sculpted by a diversity of patterns sometimes concentric,

sometimes radial, sometimes discrepantly concentric on one half and radial on the other. They formed great banks of petrifications in France and had adorned the collections of the Muséum for many years, but no one ever expected to find a living *trigonie*, any more than they might expect to find a living belemnite or ammonite. Nobody except me, thought Lamarck.

The handful of *trigonies* scattered on the desk before him were not fossils. They were dead—some broken and damaged by the action of the waves—all separated halves of the bivalve that would once have lived in the ocean depths. But they were the recently dead, the freshly cleaned bones of creatures living a week, a month, a year ago. Even in death, they represented for Lamarck the living, for these were the first, the only, *trigonies* that had ever been found *fraîches et vivantes*.

The naturalist Péron had brought them back from his voyage to New Holland. Someone said Péron had died last week—he should try to remember him at midnight mass. Such was the fate of so many naturalist-voyagers that one wit had suggested a 'martyrology of *savants*'. Péron would be a worthy candidate for sainthood. But his sacrifice had not been in vain. Lamarck did not know if Péron realised what he had found. The mountainous piles of material he had returned with were raw, unsifted, unprocessed. But coming from an unexplored continent, populated with such biological oddities, even the dross contained remarkable rarities and new species. Péron could have brought back boxes of sand and there would have been treasures aplenty for Lamarck.

And the *trigonie* was a treasure indeed, just the proof
Lamarck was looking for, that small species did not become
extinct, but survived in the far reaches of the oceans and in the
deeper waters where man had yet to explore. He had published his findings immediately. The activities of man could
certainly cause larger species, like the mammoths, to become
extinct, but nature was not so wasteful. Extinction was surely
much rarer than Cuvier would have everyone believe.

Extinction was not simply a matter of species appearing
and disappearing, it was about the nature of time and life
itself. Just how long were the days of creation in Genesis,
which coincided so conveniently with the seven great epochs
of life Buffon had found evidenced in the rocks? Was a day
for God an eon, a thousand years, or five thousand or ten
thousand? For Buffon, God was just another way of saying
'the power of nature'. This was geological time, not human or
religious time. Buffon had experimentally proven the Earth
to be at least 75 000 years old on the basis of the rate at which
molten iron spheres cooled, although Buffon had told him he
thought the real figure to be closer to three million years.

But Buffon's long timescales did not suit everyone. They
did not suit those whose world was short, discrete and
unchanging. For them, God in his wisdom had created and
destroyed life five times in the course of his works—violently
and suddenly. There was no time for change or adaptation,
life was as He had made it. The Lord gave and the Lord hath
taken away.

But the Lord had not taken away the *trigonie* after all. It had survived and changed, in the far reaches of a distant ocean. This living form was not the same as any of its fossil relatives. How much it had altered to suit its modern environment would not be known until living specimens could be found, observed and studied. This one small shell was proof of life's ability to transform. The demarcations between the great epochs of life were blurred, not broken irreversibly by violent cataclysms and revolutions, but gradually extended back into the mists of time, changing, varying, fluctuating, regressing. How they did so was yet to be fully explained.

Lamarck put down the shell and blew clean a sheet of parchment. He dipped his nib into the ink, tapping it carefully three times on the edge of the inkpot. In his plain upright hand, he carefully began to print his thoughts on the paper.

In the footsteps of others:

FREYCINET (1817–1820), DUPERREY (1822–1824) AND BOUGAINVILLE (1824–1825)

*Port Jackson as Louis de Freycinet
and Hyacinthe de Bougainville would
have remembered it from their first
voyage under Baudin.*

Rose de Freycinet

Mid Pacific—en route to Port Jackson
1 October 1819

Rose de Freycinet *was born Rose Pinon in 1794. She married the aristocratic Louis Claude de Saulces de Freycinet in 1815. Rose gave the impression of being a typically vivacious and frivolous pretty girl of her class and time, but her appearance belied a tenacious loyalty and surprising strength of character. She was smuggled aboard her husband's ship the night before its departure on a voyage around the world to study the Earth's magnetism. Rose overcame her intense fear of natives and shipwrecks to survive the wreck of the* Uranie *on the Falkland Islands. The company made its way back to France, with their collections, on an American merchant vessel. Louis de Freycinet faced a court martial for the loss of his ship but was acquitted. He was never charged for taking Rose with him and she achieved heroic notoriety in France after her return (the king wryly noting that few other French wives were likely to be so loyal to their husbands as to follow her example). Rose and Louis had no children and sadly, given her commitment to protect and look after Louis, it was Rose who died first, during a cholera epidemic in Paris in 1832, leaving Louis devastated.*

The bright sunlight glanced and bounced from the fractured waters, throwing a dancing light across Rose's face, despite the careful shading of her high bonnet. A light breeze played across the calm waters, bringing cool relief from the sun and gently filling the sails. Every inch of canvas they had was stretched aloft to catch the slightest breath of air, steadily tugging at the ship like great white tethered birds straining for their freedom. The Pacific Ocean stretched its endless sapphire luminosity around them from one unbroken horizon to the other. Above, the vast southern sky arched in an unbroken correspondence of cobalt, fading into an impossibly blue paleness around the white sun itself. It was a beautiful day, just like the last beautiful day and the one before that and the one before that. Endless, unchanging, vacant serenity.

The Pacific, Rose mused, was much like an amiable person who is always of the same opinion as oneself—very pleasant to begin with, but after a while insipid, and one would prefer a few slight arguments to enliven the conversation. She fully appreciated that dear Louis must, of course, pursue this course into the vast empty spaces of ocean in order to conduct his research into the magnetic equator. She respected science as much as anyone, but such a prodigious deviation from their ultimate destination of Port Jackson was hardly likely to promote the worthy cause in her estimation.

But it was, of course, her love for her husband, not her love for science, that had brought her here, to this small floating outpost of France, a tiny pinprick in the very middle of a vast ocean. Poor Louis needed her by his side and

Providence had ordained that it was her duty to follow her husband wherever he went, no matter what the statutes of the navy required. Perhaps it was for this reason that she had been as yet denied the privilege of motherhood? She smiled now, to recall the trembling fearful girl of twenty-three who had embarked, with cropped curly hair and blue trousers, on a dark moon-shadowed night in Toulon on the voyage of her life. Gay, wild and scatterbrained. She had been agitated by a thousand fears of storms and oceans, of ships and strange lands, feared nothing more than being discovered and forced to return home. Life was too short to live without her husband, as poor Ann Flinders had realised when her embarkation on her husband's ship was discovered and she had been sent home. Flinders had very nearly lost his command after this attempt to smuggle his wife aboard.

For Louis, the risks were even greater. The Ministry of Marine expressly forbade women to travel in ships of state. Secrecy was of the utmost importance—Rose had worn her disguise of trousers and long blue coat until they were well out of European waters—not until they departed Gibraltar was it safe for her to don her own clothes.

Her elegant white satin greatcoat shone against the light green woodwork of the bridge, completely covering the high-waisted gauze dress beneath. It did not matter that they were miles from anywhere, or that it was hot and uncomfortable, decency must be maintained—as well as the whiteness of her skin. Not for Rose the dated English fashion of almost bared breasts. At Île de France she had retained her discreetly fashionable *fichu*, laughing off suggestions of hiding a disfigurement. She did not blindly follow general prejudices. She could bear criticism by the majority in order to follow her conscience—whether it involved ensuring Louis's happiness, cutting her hair alluringly short or wearing a *fichu*. In fact, there was little opportunity for excitement about dresses on board ship. Really, she hardly ever thought about them any more. Instead her dreams were filled with fantasies of how Louis and she would live on their return to France—a country retreat, castles in the air. In her fantasies they would design gardens, plant and water them, and dream up all kinds of follies.

And in her dreams the tables groaned under the weight of epicurean delights. Food! She had never before been so interested in the pleasures of the table, having only a small appetite and giving little thought to what was laid before her. But all these months of salt beef and boiled pork, roast pork and dried fish, rice and haricot beans, on endless rotation without variation! The cook tried his best to tempt her and she was grateful for the soup, little pieces of chocolate and swipe of jam, but oh, for the simple pleasures of a good fat fowl—or eggs—even fresh milk! Anything to enliven her wearied palate. Anything to break the endless monotony of shipboard life. She had feared—indeed, still feared—storms, shipwrecks and savages, but who would have thought her greatest enemy would be *ennui*?

She did her best to keep occupied. She rose at seven each morning and was served breakfast at nine in the dining room that opened out from her little cabin. She ate only with Louis and his secretary as a rule. During the day, she assigned one hour for the study of English, one for her music, one for drawing and one for needlework, dividing her time until dinner at four. Her guitar skills had improved immensely since her time on board and, in the evening, Louis would often join his pleasant tenor with her guitar in a duet, until she must beg him to allow her the honours and risks of a solo.

It was her journal, however, kept for her dear friend Caroline, and the letters she wrote home every day, that were her saviours, keeping her sane in the absence of conversation with her friends. In these 'quiet chats' with Caroline she might pour out her hopes and fears, her little everyday observations and frustrations, which she would otherwise have had no one to unburden them upon but poor Louis. And he had enough to bear already. She only wished the conversations might be more two-way. It had been two years since she had left France. Two years without so much as a letter from home—no news of her mother, her friends or her family.

At Port Jackson there would be mail. At Port Jackson there would be society, civilisation (of sorts), excursions ashore, even a house to stay in. This, her second view of New Holland, could only be an improvement on her first—it could hardly be worse. Her first sight had been almost a year ago, of the low and arid coast of Shark Bay on the far west of the continent, entirely without trees or greenery to break the monotonous sandy coastline. They had come here particularly to collect some precious artefact that Louis had seen last time he visited, with the Baudin expedition. At that time, his commander had insisted the artefact be left, but Louis was determined to preserve it for historic posterity and he had despatched the delightfully charming surgeon, M. Quoy, and some other men in a small craft to collect it.

While they waited for the men to return, she had gone ashore with Louis. To her horror, they had been accosted by some savages, waving their spears in a most unfriendly manner. The young officers, uncertain how to approach these clearly fearful and potentially dangerous natives, began to dance around and around—an activity that soon had the natives laughing along with them and, after exchanging the tip of a spear for a mirror, a *fichu* and an article of clothing from the helmsman that would best remain undescribed, the natives merrily departed.

For all that it was a desolate spot, Rose quite enjoyed her lunch of freshly collected oysters from the rocks under an awning with her plate and glass in the sand. Cancale oysters would have to strike their colours before those from Shark Bay—this was one delicacy Europe could not rival. The flesh of the enormous turtles Lieutenant Duperrey had brought back promised to make excellent broth and delicious stew. When the heat diminished she set off across the burning sands to augment her collection of shells.

But M. Quoy did not return to the ship that night, and as windy weather whipped up the shallow bay they began to fear for the safety of their colleagues, who had taken only enough water and food for the day's outing. With no prospect of water from the land, the chances of survival were slim for the stranded. The crew were unusually subdued, pondering perhaps the omen of a tragedy on the very anniversary of their departure from Toulon.

Early next morning, however, small sails were seen on the horizon, swiftly transforming their sobriety into joyous celebration. The incurably enthusiastic M. Quoy was soon aboard with tales of their privations and salvation, implausible efforts to distil fresh water from sponges inspired by the travails of St Basil and a fine collection of little birds that he had managed to stuff while waiting for the weather to improve. And, of course, they had retrieved the precious plate Louis had so coveted.

It was a plain-looking thing, just a flattened pewter plate, neatly inscribed with square printed letters that read, in Dutch:

> *1616. On the 25th October the ship Eendracht of Amsterdam arrived here. Upper merchant Gilles Miebais of Luick [Liége]; skipper Dirck Hatichs [Dirk Hartog] of Amsterdam. On the 27th ditto we sail for Bantum. Under merchant Jan Stins; upper steerman Pieter Doores of Bil [Brielle]. In the year 1616.*

This inscription was followed by another, later one:

> *1697. The 4th February is here arrived the ship The Geelvinck for Amsterdam. The Commodore and Skipper William De Vlamingh of Vlielandt, Assistant Joannes Bremer of Copenhagen Upper Steersman Michil Bloem of The Bishopric of Bremen The Hooker The Nyptangh Skipper*

Gerrit Colaart of Amsterdam Assit Theodoris Heirmans
Ditto Upper Steersman Gerrit Geritson of Bremen The
Galliot The Weeseltie Commander Cornelis De Vlamingh of
Vlielandt Steerman Coert Gerritsen of Bremen Sailed from
Here with our fleet also The Southland Further to Explore
and Bound for Batavia.

This plate put them in a lineage of explorers to this isolated place, directly from Dirk Hartog in 1616 who had placed the first plate here on a pole to commemorate his visit, to William Vlamingh who had found it eighty-one years later and retranscribed it on to a new plate with his own details added, to the English privateer William Dampier in 1699 and on to the French expeditions that had successively touched these shores. It was much too precious to be left here for the sands to swallow or sailors to vandalise. Far better to be taken back to the Institut National where it would be valued in their archives.

Rose was anxious to leave this forbidding place as soon as possible. She could not understand the enthusiasm some of the men had for contacting the hideous savages they had met earlier. Despite the close shave his colleague had had ashore, the other surgeon, M. Gaimard, now importuned his commander to allow him to go on a small excursion in search of natives—and promptly got lost. When a search party found only his shredded pantaloons suspended in shrubbery, they feared the worst. But with more good fortune than good management, M. Gaimard found his way back and soon recovered his health and his good humour with copious quantities of tea and wine. Even the naturalist's enthusiasm for botanising waned after this escapade.

But New Holland had saved the worst for last. Even as they were sailing away—just as Rose thought she had escaped a hell on Earth—the ship ground to a sudden paralysing halt on a sandbar far out to sea. All she could think of was the terrible fate that awaited them shipwrecked on such a terrible coast. She had written to her mother:

the water became shallow all of a sudden and, a few minutes later, although quite far from the shore, we struck a sandbank. You can imagine the state I was in at that moment, shipwrecked on such a horrible coastline without any resources. All my courage deserted me and I envisaged nothing but calamity. I thought that if the wind freshened up our poor Uranie would shatter into a thousand pieces on the rocks ...

Had it not been for kind M. Quoy, who came to reassure her they would be able to refloat the ship promptly, her despair would have been bottomless. But they had soon been refloated on the rising tide and Rose was now able to look forward to Port Jackson with an enthusiasm thrown into relief by the extremes of her prior exposure to New Holland.

Louis had told her how astonishing the colony was, despite its inauspicious origins. It had been eighteen years since Louis had last been to Port Jackson, and even then it had been a thriving little settlement.

> It would undoubtedly be difficult to imagine a colony made up of more depraved elements than Port Jackson, or one which has had to struggle, since its birth against a greater number of obstacles, but it was the exclusive preserve of British genius to overcome all these things and to change a dissolute population into industrious settlers destined one day to change the face of this part of the world.

It would surely have improved since then. The English did colonies so well. They were so organised, so industrious, and they did not seem to suffer homesickness the way Frenchmen did. It was not uncommon for French sailors to suffer homesickness so badly that they had to be sent back—and not just the Provençaux either—it was an illness that could afflict any Frenchman, or woman, thought Rose. But the English seemed to adopt new lands with the stoic determination to re-create their own little England in the new world, rather than pining for the old. Even a new little England would be delightful just now. Rose glanced despairingly over the stern towards the west, where the sun was just beginning to leave its long silvery trail, pointing the way to a promised land. How could Louis pursue this unenviable course away from the very place she so longed to be?

At least Ann Flinders had been spared this tedium, Rose thought irritably. Hastily she composed herself. No, she could never envy Ann Flinders, left alone in England, a widow in all but name, while her husband pursued glory and fame on the oceans. Even worse, waiting at home while he was imprisoned at Île de France. It was not Louis's fault that Flinders had incurred the wrath of General Decaen: Louis could not be blamed that Flinders had been kept in gaol for seven years, together with all his maps and charts of discoveries in southern Australia. Louis had not intended to pre-empt Flinders' discoveries when the account of the Baudin expedition was published in 1809 before Flinders could publish his own. It had been that naturalist, Péron, who had changed all the names on the maps to curry favour with Napoléon. Péron had laid claim to far more than he had the right to. At least Flinders himself seemed to know who was to blame:

> The English officers and respectable inhabitants then at Port Jackson can say if the prior discovery of these parts were not generally acknowledged; nay, I appeal to the French officers themselves, generally and individually, if such were not the case. How then came M. Péron to advance what was so contrary to truth? Was he a man destitute of all principle? My answer is, that I believe his candour to have been equal to his acknowledged abilities; and that what he wrote was from over-ruling

authority, and smote him to the heart; he did not live to finish the second volume.

The motive for this aggression I do not pretend to explain. It may have originated in the desire to rival the British nation in the honour of completing the discovery of the globe; or be intended as the forerunner of a claim to the possession of the countries so said to have been first discovered by French navigators. Whatever may have been the object in view, the question, so far as I am concerned, must be left to the judgment of the world; and if succeeding French writers can see and admit the claims of other navigators as clearly and readily as a late most able man of that nation [M. de Fleurieu] has pointed out their own in some other instances, I shall not fear to leave it even to their decision.

But then Péron had died—in a cow barn in the country apparently—and Louis had had to finish the second volume of the narratives himself. What was he to do with all those ridiculous names? He could hardly change them halfway through the narrative, just because the rightful king had now been restored to the throne and the upstart deposed. Louis had declared quite openly:

> Happy will it be if I have been able to convince the reader that the two celebrated voyagers whose loss science so justly deplores are, one and the other, and as much owing to their loyal characters as their useful works, worthy of all our esteem and regrets.

Louis had remained loyal to his friend Péron, for all such loyalty seemed ill-warranted to Rose. But he had also given due credit to Flinders' prior discoveries. Nevertheless, still the English papers gave him no peace. At the Cape of Good Hope they had received a copy of an article in the *Quarterly* crudely suggesting that his maps were 'very like those of Captain Flinders, only *much inferior* in point of execution' and making facetious comments about a geographical *mésalliance* between the Bourbon and Bonaparte families. Louis was furious. And now Flinders was dead, tended by the ever-loyal Ann, having lived just long enough to see his own account finally printed and brought to his bedside.

Tears welled in Rose's eyes and she blinked them away. The claims of plagiarism against Louis were so unjust. He had never even seen Flinders' maps while Flinders had been imprisoned—what need did Louis have of them anyway? Flinders himself had said what a fine mapmaker Louis was. But it did not matter what Louis said now. Rose knew he kept a letter repudiating the allegations against him in his breast pocket. Of an evening he would re-read it, re-work it, planning eventually to send it to the *Quarterly* and to redeem himself. But with Flinders dead, Louis could only truly redeem his good name through actions—proving once and for all that he was a master mariner and a master cartographer in his own right. And who could doubt it? When they returned to France, all would see Louis just as she saw him, as a great man and a great commander.

A shout and muffled laughter from the foredeck recalled Rose to her present circumstances. She had been on deck for long enough. No matter how much they tried, the men's natural ribaldry could not be suppressed for long and she knew her appearance disrupted the running of the ship. She tilted her face down to watch the ship's wake churning beneath her, her elegant profile and figure highlighted by the setting sun. Pretending not to hear the perfectly audible comments emanating from the foredeck, she gave one last poignant glance at the western horizon before retiring, with twinkling eyes modestly downcast, to her cabin below.

19 November 1819

Ah! what a happy morning already! and what pleasure to describe it for you in detail! After so many days and nights troubled by a thousand thoughts and a thousand uneasinesses you will easily guess that I would sleep peaceably enough during this last one, spent in a tranquil harbour, where calm was no longer an obstacle but a proof of success. That is what I did; but I did not fail to wake with the first rays of the sun. We moored too late yesterday for me to be able to see anything beyond the ship. That wretch of a Louis, who knew

the surroundings perfectly, wishing to
enjoy my surprise, had not told me that
we were in full view of Sydney. Imagine,
then, what was my astonishment this
morning to find myself quite close to a
town, and a town whose houses were built
in European style! It is eighteen months
since I saw anything of the sort, and it
was a very great pleasure to me.

Rose de Freycinet

The coast that borders the spacious
harbour of Port Jackson is a curious
spectacle; a novel and vigorous vegetation is
there intermixed with small houses, the
European architecture of which strikes our
eyes and excites our admiration. We see
only the advanced posts of a city and are
struck with astonishment: we are scarcely
arrived and ask how many ages this colony
has existed?

I cannot describe the city I have just
visited; I am in a realm of enchantment,
and I prefer to let my admiration rest.
Magnificent homes, majestic castles, houses
extraordinary by their taste and elegance,

fountains adorned by sculptures worthy of
the chisel of our best artists, spacious and
lofty apartments, expensive furniture,
most stylish carriages, horses and gigs,
immense stores; could one expect to find
all this four thousand leagues from
Europe?

Jacques Arago

René Lesson

Blue Mountains, New South Wales

3 February 1824

He sat motionless as a heron, patiently watching the surface of the creek. Dragonflies skittered nervously across the mirrored water while a cicada striated noisily from a nearby grass tussock. The still air was filled with the low humming drone of busy summer activity. Even under the dappled shade of the gum trees, the air was warm and soporific.

René Lesson stretched and wriggled a little to relieve the numbness. He had been sitting here at Fish River for hours, hoping to see one of the famous *Ornithorhynchi* watermoles emerge from their underwater burrows. So far he had seen nothing move in the river, not even any fish unless you counted a few tiny fingerlings. Certainly there was no sign of the huge perch found in nearby rivers, upon whose delicate and choice flesh they had often dined.

The bed of the river was composed entirely of thick layers of hard black granite, interposed with thinner layers of grey. Extended dry weather had reduced the river's flow, leaving deep still pools in some places and murmuring sheets of water in others. The great uneven granite boulders strewn in the river formed fords across which one could walk from one side of the river to the other. The same granite formations extended into the surrounding landscape and up into the mountains, which shimmered in the characteristic blue haze for which they were named. Just yesterday, he had gathered an impressive collection of granite samples from Cox's River, all with the same traces of felspar, rose quartz and mica.

It was pleasant enough to sit on the banks of Fish River, yet the place was afflicted with the same monotony that

René Primevère Lesson was born on 20 March 1794 at Rochefort. At sixteen he entered the Naval Medical School and served in the French Navy. He changed his classification to pharmacist in 1816 and in 1822 embarked on the Coquille *under the command of Duperrey. Lesson was charged with collecting natural history specimens, a task he shared with Lieutenant Dumont d'Urville, whose particular interest was botany. While he initially got on well with Dumont d'Urville, their friendship later cooled. Dumont d'Urville was a hard taskmaster with little time for the medical profession and Lesson did not enjoy the best of health. On returning to Paris in 1825, Lesson spent seven years preparing the vertebrate zoological section of the official account of the expedition. Lesson's first and abiding love was for birds. He published numerous ornithology books, being the first European naturalist to see living birds of paradise, and he controversially named a hummingbird after the beautiful Duchess of Rivoli, Anna de Belle Massena. Lesson married the daughter of ornithologist Charles Dumont de Sainte-Croix. He was made chief naval pharmacist in 1839 and received the Légion d'Honneur in 1847. Lesson died in Rochefort on 28 April 1849. His brother, Pierre-Adolphe Lesson, with whom he is often confused, sailed as a surgeon with Dumont d'Urville in 1826 and became chief surgeon of the navy.*

characterised all Australian vegetation. The twenty or so species of eucalypt found in the area all looked the same—without variation. Hardly any species were to be found other than acacias and tea-trees. A scattering of familiar European species on the water's edge offered some relief from the sombre greys and greens of the native vegetation, whose similarity was exacerbated by the uniformity of their leaves. Their simple, dry, stiff foliage all fell obliquely at the same orientation, perhaps so as to collect as much oxygen as possible in the hard, dry climate. Even the acacias conformed to these traditional leaf shapes, although in the rest of the world acacias were characterised by their feathery, fern-like juvenile leaves; here a great many (although not all) developed mature leaves.

And few of the trees had edible fruits. There was a native raspberry that made a tolerable preserve, but for the rest the native fruits were hard, tough and woody. How unfortunate for the Aboriginals, Lesson mused, forced to be hunters, fishermen and nomads on a constant quest for food. Small wonder they could not progress in civilisation to the same limited extent as the inhabitants of the Polynesian islands, with the latter's abundant supply of fruit and root crops.

The medicinal possibilities of the Australian trees, however, offered greater potential. The bark of many of the acacias had proved a rich source of tannic acid—a useful commodity for the British nation so dependent on overseas supplies to feed her local consumption of the product. A pretty acacia, *Mimosa decurrens*, exuded a transparent gum usefully employed by local doctors as a substitute for African gum arabic, which was dissolved in water as a tonic for inflamed mucous membranes—although settlers apparently found it a useful solution for diarrhoea as well.

Only the bark of the eucalypts offered any particular beauty. Lesson rubbed his back on the smooth satiny trunk of the old eucalypt he was leaning against. Long tangles of bark hung from the branches above like ropes and, on a windy day, produced a most eerie sound. The exposed trunk beneath was creamy white, shot through with delicate pastel shades, flowing in smooth, sensuous curves. With white branches upstretched, the trees might appear to the vivid imagination, late of an evening in an isolated spot, to resemble half-clothed spirit-women stretching their arms towards the heavens.

A flurry of tiny parrots shot overhead, flashing green and red reflections across the pool, their chattering cries ricocheting across the valley. Lesson was immediately diverted. Birds were his real fascination, despite the fact that as the shipboard pharmacist his traditional duties should focus more on botany. Although he had qualified as a surgeon at the Naval Medical School, Lesson had recently switched to pharmacy. There was ample opportunity to indulge his passion for natural history in both professions. Pharmacists, like the *savants* at the Muséum d'Histoire Naturelle, were among the few professionals who had managed to retain their society through the upheaval of the Revolution, and had successfully transformed their College from an elitist, royalist establishment into one upholding the principles of *liberté*

and *égalité*. As the College had put it to the National
Assembly in 1790, without the enlightened cooperation of
the pharmacists 'medicine and surgery often could not hope
to achieve consistent and salutary results'. After a brief, dis-
astrous flirtation with the free practice of pharmacy, which
had resulted in some horrific abuses by unqualified herbalists
and charlatans, the National Assembly had agreed, and
retained professional credentials for pharmacists. There were,
it seemed, limits to how much liberty was a good thing.

But despite his professional interest in botany and its
medical applications, on this voyage Lesson's services in the
area were not required. Botany was the special interest of
Lieutenant Jules Dumont d'Urville, second in charge on the
Coquille, a duty he fulfilled industriously and with great
talent. With the botanical work taken care of, Lesson was free
to concentrate on the geological and zoological collections—
which is precisely why he now found himself sitting on the
edge of a river on the far side of the Blue Mountains waiting
for a watermole, while his companion d'Urville scoured the
same countryside for plant specimens.

Lesson had been happy to accompany Dumont d'Urville
on this inland expedition, while their commander Duperrey
remained on the *Coquille* at Port Jackson. Duperrey and a
number of the other officers had hastily arranged an alternative expedition, a pilgrimage to the site of Lapérouse's last-
known campsite at Botany Bay. They had no desire to
accompany their hard-driving lieutenant on a 300-mile return
trek when a pleasant day's ride to Botany Bay could be had.

But Lesson did not find Dumont d'Urville quite so difficult to deal with as some of his colleagues did. D'Urville
certainly had a brusque manner (to use a polite expression)
but this seemed to be exacerbated on board ship and when
dealing with his fellow officers. Many of the younger officers
had evinced a deep dislike for the man, it was true, but as
pharmacist, Lesson occupied a privileged place in the ship's
hierarchy and perhaps felt the weight of d'Urville's authority
less frequently.

There was no doubt that, despite the fact that he was not
in command of the expedition, Dumont d'Urville carried a
great deal of authority. The Captain, Louis-Isidore Duperrey,
freely admitted that he had drawn up the plans for his expedition jointly with d'Urville. And it seemed quite likely that
the support of this famous young officer had been as important in gaining approval for the expedition as had Duperrey's
own solid and reliable past performances.

Duperrey and Dumont d'Urville had served together in
the Mediterranean. It was there that Duperrey had developed
his interest and expertise in hydrography while Dumont
d'Urville had turned his attention to botany, earning a reputation among his fellows as being rather unsociable and scholarly in nature. Both men had applied to sail with the de
Freycinet expedition, but Dumont d'Urville's application was
rejected, much to his irritation. So while Duperrey sailed off
to the Pacific under Louis de Freycinet, d'Urville had been
forced to seek his own fame in the Aegean. Here he had been
of a party that had discovered a statue of a beautiful woman

'Kanguroo à bandes'
Banded Hare-wallaby
(*Lagostrophus fasciatus*)

1. 'Plectropome rouge et noir'
Banded Seaperch (*Hypoplectrodes nigroruber*)
2. 'Plectropome à grosses dents'
Harlequin Fish (*Orthos dentex*)

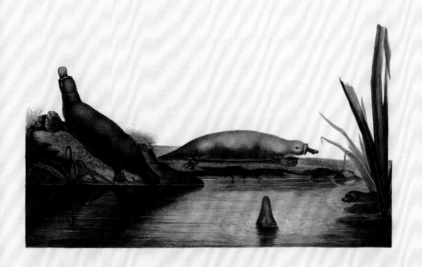

'Ornithorinque'
Platypus
(*Ornithorinchus anatinus*)

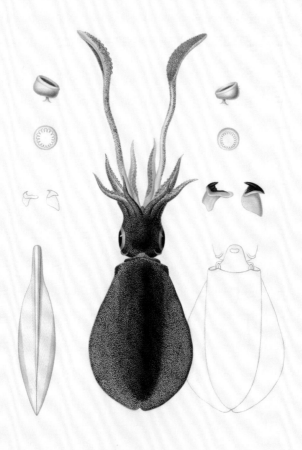

'Sépioteuthe de Lesson'
Oval Reef Squid
(*Sepioteuthis lessoniana*)

on the Greek island of Melos. Apparently, d'Urville had been instrumental in ensuring that the statue was purchased for France instead of by Turkish officials. The *Vénus de Milo* arrived in Paris at an auspicious moment, her beauty and elegance allowing officials to create a new cult of classicism to conveniently cover the embarrassing repatriation of the *Medici Venus* back to Italy, whence Napoléon had abducted her. Dumont d'Urville stood close by, bathing in Venus's limelight, and the reflected glory stuck. Dumont d'Urville earned the Legion of Honour and the recognition of the Academy of Sciences.

So when Duperrey returned to Paris, eager to command his own Pacific expedition, it was natural for the two old friends to join forces. But despite their friendship, it had not taken long for their relationship to become strained. D'Urville could not help uttering caustic and unrestrained criticisms of his commander. Duperrey was an impulsive and impressionable leader, uncomfortable in the face of Dumont d'Urville's cold, tenacious and assertive character. While Duperrey was content to focus his efforts on his magnetic and hydrographic research, d'Urville had often confided in Lesson about the importance of investigating sites for potential French colonies, a subject Duperrey entirely neglected.

For all Lesson appreciated Dumont d'Urville's endless enthusiasm for his botanical work, he could understand why people found him tiring. He was a tall, strong man, rarely put out by the most strenuous of physical activity. He had no use for surgeons and was rarely ill. He set a cracking pace on inland expeditions like this one from Port Jackson over the Blue Mountains to Bathurst. Lesson himself was no slouch, but his health often suffered from d'Urville's unrelenting zeal. Indeed it had been a rare treat, on this journey, to have d'Urville indisposed, enabling a more moderate pace.

The shrill tinkle of the parrots heralded their return, landing as a noisy mass in a tree opposite, perhaps preparing to shelter from the hottest part of the day. Lesson slowly stood up and stretched his aching limbs. He had been here three hours and it did not seem likely that the watermoles would emerge now. Disappointed, he prepared to walk back down the creek to their campsite. At least they had managed to acquire a live echidna, which even now his fellow surgeon, released from the expedition through ill-health, was preparing to return to Paris. Lesson had also captured a turtle common to the area, which had a flat black carapace and a long neck that it curiously put to one side instead of pulling into its inner fold. At the same time, he'd found a pretty golden frog and, floating on the water, two exceedingly fragile and perfectly transparent river snails.

But it was the birds that had kept him truly satisfied. In the last few days he had seen numerous cockatoos—white with yellow crests and black with red tails—each as noisy and conspicuous as the other. Just as vocal was the giant kingfisher whose raucous call had earned it the unlikely local name of 'Laughing Jackass'. Parrots appeared in all the colours of the rainbow—red, yellow, green, blue, and purple—while the trees were filled with the activity of honeyeaters—some delicately probing into flowers while others crashed noisily about in the treetops.

Lesson still hoped, on this journey, to see the handsome bird called the lyre, which his predecessor M. Quoy had described on a journey five years ago through the Blue Mountains. M. Quoy had also been a surgeon–naturalist, aboard the Freycinet expedition, and Lesson had heard much about his work. Who could fail to be impressed by his description of the splendid lyre-tailed pheasant, once so abundant in these forests and already hunted to scarcity?

Lesson's collection was filled with the grand, the obscure and the magnificent. Row upon row of tiny packages in his cabin contained the delicate bodies of diminutive humming-birds from South America. Carefully laid out, so as not to damage their plumage, were the spectacular birds of para-dise—the very birds whom, legend had it, fed on the wind, dwelt in the heavens and never even landed on the Earth itself. He had work enough for a lifetime already, without even con-sidering his professional pharmaceutical obligations.

And yet Lesson would find time for both. He would fulfil his duty as pharmacist, conscientiously and construc-tively, while still managing to satisfy his passion for birds, and bring these spectacular creatures back to life on the book-shelves of Europe. The smoke from the campfire drifted towards him as he made his way back to his companions. The watermoles might have eluded him this time, but the birds would not. To them he would dedicate his greatest works.

Georges Cuvier

Muséum d'Histoire Naturelle, Paris
18 July 1825

Carefully straightening the green-embroidered lapel on his long coat, Georges Cuvier scrutinised his reflection in the gilded mirror of his salon. The official uniform of the Academician suited him well. The cocked hat with its patriotic ribbon tamed his unkempt mane of red hair, the black feathers disguising its slightly faded hue. He straightened his back, putting one leg forward and standing at a half turn so as to best display the mother-of-pearl hilt of his ceremonial sword. He frowned imposingly at himself. There was no doubt he cut an impressive figure. Secretly he enjoyed the uniform almost as much as the actual prestige carried by his position in the Academy. That appointment had been so long ago in any case—he had always been a leader, always in charge, always right, so it was only natural that the Academy of Sciences had recognised his talents at an early age.

Cuvier glanced down at the report he was about to take to the Academy meeting. He had been as tactful as he could, but what on earth had Geoffroy been thinking of to leave all the collections to a man like Péron?

> The Baudin expedition to New Holland where Messrs Péron and Lesueur made immense collections ... did not give us, for science proper, fruits proportional to the rich materials it procured. The late M. Péron, a man with a vast capacity and an industry astonishing in such a weak body, made an infinity of searching observations, and accumulated the most valuable and the most thorough detailed notes ... But in a most natural desire to assure

Léopold Chrétien Frédéric Dagobert Cuvier was born in 1769 in the French–German province of Montbéliard. A child prodigy, he assumed the name of his dead father and older brother, Georges. Educated in Stuttgart, he tutored in Normandy where his biological works came to the attention of savants at the Muséum d'Histoire Naturelle. Geoffroy Saint-Hilaire invited Cuvier to Paris, where he soon became a professor and founded the study of fossils and comparative anatomy. His systematic modification of the Linnaean classification system enabled it to be usefully applied to animals. Cuvier was a talented anatomist and illustrator as well as a persuasive and compelling speaker and was hugely influential in French science. With his red hair and confidence, he was a natural leader and celebrity. He was, however, vitriolic and ruthless in criticising fellow scientists (such as Geoffroy and Lamarck). A classic empire builder, Cuvier did much to consolidate French superiority in the biological sciences, particularly through the promotion of collections and detailed anatomical laboratory work. Cuvier died in 1832.

for himself the sole glory for his discoveries, a desire
which the administrators [of the Muséum] left him the
most complete latitude to pursue, he kept carefully to
himself all the manuscripts, and even all the pictures
accompanying them, though he could not claim they
were his own work; and since his death, no one knows
where all his precious compilations have gone . . .

The Muséum had acted hastily, on Péron's death, to seal up
his apartment and ensure that the precious specimens did not
disappear. But somehow the paperwork associated with the
collections had become separated from them. Without prove-
nance and the interpretations of the collector himself, the
specimens were all too often worthless.

And then there were the botanical collections upon which
sat Labillardière, like an elderly ill-tempered spider. During
the upheaval of the Revolution, Labillardière had managed to
secure the return of his New Holland collections from the
English by the artifice of claiming them to be his own private
property. 'It would be necessary to have them considered as
private belongings,' he had explained artfully to Thouin, 'on
account of our being at war with them, there is a strong argument against national property.' The ruse had worked. With
the ever-reliable assistance of Joseph Banks the collections had
been returned to Labillardière, who ever after had guarded
them ferociously as his personal possessions.

In the absence of a botanist surviving from the Baudin
expedition, it had seemed only natural that Labillardière

should be given the task of ordering and analysing the vast collections Banks had returned. Who else had the expertise to interpret the Australian material? Labillardière had an excellent record of publications in his younger days, reliably producing a significant paper every year or two. His *Relation du voyage à la recherche de La Pérouse* had been an international hit (cashing in on the seemingly insatiable passion for anything—fictional or factual—relating to the famously missing sea-captain). His two-volume *Novae Hollandiae plantarum specimen* had appeared promptly just a few short years after his return to France—a most comprehensive work, if a little dependent upon the composition of fascicules. Still, it had beaten the official narrative of the voyage to publication by several years. There seemed no reason to doubt that Labillardière would likewise make good use of the Baudin collection.

But of recent years, Labillardière's pace had slackened. Promised publications were slow in coming—it had taken until last year for his latest work on Pacific material, *Sertum austro-caledonicum,* to appear. However, there was no doubt that it was a beautiful production and a valuable contribution to southern botany. Cuvier had, at least, prevailed upon Labillardière to finally abandon the simplistic Linnaean classification of his earlier work for the comprehensive natural system he himself had developed, but traces of Linnaean simplicity remained in descriptions so brief as to be useless for anyone wishing to classify on the basis of a different character than the one Labillardière had chosen. Cuvier was not really surprised by this. He had seen some of Labillardière's notes on specimens and had been horrified by their brevity. They would make sense to no one except as a prompt to the collector's memory and, with the years passing, Cuvier wondered if even Labillardière could recall the meaning of the cryptic annotations. Not everyone, mused Cuvier, had been blessed with his own faultless memory.

Small wonder then, that Labillardière would let no one else near his collections. He had become increasingly irritable and unsociable in his old age. Estranged from his wife for many years, after her death he lived alone and certainly unloved. Some said his 'sullen misanthropy' led him to live on the seventh floor to dissuade unwelcome visitors. In such intellectual and social isolation it seemed unlikely to Cuvier (a great believer in the importance of an actively intellectual social life) that anything more of productive value would come from the botanical collections of d'Entrecasteaux and Baudin. It had been clear: a new expedition, and new material, was needed.

Cuvier had worked hard to promote the Duperrey expedition and he was pleased with the results. The fifty-three new maps and charts that had been drawn would rectify many grave errors. Over twenty-one months, the expeditioners had amassed a valuable array of meteorological data from their six daily observations of sea temperature and air pressure. A significant contribution had been made to the vexing problem of Earth magnetism. For the Muséum itself, Lesson had collected about three hundred rock samples,

while Dumont d'Urville had made noteworthy botanical collections; the pair had also returned with 1200 insects, 264
birds and quadrupeds, 63 reptiles and 288 fish—a great many
of which were new to science.

It was clear from both this expedition and the de
Freycinet expedition that naval personnel, rather than dedicated naturalists, were more than adequate to fulfil the
requirements of the Muséum in collecting specimens. Indeed,
many of the civilian scientists sent on expeditions had proven
less than satisfactory. Should they survive the rigours of travel
(which many did not), on their return they invariably wanted
to analyse and publish their findings for themselves, a task
to which not all were well suited. It stood to reason that the
physical skills required to collect and preserve specimens in
the field were not necessarily the same as the intellectual skills
required to interpret those specimens within a scientific
framework. Certainly a collector had the right to name and
describe new species he discovered, but beyond that, the
specimens needed to be available to *savants* as soon as possible so that they could be used to address the fundamental
issues of the day.

The Muséum had attempted to address the problem of
naturalist-voyagers by setting up its own school to specifically
train *savants* in the skills necessary for collecting abroad.
Perhaps, in the grand tradition of Linnaeus, scores of young
acolytes might set out across the world sending back specimens for their masters at the Muséum. But the vision was not
to be. The first two candidates despatched met untimely deaths

and the remainder proved far less prolific than the Muséum had hoped. The experimental school soon fizzled out.

After his experiences on the Baudin expedition, Louis de Freycinet had argued vehemently that everyone aboard his expedition should be in the service of the navy and under his direct command. Geoffroy Saint-Hilaire had been vocal in his concern that the Muséum's interests would be overlooked but, as usual, his fears proved unfounded. On de Freycinet's expedition both the physician on board, René-Constant Quoy, and the surgeon, Paul Gaimard, had proved enthusiastic and skilled collectors, just as the pharmacist Lesson and Lieutenant Dumont d'Urville had been on the recent Duperrey expedition.

Cuvier had never believed it was necessary to see the creatures he studied in their own environment. Within the confines of his own laboratory, the entire fauna of the Earth could range before him, such as it never could before a naturalist in the field. Indeed, within his collections species past and present, local and distant, paraded themselves before him, a vision no field naturalist, no matter how heroic his circumstances, could hope to match. It was a waste of time for the field collector to engage in speculation and analysis—far better to leave this to the experts at the Muséum.

'It is a great error,' he had written in his report,

> while on a voyage, to do anything but collect the raw
> material for study, either by preparing specimens or by
> drawing what cannot be preserved, or finally, by writing

down the ephemeral details that the specimen does not retain. It is likewise a mistake to waste time with descriptions, or, in the search for nomenclature, work which will have to be started afresh once back in the laboratory.

And not just any laboratory, of course—his laboratory. He could not prevent his colleagues from accessing specimens, but sometimes it seemed such a waste given the pointless uses to which they put them. Take Lamarck, for example, a man with a quick and ardent mind, who had made so many significant new discoveries, and yet failed to scrutinise the real evidence and persisted in mingling fanciful concepts with fact and constructing vast edifices on imaginary foundations. If he would only confine himself to the small facts of the case, instead of insisting that 'big facts' should also be speculated upon. It was patently absurd to consider that animals could in some way direct their own transformation by a manifestation of will (or was it need?). By that argument it was not the nature and form of the organs that determined the behaviour of the animal, but the behaviour of the animal that determined the nature and form of the organs.

For a physiologist like Cuvier, such a notion was insupportable. Show me a tooth, he thought, and I will describe to you the diet, the alimentary system, the physiognomy, the lifestyle and the habits of the animal, without ever having seen it. These things were unchangeable, indisputable and predictable. If a creature has wings, it will fly. Tearing claws and teeth always belong to a carnivore, while a hoofed foot

and grinding teeth must belong to a herbivore. The basic rules
of physiology dictate the form a creature must take and the
life it will lead.

Even the astonishing New Holland paradox, the
ornithorynchus (or platypus, as the English termed it)—with
feet like a seal and a mouth like a duck—must conform to
these basic principles. No matter what some people said, it
was not some kind of transitional form between mammals
and reptiles, or between mammals and birds. The vast bulk of
its physiology pointed to it being a mammal and so a mammal
it must be, with all the defining features of a mammal—feeding its young with milk and giving birth to live young. Of
course, the similarity of the animal's reproductive tract to that
of birds must, by necessity, mean a somewhat unusual system
of birth—perhaps they had eggs which hatched internally
before the tiny premature young were born? New Holland
was a land of anomalous creatures. Who would have thought
that the echidna—so superficially like an anteater that he
himself had initially classified it in the Edentata—was actually more similar to a platypus? The mysteries of the marsupials with their pouches and tiny young glued to nipples
larger than themselves still remained unlocked and would
undoubtedly puzzle naturalists for years to come.

Cuvier did not concern himself overly with the anomalous platypus—its place in the system of nature would be
decided eventually. His student, Henri de Blainville, had produced an excellent dissertation on the species and continued
to bring anatomical rigour to the debate, as did the promising

young Englishman Richard Owen. Against them raged Geoffroy Saint-Hilaire, who insisted that the platypus and echidna be classified as Monotremata ('one-holed', by virtue of both species having a cloaca that combined the final passage of the reproductive and digestive systems). Lamarck encouraged him in this unnecessary embellishment to the simple traditional scheme of classification by granting Monotremata its own class, separate from that of mammals. Lamarck had written:

> These animals are quadrupeds, without mammary glands, embedded teeth, or lips; they have only one orifice for the genital organs, excrement, and urine (a cloaca). Their bodies are covered with hair or bristles.
>
> These are not mammals at all, for they do not have mammary glands and are very obviously oviparous.
>
> They are not birds, for their lungs are not pierced and they do not have limbs shaped into wings.
>
> Finally they are not reptiles, for their heart with two ventricles necessarily distances them from the reptiles.
>
> Thus they belong to a special class.

But Geoffroy, and Lamarck, were wrong. A young German anatomist had recently demonstrated that the platypus did indeed have mammary glands. And if an animal had mammary glands the females must give birth to live young. Not that Geoffroy would agree to this obvious fact. He persisted in believing that the platypus laid eggs and, given that an egg-laying animal could not possibly feed its young milk, he rejected the evidence for mammary glands, claiming instead that they must be sweat glands or some other such thing. Poor Geoffroy—on the losing end of the argument yet again. Richard Owen countered every one of his points carefully and logically while Geoffroy wound himself up into more and more emotional and irrational responses. But the facts would prevail in the end. It was only a matter of time before the myth of an egg-laying mammal would finally be laid to rest by the discovery of a pregnant female, or female with newborn young.

It was in physiology, in detail and in facts that the future of science lay, not in this vague premonition of patterns and fluctuations barely comprehensible to the human mind. There was enough room for wonder in fossils and physiology for Cuvier, without needing to stray into the realms of the metaphysical. Leave these things to God, thought Cuvier, and keep science separate within the realm of man.

The cheerful chatter of his step-daughter Sophie entering the library brought Cuvier back to the present. Smiling, he took her arm and headed down the stairs, gaily discussing the guests at this evening's weekly salon and gently teasing her about the handsome young writer who had taken her fancy. The usual crowd would be there. The writer Stendhal would be busy charming de Vigny's new English wife. Mérimée, sombre and intense, would disapprove. The eternally elegant Talleyrand would be carefully sowing intrigue and gossip about the Court of Charles X in the ear of the

general, Etienne Maurice Gérard. The brilliant composer
Rossini would endear himself to all with his charming and
self-deprecating Italian ways—his tales of being locked in a
room by an irate director until he produced the required piece
of music for the evening performance had everyone in gales
of laughter, for all Cuvier could barely repress a shudder at
the thought of having to work with someone so irrepressibly
capricious. And of course, Humboldt and some of the other
savants from the Muséum would be there. Cuvier's salon was
the place for the serious young intellectuals of Paris to see and
be seen, and Cuvier revelled in their company. From the
centre of his empire, surrounded by family and influential
friends, a recognised leader in French science and society, just
as Buffon had been, Cuvier was a contented man.

1. 'Martin chasseur de salusse'
Blue-winged Kookaburra (*Dacelo leachii*)
2. 'Acténoïde variée'
Blue-capped Kingfisher (*Actenoides hombroni*)

'Perruche à tête pourpre'
Red-capped Parrot
(*Purpureicephalis spurius*)

'Mimosa longifolia'
Sydney Golden Wattle
(*Acacia longifolia*)

'Kennedia rubicunda'
Running Postman
(*Kennedia rubicunda*)

Hyacinthe de Bougainville

Port Jackson, Australia

24 September 1825

Hyacinthe de Bougainville was born at Brest on 26 December 1781, privileged son of famous navigator Louis-Antoine de Bougainville. He studied at the Ecole Polytechnique from 1799 and was appointed midshipman on the Géographe under Nicolas Baudin. After his return to France from the Baudin expedition, where he did not acquit himself to the satisfaction of his commander, he served on various naval vessels before being made lieutenant in 1808. He was promoted to captain in 1811 and inherited his father's title of baron in the same year. Bougainville lived in his father's great shadow and his achievements were never recognised for their true worth. He led the expedition of the Thétis and the Espérance in 1824–26 and rose to the rank of rear admiral before his death at the age of sixty-five in 1846. Despite his reputation as a lady's man, Bougainville never married. Bougainville was made a commander of the Légion d'Honneur and served at the Ecole Royale Polytechnique as well as on the Admiralty Council.

Hyacinthe de Bougainville leant despondently over the gunwale of the *Thétis*, gazing morosely at the Sydney shoreline. From here, the neat array of sandstone houses with their little front flower gardens looked very fine nestled against the hills of the harbour. The low flat rocks lining the foreshore provided a break against the deep blue of the waters. Numerous indentations and bays opened out on all sides, promising a seemingly limitless overflow of sheltered harbours. Towards the sea, tall red cliffs rose fortress-like against the waves. A covering of fine grey-green vegetation stretched down to the warm yellow rocks, enclosing the town in a verdant mantle, only partially cleared by the labours of its inmates. Such a fine location could hardly help but produce a beautiful town in time.

But for all its trappings of civilisation, it would be many years before Sydney could rival even a third-rate town of France or England. Its wide streets were unlit and unpaved—either clouds of red dust or rivers of mud. The buildings, while made of an attractive local stone, were rather garish and short-lived, their taste being as poor as their construction. The streets and parks were unsafe at night. Even the *Thétis*'s bursar had been mugged during their stay here. Clearly little had improved in local morality since the de Freycinets had awoken from their first night ashore to find all their silverware and plates stolen while they slept.

Only the enthusiasm and hospitality of the local society could not be faulted. They drank hard, gambled, sang and danced with vigour, if not panache. Bougainville rose to the challenge with gusto—drinking the menfolk under the table and entertaining their wives with a captivating Gallic charm. But the charm had not gone all one way.

Bougainville sighed deeply. As he gazed across the waters he could see again Harriott's teasing brown eyes, flirting beneath sultry lids. He could see her curls glinting red and gold in the sunlight as they explored the sea baths together just a week ago, her delicately arched eyebrow mocking yet enticing him. He could feel the curve of her soft white breasts, the warmth of her breath as she agreed to a midnight rendez-vous on the *Thétis*. How he ached to hold her once more! If only he had met her earlier. If only he were not obliged to leave—he had stayed too long already.

Harriott's letter, foregoing their rendezvous and pleading a prior engagement at Newington, had struck despair in his heart. The prior engagement was clearly the jealous husband. She longed to see him again, she wrote. She would dine at the sheriff's house on Monday. And she had—demurely seated next to her angry husband who was constrained from notic-ing the French officer casting sorrowful glances at his wife only by his Englishness. Such constraint might not be forth-coming on future occasions and Bougainville had decided to avoid further contact. It would be futile to try to see Harriott again and it would do no one any good, least of all himself.

Had he learnt nothing from his last near-disastrous visit to Port Jackson? It had been a quarter of a century since Bougainville had last visited this harbour. And how different were his circumstances then, as a midshipman on his first voyage. The cruelty and rudeness of his commander, Nicolas Baudin, had driven him to seek any escape. His request to be transferred to the *Naturaliste* had been brusquely denied. But on discovering that the *Naturaliste* was due to return to France, Bougainville had been driven to desperate means. Feigning severe illness, he had persuaded local doctors to tell Baudin he would be unable to continue the expedition. Baudin was not fooled—Bougainville had never forgotten his contemptuous sneer as Baudin signed to transfer the sick and unruly to the *Naturaliste*, back to France. It was a poison he was glad to be rid of, Baudin had said vindictively.

Looking back to the impetuousity of his youth, Bougainville could see that his behaviour on Baudin's expedition might not have been ideal. He did not forgive Baudin his ill-humour, poor decisions and cruelty, but he had a better understanding now of the challenges of command. They had all been so young at the time and had joined the expedition with such high spirits, such an expectation of camaraderie and excitement. At first, Baudin had been content to let such high spirits, such expressions of individual will, go unchallenged. And later, by the time it was necessary for Baudin to enforce discipline, the opportunity to impose his will on his officers had been lost. He had lost their respect and their allegiance and could not regain it.

Then, as now, Bougainville had left Port Jackson with mixed emotions. Elation at finally escaping his tormentor and returning home was combined with adolescent despair at leaving the pretty young girl he'd met and fallen in love with.

And always lurking in the back of his mind was the burden of his father's disappointment. His father, the great Pacific explorer Louis-Antoine de Bougainville, whose tales of tropical paradise and burnished beauties had inspired a generation. His father, so influential and powerful, so old and fragile, who had pulled so many strings to get his son a place on the Baudin expedition. His father would read Baudin's damning report. He would shut himself in his study, his silence more painful than recriminations, before emerging to forgive his erring son yet again and set about reviving his blighted career. A friend of his father's had once warned him:

> Never forget that, because you are your father's son, you will be expected to achieve even more than others. Perhaps the son of Buffon would have been deemed an eagle, had he not had the acclaimed naturalist for a father.

Bougainville turned and surveyed the decks of the *Thétis*, everything neatly stowed and prepared for sea. Fit, healthy men busied themselves with preparations for getting underway. A fine collection of plants and animals was carefully stowed aboard. It was a ship to be proud of, an expedition to be proud of—small, but without fault. He wished his father could see him now. But his father had died years ago and would never see what he had achieved, would never be able to give him the recognition he craved.

He wished his father could have seen him as he'd sailed into Port Jackson two months ago. He wished Baudin could have seen him. Twenty-five years ago, the *Géographe* had limped into port, barely able to muster enough men to sail the ship. Men lay sick and dying of scurvy and neglect. The English crew of the *Investigator* had barely been able to conceal their horror as they'd leapt aboard to assist their French comrades into port.

In stark contrast, the *Thétis* and the *Espérance* had sailed triumphantly into Port Jackson as fresh and as sprightly as if they had just set out from Brest. Just over a year into their expedition and they had adhered to their planned itinerary with a precision numbered in days. While contrary winds had prevented Bougainville from achieving his long-cherished dream of stepping in some of his father's footsteps across the Pacific, he had fulfilled to the letter the terms of his instructions, diligently and conscientiously. Even without naturalists, without artists, he had managed to acquire the specimens and observations requested by the Muséum by paying local hunters, sometimes out of his own pocket.

The French taste for expeditions was waning, as Bougainville himself knew. His own expedition had only finally departed because of fortuitous political events in China that demanded some parading of the French flag in the surrounding oceans. The politicians now wanted concrete outcomes, not just the glory of discovery and exploration. 'What is in it for France?' they had asked—commerce, colonies, a convict settlement? They did not seem content to fund expeditions purely on the basis of science any more, or to chart more thoroughly the coasts so briefly visited by others before them. They had no eye for detail, these men of money and power, but an eye for future fame and fortune. It had taken all of Cuvier's support to get Duperrey's expedition approved and without the backing of the charismatic Dumont d'Urville it might never have left France.

Duperrey's expedition had delayed Bougainville's by several years and Duperrey was due to return as they were setting sail to leave. Perhaps they had crossed paths off the African coast, or perhaps Duperrey had sailed into the shelter of the Mediterranean just as Bougainville's expedition had sailed down the French coast on its eastward circumnavigation. Wherever they were now, he knew that Duperrey had been anchored here in Sydney, just where he was anchored now, a mere eighteen months before. His crew had followed, at least partly, in the footsteps of Duperrey, also revisiting the site of Lapérouse's camp at Botany Bay. The site, known locally as 'French Garden', was near an exposed plateau at the tip of the second headland on the starboard side of the entrance to the bay. It sloped down slightly to the sea and you could still see the holes dug for posts to hold up the barricades. Nearby was the tree where Duperrey's men had carved a small epitaph to Lapérouse's chaplain:

NEAR THIS TREE

ARE THE REMAINS OF

FATHER RECEVEUR.

VISITED

IN MARCH

1824

The humble memorial gave Bougainville an idea. He would erect a monument to his illustrious and unfortunate compatriot on the very spot where Lapérouse had composed his final message. The tribute was long overdue. Governor Brisbane had recently erected a rather inaccessible monument to Captain Cook on the opposite side of the bay. Surely such a friend to France (a corresponding member of the French Academy of Sciences, no less) could be enlisted to support the proposal? As Bougainville had sat on the headland eating freshly baked bread, he could see the monument rising—an elegant, classical column gleaming white and visible to all from land or sea.

A warm glow of satisfaction filled Bougainville as he considered the successful progress of the monument. Governor Brisbane had kindly donated the land on which the monument was to stand (in addition to a further seventy square yards surrounding Father Receveur's grave) and had put the government architect at Bougainville's disposal. Bougainville had left the sum of 736½ *piastres* with his good friend Captain Piper to cover the expenses of construction. In four years, he was confident, the monument would be complete. He could leave Sydney knowing that this legacy to France would be in safe hands.

The sun-warmed air spilled as the cotton duck sails rose steadily into the sky. As the sails filled, the ships began their sedate progress across the harbour. The heaving of the anchor gave way to the steady thrust of the bow wave. Sunlight rippled on the waters as they farewelled Sydney for the southern islands of New Zealand and then on to South America.

Bougainville stood to attention, tugging his dress coat straight, its brass buttons gleaming in the sunlight. He gave the order for a 21-gun salute, which was duly echoed across the bay by a return cannonade. As they sailed past Captain Piper's residence another 21-gun salute rang out across the bay. Bougainville ordered a nine-gun salute with topgallant sails and royal sails brailed up by way of response. The corvette gave an eleven-gun salute as she sailed past. The French ships would be missed in the colony almost as much as the French officers would miss Sydney.

At midday, they were at North Head. By 4.30 p.m., they lost sight of the lighthouse from the topmast and, a little later, of the land from the deck. As Sydney faded into the distance Bougainville realised that he would never again set eyes on those shores. His heart sank and he almost wished that they had sailed a month earlier, that he had never met Harriott, that those fleeting happy days had never happened and that this painful parting that was bound to last forever might not have to be borne.

Bougainville turned and headed below decks. Released from the constraints of formal attire, he threw his captain's hat to one side, rubbing his hands through his unkempt brown hair. Unbuttoning his coat and pulling the cravat from his throat, Bougainville threw himself into the nearest armchair, his long legs sprawling across the painted canvas floor. He surveyed the neat, comfortable cabin that would be his home yet again for the next four months. The panelled bulkhead was lined with books, including copies of all the reports of recent voyages to Australia and the latest works of natural history, navigation, astronomy and geology. A stack of newly published additions, sent from Paris to meet him in Port Jackson, lay stacked nearby, waiting to be shelved. On his desk lay his journals, filled with his careful observations, and hundreds of pages of transcriptions of reports he had found on the British colony which might be of value to his superiors in France. Not all of his time had been spent on romantic pursuits. Now, the time for gay society had certainly passed.

He had reports to write, accounts to prepare, paperwork to complete, on the plants and animals he had seen and their scientific and commercial value, on the defences and fortifications of Sydney, on the convict settlement and its application for similar French endeavours, on the natives and their sad degeneration, on the English and their progress and endless plans for expansion, on the Lapérouse monument.

His expedition might not be as grand as his father's—there were not so many opportunities for discovery now—but he would leave no task incomplete, no account unwritten, no sailor unacknowledged. He had fulfilled every instruction to the letter, exceeded every expectation. But in the end, would it be enough? Would his achievements be enough to put his name alongside that of his father's in the history books? Would the fruits of this expedition bring happiness or would the results be more bitter than sweet? Who could tell?

Bougainville shrugged, '*Sic voleure fata!*—Thus fate turns!'

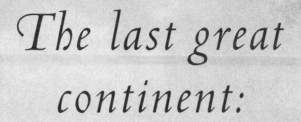

The last great
continent:

DUMONT D'URVILLE
(1826–1829
AND
1837–1840)

The discovery of Adélie Land

on 19 January 1840 by

Dumont d'Urville's expedition.

Jules Dumont d'Urville

Vanikoro Island, Santa Cruz Islands

17 March 1828

Jules Sebastien-César Dumont d'Urville was born in Normandy on 25 May 1796 into an old noble family. His father died when d'Urville was seven; his mother was a contrary and domineering figure. D'Urville had a stoic constitution and a talented intellect. He joined the navy at seventeen, studying astronomy, navigation, languages and botany. He married Adèle in 1816 and they had four children, only one of whom survived infancy. After helping recover the Vénus de Milo, *Dumont d'Urville served as a lieutenant on the Duperrey expedition to the Pacific. He commanded his own expedition to the Pacific (1826–29) where he discovered the remains of the Lapérouse expedition. His third expedition, to the Pacific and Antarctica (1837–40), landed the first men on Antarctic soil. Dumont d'Urville's steely determination and contemptuous attitude towards lesser mortals did not always endear him to others; however, his achievements did earn him popular accolades. He, his wife and son were tragically killed in a horrific train accident in 1842.*

The warm, turbid air hung in the cabin like dirty washing. The windows were open to the early morning but no breeze dared enter to dispel the filthy miasma. The squall that had swept over them at midnight had passed, leaving everything waterlogged in its path. The uncertain weather disturbed everyone's sleep with anxious nervousness. Even the sick had lain wakeful and tense, listening to the waves crash ominously over the inshore reefs to leeward. Everyone knew their peril.

If we let this day pass without moving, thought Dumont d'Urville, tomorrow it will be too late to attempt to leave Vanikoro.

Despite the heat, the commander shivered uncontrollably. Waves of fever swept across his body, weakening his legs and dimming his sight. Gulping down some yellowed water, barely registering the minuscule creatures wriggling within it, Dumont d'Urville refocused his attention on the chart before him.

They had been at this hellhole for almost a month now. Vanikoro—the fever island. They had been warned they would all die here, but a sacred duty had drawn them to this fatal place.

Yet their journey had started so well. After the success, and limitations, of his voyage with Duperrey, King Charles X had given Dumont d'Urville command of the old *Coquille*, renamed the *Astrolabe* in honour of Lapérouse's famous ship, to 'explore some of the principal archipelagos of the Southern Ocean which *Coquille* only rapidly passed by ... to augment the mass of scientific documentation which resulted from [that] voyage'. Furthermore, the Secretary of State for the Navy and Colonies had written, 'interest will accrue to your voyage should you manage to discover any trace of Lapérouse and his companions in misfortune'. There had been rumours that an American captain in the area between New Caledonia and the Louisiade Archipelago had seen French artefacts that might have come from the Lapérouse expedition.

By the time they had reached Hobart Town, fresh stories were circulating. A reprobate English captain in the employ of the East India Company claimed to have found remains of the Lapérouse expedition on an island by the name of Vanikoro, near Tikopia. Captain Dillon was not liked in Hobart Town and had even been imprisoned for his misdemeanours. Everyone dismissed him as a madman and adventurer and his Lapérouse story as just another of the fanciful myths that had circulated for forty years through the Pacific.

Disturbed but not dissuaded, Dumont d'Urville pursued his enquiries. He sought out any who had met Captain Dillon and diligently read all the newspaper accounts, court proceedings and reports of his activities. The man was probably brutal and abusive, but that seemed to be no reason to doubt his honesty. Furthermore, Dillon was illiterate and clearly incompetent as a navigator, so much so that it seemed unlikely that he could have had either the skill or the nous to fabricate such a story with any reliability. As Dumont d'Urville read the accounts, impressed by the accuracy of details that only an experienced sailor could gauge, he felt a veil lifting, revealing the tragic fate of Lapérouse and his companions. He imagined himself on the scene of that great calamity, giving to the shades of his luckless compatriots the final testimony of the sorrow felt by the whole of France. Such a momentous discovery could not be left to a disreputable Englishman, who might at this very moment be at the scene of the tragedy, raking it over for trinkets and mementos!

Dumont d'Urville had resolved to leave direct for Tikopia. Resolutely setting himself against the prevailing views of his officers and crew—and, indeed, all of Hobart Town, which viewed any talk of Tikopia or Vanikoro as a great joke—Dumont d'Urville prepared to set sail. Dillon might have been deliberately vague on the location of Vanikoro, but for an experienced sailor the direction 'two days distance to the leeward from Tikopia by canoe' was enough. Given the prevailing winds, the island must lie forty to fifty leagues either north-west of Tikopia (in the Banks group) or south-west (in the Santa Cruz group). Only time would tell if Dumont d'Urville had given up the opportunity to do valuable work in New Zealand to follow a madman's fantasy.

They left the young town of Hobart in good spirits. The nascent colony had made an enjoyable base, with its neat little houses and English commitment to being 'pleasant' and 'comfortable' (even under conditions that were patently the reverse). French ships could surely be assured of a warm welcome and hospitable base for future voyages here. All on board the ship were in good health, with not a single sailor seriously ill. After the obligatory Tasman gales they rounded the northern tip of New Zealand and headed north-west towards the tropical waters of Tikopia.

Their arrival a month later could not have been more auspicious. The weather was as good as could be expected for the season, alternating squalls and calms, but manageable nonetheless. The Tikopians, from whom they sought assistance to locate Vanikoro, were a charming, friendly people who rapidly won the respect even of the sailors. A number had offered to accompany them wherever they wished to travel—although their enthusiasm diminished considerably when their destination was revealed. But the Tikopians came anyway, skilfully guiding their way across the empty horizon by the stars. And the crew were cheered by the prospect of an abundance of pigs and poultry on Vanikoro.

With his carefully garnered repertoire of Polynesian vocabulary, Dumont d'Urville quizzed the Tikopians on their destination, patiently referring them to the charts of the area so diligently compiled by the d'Entrecasteaux expedition. Patiently, insistently, the Tikopians deflected his questions, either through boredom or ignorance, showing no interest in the squiggles and lines on the paper before them, looking instead to the water and horizon outside. Dumont d'Urville gave up. He could see for himself where they were headed. D'Entrecasteaux had been in these waters before.

With a sinking heart, d'Urville realised that the island they were headed for had a French name as well as a local one: Vanikoro had once been called Recherche Island.

The expedition sent to find Lapérouse had sailed past the island that might even then have harboured survivors, and had named it after the very search in which they were destined to fail. The irony was painful.

Dumont d'Urville had first caught sight of the highest points of Vanikoro at sunset on 11 February 1828. How well he could recall his feelings on this momentous occasion.

> At this sight, our hearts were beating faster from an indefinable impulse of hope and regret, of pain and pride. At last before our eyes we had the mysterious place that had so long kept hidden from France, from the whole of Europe, the wreckage of a noble and generous enterprise; we were going to tread this fatal soil, explore its coasts and question its inhabitants. But what was to be the outcome of our efforts?

It had been difficult to find a safe anchorage—somewhere within the labyrinth of reefs protected from the ocean swells, yet deep and wide enough for the ships to manoeuvre safely and be able to leave when required. The Vanikorons had watched the proceedings carefully. Such unwieldy vessels as these had passed their shores before and some had never left them. Dumont d'Urville felt vulnerable as he searched for a safe anchorage, as if these people knew white men's weaknesses too well.

The island itself was fertile with majestic forests, superb plant life and an abundance of insects and butterflies which bore a striking affinity to those of New Guinea, New Ireland and the Moluccas. The forest was dense and forbidding, however, and allowed little access from the shore. The natives were ugly and unlikeable, and offered nothing interesting or good to eat. The trader Dillon had flooded them with goods far in excess of anything a naval ship could hope to offer. Without the ability to trade for information, Dumont d'Urville was dependent upon goodwill and generous spirits—neither of which seemed abundant in the nature of these people.

Of all the islands of the Pacific, what unfortunate fate had cast the great Lapérouse here? Among the Tahitians, the Tongans or the Tikopians, a shipwrecked sailor would have had some hope of being treated with respect and care. Even the cannibals of New Zealand had been known to show hospitality to shipwrecked sailors on occasion. But the Vanikorans lacked any such virtues. Lapérouse could have found only greed, barbarism and treachery here.

On the subject of possible French shipwrecks, the Vanikorans were almost uniformly evasive and contradictory, their fear of reprisals surely indicative of guilt over past actions.

'I don't know ...'

'I didn't see anything ...'

'That happened a long time ago ...'

'We heard about it from our fathers ...'

It was only the Vanikorans' insatiable desire for red cloth that finally led the Frenchmen to their long-awaited destination. Their guide, enchanted by the prospect of this beautiful material, took them to an opening between the reefs, and directed them to look down into the water. The crystal green waters fractured their gaze but there, seemingly just within reach, lay scattered lead plates, cannons and balls, encrusted with coral.

After so much anticipation, after so much hope and enthusiasm, the sight of this pathetic remnant of Lapérouse's brilliant expedition struck silence in their souls. One after the other, boatloads of crew made the weary pilgrimage to the site until every last man had paid his respects. After forty years, the great mystery was solved. There remained nothing more to do but pay a sorrowful tribute to the memory of their unfortunate compatriots.

The men had attended to the task of building a memorial with bitter determination. While they worked, the surgeons Quoy and Gaimard documented every detail and collected every species for their painstaking studies on the construction of coral reefs, their pale skin burning red even beneath their broad-brimmed hats.

Every day that passed rendered this place less and less hospitable. The shifting deceit of the natives convinced everyone that they had treated their shipwrecked comrades with treacherous barbarism. Everyone knew that the fate of Lapérouse could easily have been—could easily still be—their own. Only one of the Vanikoran chiefs seemed to show any civility or any honesty. Dumont d'Urville culti-vated Moembe's goodwill, honoured his gods, but doubted his reliability.

From numerous sources, some reliable, some not, the fate of Lapérouse and his men now seemed clear. One ship had been stranded off the island during a night of bad weather and the other ship, on standing by to assist her stricken comrade, had suffered a similar fate. Some seventy or eighty men had come ashore at Païou and over several months had built a small boat on which they had departed. Their stay on Vanikoro had not been peaceful. There were varying accounts of brawls and deaths on both sides. Some said that two of the Frenchmen had stayed behind when the others left.

One report had it that the last Frenchman had died only the year before this. Perhaps this man had still been alive when d'Entrecasteaux's frigates had sailed past? The natives had seen them, they knew of every European ship that had passed by this way. Had this sole survivor seen them appear and then disappear on the distant horizon—his last hope of rescue surely evaporating with them? Dumont d'Urville shook off the mournful fancy. It was unlikely any Frenchman could survive long on this island. Death stalked here relentlessly. Gaimard had pleaded to be allowed to stay ashore with the natives. The jovial doctor was popular among all people, wherever he went. But after a few days he had returned, irritated and annoyed with poor treatment and ill with painful boils and a fever. It was a sign of things to come. The next day Dumont d'Urville recognised signs of dreaded sickness in himself. He had suffered its curse before, in Greece. Within a week, men started to drop like flies.

At last, the cenotaph was complete—a six-foot-high coral pillar topped with a wooden pyramid made from the kauri bought at Kororeka in New Zealand. No nails or iron were used in its construction—just a small lead plate engraved with a simple message:

A LA MÉMOIRE
DE LAPÉROUSE
ET DE SES COMPAGNONS,
L'ASTROLABE
14 MARS 1828

The 21-gun salvo shattered the peaceful quiet of the island, sending the savages scurrying for cover. The salute echoed from the mountainside, these same mountains that had witnessed the deaths of their countrymen from fever and savagery so many years ago. From the shore, Dumont d'Urville could see a canoe being launched hastily, anxiously. He had not warned the natives of the ceremony. A bit of fear was a good thing.

Moembe came aboard first, confident in his friendship but uncertain nonetheless. Respectfully he kissed the back of the commander's hand, anxious for reassurance that the visitors were not declaring war on his people. Dumont d'Urville looked down on the native sternly, not willing to dispel this notion entirely.

'The shots were fired in honour of the *Atua Papalagui*, the god of the Europeans, that we have just placed on the reef,' he explained. 'You must promise that your countrymen will respect the house of our god and not seek to destroy it. If ships come to your island after us and see this house intact, it would be a warranty of our friendship . . . if the monument is overturned the whites will be very angry and will take a heavy revenge for this outrage.'

Moembe looked uncomfortable, perhaps wondering what his own gods would think of a European god setting up house on their shores.

Dumont d'Urville took another tack. 'We have placed ours on the reef, surrounded by water, away from the Atuas of your country, Banie and Loubo, as a precaution to avoid any conflict of powers among these different gods. Please accept these gifts for Loubo and Banie to appease them.'

Moembe brightened visibly at this and accepted the lengths of red cloth and cleavers readily. 'I swear by everything I hold most sacred', he said solemnly, 'that the *Atua Papalagui* will be equally respected with Loubo and Banie. We will see to the preservation of his house, *fare Atua*, and we will treat as an enemy anyone who attempts any desecration.'

As Moembe left, Dumont d'Urville leant on the rail, his failing strength taxed by the display of commodorial authority. He did not doubt Moembe's sincerity, but did not trust the natives to keep their word. He only hoped that their natural indolence would reduce their inclination to expend effort destroying something that contained nothing of value to them.

There was nothing more they could do but leave before more men succumbed to the fevers wracking the ship. It was while they were occupied raising the anchors—painful work, with forty men confined to their sickbeds—that the canoes arrived. They came to trade coconuts, the natives said, laughing slyly. They had no coconuts, only bows and arrows. A few sauntered on board, glancing down at the sick men on the orlop deck, their evil grins extending.

Dumont d'Urville drew himself up to his full height, rallying the last of his strength for this final performance. 'Leave this ship at once,' he commanded.

The natives just stared at him, smirking insolently. Dumont d'Urville stared back, his eyes icy with dislike. His thin lips tightened. Silently he motioned for the armoury to be opened. The natives' eyes widened at the sight of the gleaming muskets. D'Urville's gaze did not waver. With one hand he pointed at the armoury and with the other he pointed menacingly at them, and then to their canoes. Backing quickly, they tumbled into their canoes and away.

A wave of murmuring approval swept the deck in appreciation of d'Urville's performance. The commander turned away, feeling cold and clammy again and not just from fever. It was well the men did not appreciate how dangerous their position had been. While the sight of a pistol might put twenty savages to flight, reflected Dumont d'Urville, they could equally be capable of hurling themselves like wild animals at a whole detachment firing at them. The ships must leave this place and quickly.

The *Astrolabe* piled on her canvas to flee this miserable prison, but Vanikoro did not release her victims lightly. No sooner were they in the narrow channel leading out through the reef than rain began to fall, as torrential as only Vanikoro rain could be. A wall of water encircled them. They were blind and helpless. One false move would be the death of them all. Dumont d'Urville strained to see the white of the breakers lining the channel but the fever returned ferociously, blurring his vision and striking him with a sickening dizziness.

He gripped the rail again. 'M. Gressien,' he rapped firmly, as though nothing were amiss at all, 'you will pilot the ship to clear water.' The officer nodded, taking his lead from the captain. Calmly and coolly he followed his captain's orders and after a few anxious minutes, they were finally clear of the treacherous reefs.

A cheer went up from the lower deck, and smiles of intense relief spread across the officers' faces. Their mission had been completed, at last they could set their sights on their homeland, six thousand leagues away.

Dumont d'Urville slid senseless to the deck as the fever finally overwhelmed him.

Elisabeth~Paul~Edouard
de Rossel

Ministry of Marine, Paris

14 May 1829

Rear Admiral de Rossel paused to catch his breath on the steps of the Ministry of Marine. A sharp pain caught his left side, reminding him that he was not as young as he used to be. Supporting himself against one of the pillars at the entrance, he turned and gazed across the square, waiting for the spasm to pass.

The terracotta statue of Liberty sat impassively, surveying the octagonal plaza, as unmoved by the bustle of people going about their daily business as she had been by the thousands of deaths she had witnessed under the guillotine. This square had seen so much blood in its short history. It was said that a herd of cattle had refused to cross it during the Revolution, petrified by the smell of the blood that had soaked into every crevice and stone.

Those days, of course, were long past. The square was no longer the Place de la Révolution, nor even the Place de la Concorde. With the restoration of the Bourbon kings to the throne of France, it had briefly reverted to its original name of Place Louis XV. Now the square honoured the king whose execution it had witnessed, Place Louis XVI. It had even been suggested that the statue of Liberty be replaced by a monument to Louis XVI, perhaps reminiscent of the grand effigy of his grandfather that had been destroyed during the Revolution.

Louis XVI, whatever his political failings, had been hugely influential at the Ministry of Marine, along with his advisor Comte de Fleurieu. It was they who had launched the famous Lapérouse expedition that had disappeared all those

See page 62 for a biography on Rossel.

years ago to an unknown fate. And it was in search of
Lapérouse that Rossel's naval career had flourished, as a lieutenant on the d'Entrecasteaux expedition. He could not have
imagined, when he first embarked upon the *Recherche* so
many years ago, that he would have come this far. With the
deaths of so many senior officers, it had fallen to Rossel to
bring the remnants of the expedition home. Revolution at
home and war at sea had not made his task any easier. After
being imprisoned by the Dutch in Java, he had managed to
return to Europe with the expedition's precious records and
collections intact, only to be captured in the Atlantic by the
British.

To be fair, the British had treated him well, allowing him
full access to his charts and hydrographic records. His seven
years as a prisoner had not been unpleasant and the work he
completed was well received when he finally returned home
to France after the Peace of Amiens in 1802. It was only
through this delay that the botanist Labillardière had been
able to beat the official account of the voyage into publication,
which Rossel had attended to on his return. D'Entrecasteaux
would have been annoyed by the botanist's duplicity—he had
suspected him all along of attempting to pre-empt the official
narrative with his own material.

Over the years Rossel had continued to produce clear
and carefully researched sailing manuals for various sections
of coasts, as well as guides to signalling techniques such that
anyone requiring this information would find it both acces-
sible and understandable. Navigation in the modern era was

a science, not an arcane art, and the knowledge necessary for its safe practice should be readily available.

His painstaking work had been well rewarded. Now, at the age of sixty-four, Rossel was a respected member of the Academy of Sciences and the Bureau of Longitude. He had been promoted to Rear Admiral and was the Director of the Hydrographic Office. He had come along way from the stumbling, gauche youth so eager to impress his seniors on the d'Entrecasteaux expedition.

It had been Rossel's one regret from those long-gone days that they had failed to ascertain the fate of Lapérouse. But now the return of the Dumont d'Urville expedition from Vanikoro had finally laid even that mystery to rest.

> May I be allowed to express the regret that must be felt by those who took part in the expedition in search of La Pérouse, and which affects me as sharply as any other. On the 19th of May 1793, the frigates *Recherche* and *Espérance* first saw the summit of the island of Vanikoro; it was then fifteen leagues to windward. The name Recherche was allotted to it, and this island then became merged in our view with the multitude of other islands we had seen, and which it had been impossible for us to examine closely. We were far from thinking that it was there that would be found the goal and the end of our search and of all our wishes . . .
>
> From the information obtained and conveyed by M. d'Urville one must suppose, if not with entire certainty,

'Naturel de Manève'
Vanikoran Man

1. and 2. 'Papilio Urvillanus'
D'Urville's Birdwing (*Ornithoptera urvillianus*)
3. 'Papilio Euchenor'
Euchenor's Swallowtail (*Papilio euchenor*)

1. 'Plectropome ponctué'
Marbled Coralgrouper (*Plectropomus punctatus*)
2. 'Ophisure alternant'
Harlequin Snake Eel (*Myrichthys colubrinus*)
3. 'Baliste pellion'
Prickly Leatherjacket (*Chaetoderma penicilligerus*)

'Perruche érythroptère'
Red-winged Parrot
(*Aprosmictus erythropterus*)

that Rear Admiral d'Entrecasteaux must have arrived too late to save the life of any of the unfortunate castaways, since two years after the loss of the ships not one of them remained on the island.

He knew now that survivors from the wreck had probably built a small vessel to sail to the Moluccas, or perhaps back to New Holland. Their fate remained a mystery, perhaps they perished on some unknown reef in uncharted seas. There was nothing they could have done for them all those years ago. Dumont d'Urville was certain there had been no survivors on the island when the *Recherche* and the *Espérance* had sailed past. But still there were rumours, suspicions. Perhaps one or two men had remained. If only they had stopped, if only they had checked, if only he could be certain.

Dumont d'Urville suffered no such uncertainties. After unloading his ship in Marseilles, sending his impressive collections to the Muséum and visiting his family, he had emphatically arrived in Paris. Already, the disturbing ripples of his presence had been felt through the Ministry of Marine. There was no doubt this expedition, like so many others in the past, had undergone great hardships. The toll from sickness and fever had been heavy. There was no doubt the expedition's achievements had been great, but the days when captains could award promotions to their own officers were long gone. Dumont d'Urville might style himself in the mould of the great explorers of the past (Bougainville, Lapérouse, d'Entrecasteaux, even Baudin) but the glory days of French exploration were over and it was not easy to gain just rewards for those men who had put their lives at risk in the pursuit of science and knowledge.

Rossel had done his best to promote the results of the expedition within the Ministry, and within the Institute, but he had received a chilly reception from many. Dumont d'Urville argued his case with the passion and arrogance of a man who believes himself to be absolutely in the right. He dismissed those who disagreed with him, snubbed those he regarded as unworthy of his attention, bullied those who might have been persuaded to assist him and irritated nearly all of his superiors. Dumont d'Urville was exceptionally gifted in so many areas—navigation, leadership, natural history, stoicism, anthropology, determination—and yet he was so utterly deficient in those vital skills of diplomacy, tact and humility. He took every delay, every neglect as a personal slight. It hardly mattered to Dumont d'Urville that many in the Ministry were preoccupied with the difficult and challenging political climate in which they now operated. The throne of Charles X might be teetering on the edge of an abyss, but Dumont d'Urville would still demand the full attention of his superiors.

Rossel took a deep breath. The pain in his chest had passed again and he could breathe a little easier now. The square looked so serene, so peaceful. It was hard to imagine that it could ever have been the setting for such horror. It was impossible to think such political turmoil could ever be visited on France again. He turned to head into the Ministry.

For all Dumont d'Urville's personal foibles, his achievements deserved acknowledgement and Rossel would do his best to support him. After all, glory would not accrue to France through the efforts of bureaucrats, politicians and courtiers, but only through the efforts of brave and great men like these explorers.

Charles Darwin

Blue Mountains, New South Wales

18 January 1835

Splinters of sandstone flew out from behind the horse's racing hooves as she galloped effortlessly along the ridge top. The red earth pounded beneath her feet as Darwin urged her forward, up the steep incline to the rocky plateau ahead. Through the sparse trees he caught glimpses of sky, as if he were on top of the world, instead of the bottom. The eucalypts were more open here than further down. He could see the view from Govett's Leap would be as good as he'd been told.

The wide path came to an abrupt end at a small stream, and Darwin pulled his mount to a standstill. The mare snorted and shook her head as Darwin dismounted and left her to refresh herself at the water while he walked the remainder of the way down the little valley along the dry edge of the creekbed.

No doubt in wetter years the stream would be filled with water, but drought gripped the country at present and the creek was no more than a trickle. Dry winds filled with dust had buffeted them since their arrival on the *Beagle* in Sydney, but there was no indication that the season had been hard in the bustling township itself. Sydney was a magnificent testimony to the power of the British nation. Darwin had written, with pride, in his journal:

> Here, in a less promising country, scores of years had done many times more than an equal number of centuries have effected in South America. My first feeling was to congratulate myself that I was born an Englishman ... The streets are regular, broad, clean, and

Charles Robert Darwin was born in Shrewsbury in 1809. After studying med-icine, Darwin used his independent wealth to pursue an interest in science. He was appointed naturalist on the Beagle, *1831–36, which his father dismissively hoped might give him some focus in life. On his return he became sec-retary of the Geological Society and a Fellow of the Royal Society. He married his cousin Emma Wedgewood, who bore him ten children. Darwin was often confined to his bed, suf-fered from both paralysing doubts and absolute conviction about his work. Like Geoffroy and Lamarck, his greatest talent lay in seeing the big picture. His scientific credentials were established by his work on coral reefs, published in 1842. Darwin worked on his theory of the mutability of species for twenty years until prompted into publication by Alfred Wal-lace in 1858, who proposed a nearly identical system. In 1859 Darwin published his most famous work,* On the Origin of Species by Means of Natural Selection, *followed by* The Descent of Man *in 1871. After suffering ill-health for many years and anxiety about the theological implications of his work, Darwin died in 1882.*

kept in excellent order; the houses are of good size, and
the shops well furnished. It may be faithfully compared
to the large suburbs which stretch out from London and
a few other great towns in England ...

It seemed so strange to be in the middle of such an English
town in a landscape that was so very un-English. And the further he travelled inland from Sydney, the less familiar the
landscape became. The open woodlands that seemed to dom-
inate New South Wales were nearly all of the one family, with
scanty pale-green leaves drooping vertically and offering little
shade from the scorching sun. The grass beneath was dry and
thin, without the slightest hint of green. The uniform appearance of the vegetation apparently extended throughout the
year, with no glorious burst of exquisite green in spring. The
landscape could not contrast more with the vibrant tropical
forests of South America he had explored so recently.

They had passed a score of Aborigines last evening, car-
rying bundles of spears and other weapons. In return for a
shilling they had stopped and provided demonstrations of
their skills. They did not seem to Darwin to be so degener-
ate as some had made them out to be. They were skilled
marksmen and trackers and several of their comments
revealed sharp minds. They were much to be preferred to the
savage New Zealanders, with their wars and slaves and dirt.
Darwin could not help but feel sorry for these friendly, harmless men, welcoming the white people, who would inevitably
be the cause of their destruction, on to their lands. Alcohol,

disease and the loss of their food supply had already caused a dramatic decline in their numbers.

The path suddenly turned, and to Darwin's surprise an immense gulf opened up before him. A drop of some 1500 feet fell away like a sea cliff overlooking a vast blue ocean of forest. The sandstone crag on which he stood extended horizontally to either side, presenting a series of little headlands. Darwin picked up a stone and threw it off the edge, watching it plummet directly down in the trees far below. The view was spectacular and magnificent—quite unlike anything Darwin had ever seen before.

The correspondence of vertical strata on each side of the valley and the great amphitheatre between gave the impression that the valley had been hollowed out by water. But on reflection Darwin realised that it was impossible for that quantity of rock to have been removed by a river through the narrow gorges and chasms that led from here towards the sea. Perhaps the answer lay in subsidence of the Earth's crust? But that could not explain the pattern of irregular valleys and protruding promontories. His first impression stuck—the scene resembled nothing quite so much as the sea coast. He half closed his eyes, the hazy blue of the forest below transforming into water. The resemblance to Port Jackson was remarkable, with its sandstone promontories, narrow entrances and vast river inlets. The precise geology remained a mystery, but rising and falling sea levels were surely the key, just as they were to so many other great mysteries he had seen on the *Beagle*'s voyage.

Darwin was, by inclination, a geologist, albeit with a passing interest in beetles. This voyage was his opportunity to make a decisive change in his life, to move beyond the vacillating indecision that had haunted his early life and embark upon an honourable career, like his father. Not that his father was really convinced that a voyage around the world would settle him down. 'You care for nothing but shooting, dogs and rat-catching, and you will be a disgrace to yourself and your family,' he had once shouted at his son in a temper. Still, he had finally been persuaded by uncle Josiah that the voyage would not be a waste of time, and that Charles might actually make good use of it, despite the fact that a great many men had declined the opportunity before it had been offered to Darwin. He had been selected in the end, one of his professors gravely explained, not because he was 'a *finished* naturalist' but because he was 'amply qualified for collecting, observing and noting anything worth to be noted in Natural History'.

And indeed, his love of geology and curiosity about nature had been transformed into a passion by the voyage. The great shunted rock formations of South America, with their clear evidence of upheaval and subsidence, had fascinated him. The strange oceanic islands created entirely from tiny sea creatures had puzzled and inspired him. As they had sailed through the Pacific, it had astonished Darwin to think that such fragile coral invaders could defy the all-powerful and never tiring waves of the great Pacific Ocean. But while his professor might have envisaged him merely as a good and observant marksman, the voyage had revealed a hidden talent that not even the most kindly of his professors might have imagined—a talent for making sense of things.

He had been obsessed by the problem of coral reefs for the last year or so. It had once been thought that the creatures that built these structures did so in a great circle to protect themselves from the actions of the ocean on the outer parts. Certainly the largest and strongest corals were found on the outer edge. The French scientists Quoy and Gaimard had completed detailed studies of many of the species comprising a reef and had noted that they did not believe the main reef-building species could survive the full pounding effect of the ocean. And yet what conditions were most favourable to coral formation? While the outer edge supported the biggest, strongest specimens, Quoy and Gaimard had found that the inner edge in tranquil waters supported a far greater diversity of species. If anyone should have produced a conclusive theory of coral-reef formation, it should have been these men who had visited so many different Pacific islands, and yet surprisingly their discussions focused solely on fringing reefs.

This deficiency had puzzled Darwin until he had retraced the steps of their voyages to find that by pure chance every single one of the islands they had visited had been characterised by a fringing coral reef. What was needed was a theory that could explain the development of all reef structures—those surrounding islands, those fringing continental landmasses, those forming coral atolls and those strange islands constructed entirely of dead coral. The answer, he was sure, lay in gradual subsidence and upheaval, or equally gradual changes in sea level. Recalling again the exquisite drawings the French scientists had produced from the de Freycinet expedition, Darwin rued yet again the poor language skills that made him so dependent on translations of French and German work and caused him to labour so painfully through even those texts he most admired.

It was fortunate that his friend and mentor, Charles Lyell, had such a fine grasp of French science. It had been his task to rebut the cataclysmic claims of Cuvier and support the more gradual, uniformitarian position of gradual subsidence and upheaval along with the raising and lowering of sea levels. As Darwin looked out across the spectacular vista, he marvelled at how the combined power of the ocean and time could achieve such remarkable feats. He turned back along the path. It had been worth the walk, but they still had a long way to travel that day. He wanted to get to the farm of Walerawang by nightfall, where the superintendent had promised to take him kangaroo-hunting.

20 January 1836
The open woodland offered a pleasant ride. The large well-spaced trees with their green grassy underlay were as pretty as those in a park, for all they carried the scars of a recent fire. The valley with its gently undulating grassy hills provided the most picturesque of scenery, even for someone thinking only of England. Darwin had descended from the sandstone

plateau the previous evening via the pass of Mount Victoria. An enormous quantity of stone must have been removed to make the road, which was well built and designed. The value of convict labour could not be more apparent, for all it made Darwin uncomfortable to see men enslaved, without even the right to compassion.

The greyhounds ran a small kangaroo rat into a hollow tree, but the sport was poor. Not a single kangaroo was to be seen, nor even a wild dog, and before long they returned to the farmhouse. After lunch, Darwin lay on a grassy bank, sunning himself, and gave himself up to the contemplation of the strange Australian fauna. Every species seemed so different, so unique, so unlike any other form in the rest of the world, that one was almost tempted to think that they must surely have been the product of two entirely different Creators. Why on Earth would the one God have created both the kangaroo and the antelope? The possum and the squirrel? The echidna and the porcupine? It was enough to make one a disbeliever if one were so inclined.

Resting on one elbow, Darwin poked at the sandy soil with a blade of yellowed grass, noticing, as he did so, tiny sprays of sand emerging from a conical pit in the ground. Moving closer, he could see it was the pit of an antlion. A fly had fallen in and was promptly consumed by the voracious larva waiting at the bottom. As he watched, an unwary ant began to slide into the pit, setting off violent struggles in its efforts to escape. The antlion flicked sprays of sand up towards its would-be victim, attempting to dislodge it from the shifting slope, but the ant persevered and escaped.

The sceptic in Darwin's mind retreated. How could two separate Creators possibly have hit upon so beautiful, so simple and yet so artificial a contrivance as the antlion, the genus containing both the European form and the smaller Australian species?

No, the answer to diversity did not lie in separate Creators or indeed in a single act of Creation. Rather, the answer must lie in time itself and in the gradual, creeping nature of change. Great marvels could be created with nothing more than ordinary everyday events, given enough time. Govett's Leap was a perfect example of that. What amazed Darwin was how much a change in one's view of the geological history of the Earth could change one's view of the history of life on Earth. It was natural, under a sudden revolutionary, cataclysmic model, to assume that the history of the Earth had been relatively short, that life had been punctuated by great sweeping extinctions which naturally necessitated creation events to rapidly replace the species lost. By contrast, a uniformitarian view of geology posited a slow, gradual history stretching the Earth's past back indefinitely in time. Time enabled gradual change. What had seemed a sudden cataclysm in the fossil record thus becomes a long period of change and gradual replacement of some species by others—a period of transition from one era to another, from one species to another. With time, great changes could be wrought on the face of the Earth without recourse to any events more dramatic than those happening today. Perhaps, with time, great changes might even be wrought in the nature of life itself.

Just as Cuvier argued that a short geological history precluded changes in species, it seemed to Darwin that Lyell's convincing exposition of a long geological history naturally favoured a transformationist view of species. But Lyell would have none of it. He was brutal in his condemnation of Lamarck's theories. Species, he argued, were stable units over time, enabling them to be reliable geological markers. Lamarck's notion that species were variable, changing from one into another, was insupportable. For Lyell, there was evidence of a modicum of change from place to place and from time to time, but only within a limited, recognisable range.

Still, it comforted Darwin that there was at least one accurate describer of species who did not believe in the permanence of species. Lamarck's transmutationist theories might be vague and absurd in parts, but no one could doubt the quality of his work in describing species themselves. If he could see variation and interconnections between the fossil and living forms of the species he studied, then perhaps it was worth pursuing the question of the origin of species. There were times when Darwin doubted his ability to address this question where so many others had failed. His one saving grace was that he knew a few species well across a number of branches of natural history and, importantly, he could combine an indispensable knowledge of geology with what Lamarck had termed 'biology'.

At dusk, Darwin took a stroll along a chain of ponds, which in wetter weather might constitute a river. He had not gone far when a small splash in the middle of a pool caught his attention. He tugged at his companion's sleeve, pointing, and they lowered themselves behind a rock, sneaking up on the pool so as not to disturb the inhabitant. Before long, ripples on the surface provided evidence of more activity, but whatever it was kept its body well hidden beneath the surface. It was about the size of a water rat, but with a broader body and tail. Just then, a head broke the surface and another creature emerged behind, attacking the first in mock battle. The wide bill of the ornithorhynchus was unmistakable in the ensuing tussle and Darwin was delighted to have the good fortune to see such rare creatures in the wild.

They watched the animals for a little longer before Darwin's companion, Mr Browne, raised his gun and, taking careful aim, shot one in the shallow waters of the pool. Darwin was no mean shot himself, having spent hours practising with a cap in his rooms at Cambridge, but Mr Browne was better. What luck to be in at the death of so wonderful an animal, Darwin thought excitedly. Retrieving the little corpse, he extended its wide webbed feet, marvelling at its bird-like features, mammalian fur and yet knowing of its reptilian skeletal affinities beneath. He had seen a dried specimen in England, but it had not done justice to the little creature at all. He pressed back the rubbery bill, examining the grinding plates within. It was not at all hard like a duck's bill, but quite soft and sensitive. He felt through the thick soft fur, noting the apparent absence of mammary glands. They were notoriously hard to see, he knew, but they were there, perfect examples of nascent organs which, even in their most primitive form (compared to the refined and specialised udders of a cow), were no less useful and suited to their purpose.

It was an anomaly, of that there was no doubt. But it was in seeking to fit such anomalies into the broader patterns of life that one might ultimately find the answer to the origin of species. One day, he would find that answer. Of this he was certain.

'Phalanger de Cook'
Common Ringtail Possum
(Pseudocheirus peregrinus)

1. 'Pagure vieillard' Bristly Hermit Crab (*Aniculus aniculus*)
2. 'Pagure sanguinolent' Yellow-eyed Hermit Crab (*Dardanus lagopodes*)
3. 'Pagure moucheté' Blue-spotted Hermit Crab (*Dardanus guttatus*)

'Hibiscus heterophyllus'
Native Rosella
(Hibiscus heterophyllus)

1. 'Dasyramphe d'Adélie'
Adelie Penguin (*Pygoscelis adeliae*)
2. 'Corfou antipode'
Yellow-eyed Penguin (*Megadyptes antipodes*)

Jules Dumont d'Urville

Antarctica

20 January 1840

It was four in the morning and the sun streamed down through the misty air, faintly warming the commander's back. He rolled his shoulders, releasing the strain of standing still and straight. While most of the crew clambered clumsily about overburdened with coats and gloves against the cold air, Dumont d'Urville wore nothing more than his habitual torn duck trousers and unbuttoned twill coat. Only his bearing betrayed his authority. Many an immaculately presented English officer had been misled by Dumont d'Urville's careless appearance—but a glance from those fierce Norman eyes, a scornful word brought to bear with the full weight of the ancient de Croisilles heritage, and there was no doubt that they dealt with an officer.

Dumont d'Urville narrowed his eyes and scanned the horizon. Huge icebergs (seventy-two at last count) drifted in the calm dark waters, slowly twisting and disintegrating before his eyes. The sun reflected on their crystal walls, creating a bright and magical world. The two ships hung above their own reflections in the still air and the uniform snow-clad mass ahead gleamed tantalisingly. No hint of black or mountain peak revealed itself, but the crew and officers were undaunted and the decks buzzed with excited reports of land, not ice, ahead.

A high-pitched cry sounded overhead, startling the commander. 'Jules!'

The sound drifted off into the distant air. It was only the cry of a gull, but for a moment, Dumont d'Urville could have sworn it cried with his wife's voice. It had been so long since

See page 214 for a biography on Dumont d'Urville.

he had seen Adèle, with her pretty brown hair and vivacious features, that even her voice had faded in his memory until recalled by the pitch and intonation of a seabird's lament. Now the cry gave life to the tear-stained words he tried so hard to forget:

D'Urville, husband, why are you not by my side ... alone, isolated, without any help in my despair ... forcing myself to stay alive for our only remaining child and for you, for whom I would give my life if need be. I am crushed by my sorrow whenever memories come crowding in ... I still hear the heart-rending screams of my baby, but cannot ever see him again ... such a tragic fate, such cruel punishment.

My little Emile, so good, so loving, who had healed my wounds ... why has he been torn from me ... why has God sent me children I adore only to take them from me so cruelly ... I am accursed ...

You will receive two letters. The first telling you how happy I was ... at that time I had saved my son ... he had returned to life and I to happiness when he was so well that I had paid the doctor ... then in the middle of the night the cholera struck ... his face was distorted, there was diarrhoea and vomiting that culminated in a terrible brain fever ... his cries were heart-rending ... during the convulsions his tongue was retracted, his eyes were staring, unseeing, he tore at and bruised his head. The fool of a doctor did not listen to me ... he didn't even sit down ... on the last day time had run out, his little head was covered in blisters. On my knees beside his cradle ... for twelve days swinging from hope to despair and back, clinging to treacherous hope until the last, crying out to that God who was punishing me ... I suffered the torments of the damned ... That cruel prophecy of your mother's ... in your old age you will no longer have any children ... I'm telling you ...

My head burns and I am always cold. How long the days are, that used to be so short. I am waiting for Jules, he thinks of nothing but his lessons ... no more childish affection, no more caresses ... d'Urville, my dear, come home straight away ... What will become of the child that is left? ... I am by myself all day, and at night I cannot sleep. I have to write about a tomb ... he was such a lovely

child ... they only left him with me for
twenty hours, they have taken him from
me ... his beautiful little hands.

When you receive this letter, you will
have finished your work in the ice and you
will be able to come home, won't you? It
is my only desire ... glory, honour,
wealth, I curse you ... the price is too
high for me.

I am to blame for this voyage ...
I too have caused the death of my son.
Why was I ever born, unhappy creature
that I am ... How beautiful my little
Emile was ... Come home I beg you
through the prayers of our children in
Heaven ... I do not pray any more, God
has cursed me ...

But he had not gone home. More than two years had passed
since Adèle had written those terrible words and he was still
in the ice, just one more season, one more attack on this icy
fortress. Tears may have streamed down his cheeks unbidden
and unnoticed when he read of his son's death, but his determination was unswayed. The Southern Continent would
yield her secrets to him. He would not return to France
empty-handed.

Jules would take care of his mother. At eleven, he would
be the man of the house in his father's absence. A smart boy—

studious, serious and stoic—just like his father. He would at least be his mother's rock even if, like his father, he did not make a very accommodating pillow. His neat tidy hand had followed his mother's distraught letter, detailing in turn his mother's decline, who precisely had visited and offered support (the good doctor Quoy, a friend from early travels, came often—others rarely) and his own success at school. Dumont d'Urville smiled at his son's naïve pride but recalled with pain his son's reprimand, 'Why have you made this voyage? We would still have the poor baby and we would all be together, whereas since you left, everything has gone to pieces.'

Jules was too young to understand. One day, when he was grown, he would bask in the glow of his father's achievements and would forgive him. Adèle understood, although she might not forgive him, not now with the loss of another child burnt into her heart. She had known the dreams that plagued him—the destiny of Cook's circumnavigations. The more he had devoted himself to his paternal duties, relishing the new baby, delighting in Adèle's company, working on his novel—the more violent and fearful the dreams became. The spirit ship always drove nearer and nearer the Pole, ungovernable, uncontrollable, forcing him into narrowing channels, rocky ravines or even dry land—and yet even here he saw himself at the helm, railing against the heavens, urging the ship onwards, ever onwards to her destiny.

Adèle had cried when he told her of this final polar expedition. Cook had made three circumnavigations—she knew her husband could do no less. But Cook had also died on that last fateful voyage, joining the ranks of so many other commanders who failed to return—du Fresne, Saint-Allouarn, d'Entrecasteaux, Baudin. But the decision had been made. Dumont d'Urville's fretful dreams ceased to disturb his sleep. Adèle set about preparing for his departure with a gallantry, enthusiasm and devotion for which he would be forever grateful. But her eyes spoke what her lips refused to say— 'What does glory matter when it must be bought at the price of such a long separation?'

The price had been paid now, and Dumont d'Urville could not return without the glory to make that sacrifice worthwhile. He did not care that the ship was weakened and rotten, that their supplies were contaminated and the men still enfeebled from the epidemic of dysentery that had plagued them since leaving Lampung Bay. The useless doctor whined ceaselessly about the conditions, as if it were not his job to care for men dying on board. If only the capable M. Quoy or good-natured M. Gaimard could have been persuaded to join him again on this voyage—but these reliable men had had their share of southern adventures.

The Southern Continent had enchanted the French people ever since Charles de Brosses had written of the need for its discovery. Kerguelen's islands, claimed grandiosely as the tip of a lush and rich continent, had turned out to be little more than windswept rocks, but even this had not dimmed the French enthusiasm for finding the great Southern Land. Cook, with his characteristic determination and temerity, sailed further south than any man had before, charting South

Georgia and the South Sandwich Islands. Ever since, tales of new lands had emerged with regularity from sealers and whalers—some reliable, many not. The English, the Russians and the Americans all claimed to have seen land there in 1820.

But the great Southern Continent had kept its secrets locked within its icy prison. Some believed there was no land at the South Pole at all, just a mass of frozen ocean. But Dumont d'Urville knew there had to be land—the ice was fresh, not salt. Ice always forms around land, never in the open ocean where the incessant movement of the waters prevents its creation. Even in the frozen south the cold was not enough to freeze salt water. There would be land, just as Buffon had predicted so many years ago.

> The discovery, however, of the southern continent, would be a grand object of curiosity, and might be attended with the greatest advantages. A few of its coasts have been recognised; but those navigators who have attempted the discovery, have been always prevented from reaching land by large bodies of ice. The thick fogs which infest those seas is another obstacle. But, notwithstanding all these inconveniencies, it is probable, that, by setting out from the Cape of Good Hope at different seasons, part of this new world might still be discovered.

Sealers claimed they had landed on the continent, but he doubted their claims, just as he doubted the claims of the Englishman, Weddell, whose reputed achievements had finally prompted King Louis-Philippe to grant his request for an expedition. Dumont d'Urville had followed Weddell's route from the tip of Chile, but had encountered conditions so vile, ice so impenetrable, it would have required astonishingly mild weather to have penetrated as far south as Weddell claimed to have done. Despite the conditions, d'Urville pushed on. With the promise of 100 gold francs for every man if they reached the 75th parallel, and an extra 20 francs for every degree further south, the men would follow him to hell and back. Indeed, many felt they had been there as they worked frantically for five days, all frost-bitten hands to picks, pincers and pickaxes to free the imprisoned ships as the ice cracked and closed the channel behind them. In the end, it had only been the weakness of his men succumbing to scurvy that had forced his return.

This season, Dumont d'Urville launched his attack from Hobart Town—a pleasant enough staging post from which to begin this, his last chance, his final season, to run the gauntlet of fearsome icebergs, fogs and foul winds, to conquer Antarctica. But Dumont d'Urville was unperturbed. Just like the search for Lapérouse, he would succeed where all others had failed. He would land on the great Southern Continent and prove it existed. Of this he had no doubt.

A cheer from the lower deck called Dumont d'Urville's attention, and he smiled benevolently as the weirdly bedecked Father Antarctic made an early appearance on deck, preparing to celebrate crossing the 60th parallel. The men had been rehearsing for days, adjusting the familiar equatorial ritual to suit the colder climes. Instead of a tropical baptism the men proposed a communion of wine. No wonder their spirits were high and their health good. Such vulgar pranks were good for the men on a ship that afforded so little amusement.

The strange figure of Father Antarctica beckoned to the captain, and with rising cheers and shouts Dumont d'Urville strode to the lower deck, showers of rice and beans falling on his head and shoulders as he went. A messenger astride a seal approached, delivering to the sovereign of one small floating kingdom a message of welcome from the sovereign of a far greater realm. Dumont d'Urville only hoped Antarctica herself would prove as welcoming as her self-appointed representative. With a gracious bow, he accepted his gift and with another cheer the festivities continued with parades, a sermon and a feast. Dumont d'Urville withdrew to his cabin to work on his journal and papers. He had had enough of the company of men. They would sing and dance all the merrier without his presence on deck.

As the sun finally disappeared after its lengthy sojourn, its rays threw into relief the contours of the beckoning land. In the half twilight, the ice masses seemed more grand, and more sinister. The night itself lasted merely half an hour and even at its depth there was still light enough to read on deck.

By early morning a light south-south-easterly breeze had picked up, inching the ships forward into the ever-increasing icebergs. The walls closed in around the small corvettes, hanging menacingly overhead while the dark waters swirled in powerful eddies near the ice cliffs, threatening to sweep the unwary to their doom. The ships crept forward into the narrow streets of giants while the voices of the uneasy waters roared and boomed from the caverns carved beneath. The shrill voices of the officers echoed eerily back and forth across the narrow corridor, but the men were otherwise silent, all too aware of their peril.

D'Urville glanced back to watch the progress of the *Zélée* following close behind and checked a startled gasp. She looked so tiny, her rigging so frail against those menacing perpendicular walls rising around her, he could barely suppress a momentary sense of terror. The vertical ice stretched on and on ahead, blocking their view of the land, leaning over them and squeezing closer and closer. The scene brought to mind the words of the English poet:

Listen, Stranger! Mist and Snow,
And it grew wond'rous cauld:
And Ice mast-high came floating by
As green as Emerauld.

And thro' the drifts the snowy clifts
Did send a dismal sheen;
Ne shapes of men ne beasts we ken—
The Ice was all between.

The Ice was here, the ice Was there,
The Ice was all around:

It crac'ed and growl'd, and roar'd and
   howl'd,
Like noises of a swound!

Suddenly an opening appeared in the ice ahead and within moments the two ships emerged into an open basin with snow on one side and the floating giants on the other. A wave of relief swept over the crew and Dumont d'Urville felt a weight lift from his shoulders. But as he gazed at the even undulations ahead he was beset by an uncharacteristic doubt. With no sign of rock nor land or soil, just a mass of snow and ice, broken into cliffs at the edges, could this be just another impenetrable wall of icebergs similar to the one they had so perilously negotiated? Could they have come so far only to have to turn back yet again without the final proof of the great Southern Continent?

A shout from the officer of the watch drew their gaze to a patch of dark against the snow, but it quickly disappeared as the ships moved. It was late in the evening, but the bright sun lit up the white world with blinding brilliance. Again! A sombre patch of dark against the snow. Dumont d'Urville hastily ordered the cutter ashore. He must have proof of land.

He kept himself occupied attempting soundings from the ship but the longest of his lines, 100 fathoms, was inadequate to the task. He was not surprised. It was quite clear, from the speed with which they shifted, that even the largest icebergs floated clear of the ocean floor. Impatiently, Dumont d'Urville awaited the cutter's return.

He had almost given up hope of this expedition. When the conservative Charles X had been deposed, he was pleased to offer his support to the new, more liberal regime of Louis-Philippe. Surely Louis-Philippe's modern views and sympathies with the people would also extend to supporting the advancement of science and discovery? But monarchs, it seemed, were never quite what they seemed. D'Urville had been happy to transport the deposed Charles X to England at the request of the new regime. And he had been equally ready to inform his ex-king that he had brought about his own downfall by his unnecessarily conservative approaches. Charles had taken the comment with equanimity. To d'Urville's surprise the deposed king was a simple, unaffected man who quite delighted in hearing d'Urville's tales of his expeditions. On his return to France, d'Urville had been less pleasantly surprised to find that Louis-Philippe's flattering platitudes and dinner invitations never seemed to result in more concrete offers. How could a system of government be based on the foibles of individual men? Surely the time for monarchy had passed.

Even once the expedition had been announced, d'Urville had feared it would be scuttled by the unscrupulous slandering of François Arago, secretary of the Academy of Sciences and the man d'Urville suspected of opposing his membership. D'Urville had written a scathing attack on this 'Sultan of the Observatory'; Arago had replied with withering finesse— 'Sailors say M. d'Urville is a botanist, botanists say he is a sailor'. Hastily Dumont d'Urville withdrew from the arena—

he had no time for such skilful salon repartee. He was a man of action. He would just have to prove them all wrong.

Dumont d'Urville raised his glass towards the shore. The naturalists had been ashore for hours. But here they came at last. The crews rowed as enthusiastically as if headed for the brothels of Hobart Town. The naturalists' cheeks were rosy and excited as they passed up their rough-hewn treasures. Here were the fragments of rock chipped from the heart of an undisputed continent. As Dumont d'Urville fingered the glistening shards of granitic gneiss, holding in his hands the proof they had battled so hard to attain, he barely heard their chattering account of discovery and he would afterwards have to use M. Dubouzet's diaries to re-create for himself that historic moment.

> It was very nearly 9 p.m. when, to our great delight, we landed on the western part of the highest and most westerly of the little islands ... We immediately leapt ashore armed with picks and hammers. The surf made this operation very difficult. I was obliged to leave several men in the boat to keep it in place. I straight away sent one of our sailors to plant the tricolour on this land that no human being before us had either seen or set foot on.
>
> Following the ancient and lovingly persevered English custom, we took possession of it in the name of France, as well as of the adjacent coast where the ice had prevented a landing. Our enthusiasm and joy were boundless then because we felt we had just added a

province to France by this peaceful conquest. If the abuses that have sometimes accompanied this act of taking possession of territory have often caused it to be derided as something worthless and faintly ridiculous, in this case we believed ourselves to have sufficient lawful right to keep up the ancient usage for our country. For we did not dispossess anyone, and as a result we regarded ourselves as being on French territory.

A cheer from the crew announced the distribution of wine to celebrate the occasion. Dumont d'Urville took a gulp from the glass he had been offered, feeling its warmth surge through his innards, spiting the icy cold. Never was Bordeaux wine called on to play a nobler role; never was a bottle emptied more appropriately. There could be no more doubts. They had at last found the great Southern Continent.

'I name this place—Adélie Land,' he proclaimed, raising his glass.

'*Vive le Roi!* Long live the King!'

Notes

PROLOGUE

Page x: '*one of the finest ... a European colony.*' Péron, 1807, p. 252. **Page xi**: '*extrapolation of the present towards the past*', G. Canguilhem, *Idéologie et rationalité*, Urin, Paris, 1970, p. 13, quoted in Barthélemy-Madaule (1982), p. xii. **Page xiii**: '*The webs of significance... Makes the past our puppet.*' Dening, 1998, pp. 208–11. **Page xiv**: '*nothing in biology makes sense without evolution*', Dobzhansky, 1973, p. 125. **Pages xv–xvi**: Many official instructions and proposals for expeditions emphasise the potential political, colonial and commercial benefits, just as modern scientific grant applications almost always seek to cure illness, redress social imbalance and/or protect the environment. The successes and failures of these expeditions need to be judged in relation to the goals the individuals involved set themselves, rather than by the customary claims for national benefit that justified their activities. Hyacinthe de Bougainville's expedition was sent as a show of force to China and to achieve diplomatic goals there. However, Bougainville's journal reveals a strong motivation to follow his father, Louis de Bougainville, whose expedition across the Pacific in 1766–69 had provided the primary impetus for many subsequent expeditions (see Rivière, 1999, and Dunmore, 1969, vol. 2, pp. 156–77).

LOUIS XVI

Page 4: For more biographical information on Louis XVI, see Hardman, 1993. **Page 5**: Louis had been imprisoned, with his family, in the Tower of the Temple, at the Royal Palace on Île de la Cité, since the attack on the Tuileries, before being taken on a two-hour carriage ride to the Place de la Concorde where he was executed. Although accounts of Lapérouse often quote Louis asking after him just before his execution, accounts of Louis's last day make no mention of this query (see the account of Henry Essex Edgeworth de Firmont, the English priest who accompanied Louis, in Hanet-Cléry, 1910; JE Milligan in Thompson, 1938, pp. 226–31; and also Hardman, 1993). Nonetheless, Louis had a strong personal interest in the Lapérouse expedition. Details of Lapérouse's fame and reputation are in Shelton, 1987, and Scott, 1912. **Page 6**: '*confined to . . . to their friends.*' Agriculture Committee and Marine Subcommittee of the National Assembly, quoted in Dunmore & Brossard, 1985. **Pages 6–7**: '*Amongst all . . . Southern Continent*', '*the discovery . . . his name by*' and '*Glory is . . . neighbours and subjects*', Brosses, 1756, trans. Callander, 1766, vol. 1, p. 65. **Pages 7–8**: Gonneville's 1504 account was first published in 1658, and republished in Brosses, 1756, and Callander, 1766 (discussed in Cannon, 1987; Marchant, 1982; Dunmore, 1969, vol. 1, pp. 1–7). For Buffon's role in South Sea exploration, see Roger, 1997, and for early French activities in the Pacific see Dunmore, 1969, vol. 1, pp. 7–53. **Pages 8–9**: Details of Bougainville expedition are taken from Dunmore, 1969, vol. 1, pp. 58–113, while Bougainville's biographical information is drawn from Dunmore, 2005, as are details of Louis de Bougainville's expedition. The naturalist aboard Bougainville's voyage was Philibert Commerson, subsequently famed for having taken Jeanne Baret on board with him disguised as his valet and personal assistant. She was the first documented woman to have circumnavigated the world (Schiebinger, 2003). Commerson named many new plant species, including the cheeky coco-de-mer (*Lodoicea*). His account of Tahiti, rather than Bougainville's, stirred French imagination about a 'society of nature'. Williams & Frost (1988, pp. 1–37) discuss the southern continent in French imagination. **Pages 8–9**: See Dunmore, 1969, vol. 1, pp. 114–65 and pp. 166–95 for summaries of Surville's and Marion du Fresne's expeditions. **Page 9**: For recent contributions to the voluminous literature on James Cook, see Williams, 2004.

Cook's fame, particularly in Australia, is near legendary, causing much debate about the extent of his achievements and failings. Contemporary French explorers, however, were unstinting in their praise and admiration for Cook. French activities were central to inspiring and supporting Cook's work (with free passage). For example, see Banks's letters supporting French scientists, Chambers, 2000, and Gascoigne, 1994. **Page 10**: Dunmore, 1969, vol. 1, pp. 196–294, summarises Kerguelen's and Saint-Allouarn's fates. **Page 11**: Williams & Frost (1988, pp. 1–37) discuss knowledge about the southern continents. **Page 12**: Louis XVI was passionate about geography and repairing clocks but was less suited to kingship (Hardman, 1993). His discussions with Fleurieu and Lapérouse about the expedition are immortalised in a 1785 painting in the royal palace of Versailles by Nicolas Monsiau. **Pages 13–14**: Milet-Mureau, 1799; vol. 1 includes instructions (pp. 4–181) and itinerary (pp. 12–24). **Page 14**: Lapérouse's thoughts reflected a French antipathy towards the earlier Spanish conquests and modern Rousseauean ideals. Enlightenment ideals also became apparent in Britain, with emancipation and anti-slavery and later concerns about the impact of colonisation on Australian Aborigines. **Page 14**: '*on all occasions . . . civility and good behaviour*', Milet-Mureau, 1799, vol. 1, p. 41. **Page 14**: See Crosland, 1992, for the history of the Royal Academy of Sciences. *Savants* were scientists, experimental and observational empiricists, distinct from *philosophes*, who were literary thinkers. *Savants* such as Buffon, however, spanned both traditions. **Page 15**: The Academy's instructions to Lapérouse (Milet-Mureau, 1799, vol. 1, pp. 119–55) resemble the research program (ranging from the useful to the farcical) outlined by French scientist Maupertuis for Frederick of Prussia, which was satirised by Voltaire. **Pages 15–16**: See Milet-Mureau, 1799, vol. 1, pp. 182–93, for equipment and books on the Lapérouse expedition. Background on measuring longitude has been popularly recounted in Sobel, 1995. Many French navigators respected English innovations in this area. Buffon and the burning mirror detail comes from Roger (1997), although the mirror's purpose on the expedition is unclear. Disagreements between Buffon and Linnaeus, both leading naturalists of their time, are also discussed in Roger, 1997. **Page 17**: Napoléon was reported to have been among the unsuccessful candidates for the midshipmen positions on Lapérouse's expedition (but see Duyker, 2003, p. 310n). **Pages 17–20**: Lapérouse expedition details are from Milet-Mureau, 1799, specifically: loss of men in America (vol. 1, pp. 376–80); d'Entrecasteaux in China (letter from Lapérouse to Fleurieu, Manila, 7 April 1787), vol. 2, pp. 462 and 468; the description of Maouna (Navigator Islands), vol. 2, ch. 24. **Page 18**: Marion du Fresne was killed by apparently friendly Maoris in New Zealand, probably after unwittingly transgressing a local law or offending a chief. Cook suffered a similar fate in Hawaii. Lapérouse noted that 'these islands were very turbulent and in little subordination to their chiefs', Milet-Mureau, 1799, vol. 2, pp. 131–2. Failure to recognise different cultural laws was a major cause of violence between early explorers and residents. **Page 19**: '*having attached . . . had suffered*', Milet-Mureau, 1799, vol. 2, p. 132. The massacre in Samoa is described in Milet-Mureau, 1799, vol. 2, pp. 134–8. Many explorers expected the idealised 'state of nature' proposed by philosophers but most were disenchanted by the end of their expeditions. **Page 19**: '*I am a thousand times . . . savages themselves.*' Final letter from Lapérouse to Fleurieu, Botany Bay, 7 February 1788, Milet-Mureau, 1799, vol. 2, p. 506. **Page 19**: French enthusiasm for the English in Botany Bay is noted in Williams & Frost (1988, pp. 161–207), while the English response to the French is described in Milet-Mureau, 1799, vol. 2, p. 179. **Page 19**: '*All Europeans are . . . from home*', Milet-Mureau, 1799, vol. 2, p. 179. **Page 20**: '*we had . . . trouble and embarrassment*', Milet-Mureau, 1799, vol. 2, p. 180. **Page 20**: Lack of botanical or agricultural expertise on the First Fleet contributed to early problems in the colony, according to Arthur Phillip. This contrasts sharply with French expeditions which included gardeners and botanists (Tiley, 2002). George III shared Louis XVI's interest in science and agricultural (Palmer, 1972). The role of Joseph Banks in the first Cook expedition can be found in O'Brian, 1989. **Page 22**: 'The Death of the King', 23 January 1793, from Hall, 1951, pp. 392–3.

JACQUES-JULIEN LABILLARDIÈRE

Page 24: For more biographical information on Labillardière, see Duyker, 2003. **Page 25**: The Declaration of the Rights of Man and Citizen was made on 27 August 1789 (see Stewart, 1951, pp. 113–15). **Page 25**: Details of Labillardière's life at this time are from Duyker, 2003, chs 5 and 6. **Page 26**: Labillardière noted that the quietness of the city was due to the National Guards in a letter dated 26 June 1791. The issue of priests and their oaths of loyalty was of general public interest, but particularly for Labillardière, whose brother Michel had readily acquiesced to the revolutionary demands, incurring the long-standing enmity of many of his rural parishioners, who defended traditional values (Duyker, 2003, p. 10). Similarly Marat, in addition to his general political persona, may have been of particular interest to *savants* because of his scientific and medical credentials. Marat later abolished the Royal Academy and replaced it with the Institut National. **Pages 26–7**: Labillardière's early botanical career is outlined in Duyker (2003, chs 3 and 4) with nomination for Academy membership and friendship with L'Héritier on p. 62. For publication details of *Plants of Syria* see Labillardière, 1791–1812. **Pages 27–8**: Details of the Jardin des Plantes (previously known as the Jardin du Roi), its trees and their history have been taken from Van-Praet, 1991. **Pages 28–9**: See Roger, 1997, for a biography of Buffon and his legacy to the Jardin des Plantes and French biology. As part of a broader Enlightenment interest in collecting and nature, Buffon was influential among European scientists and the public, as evidenced by his book sales (see Burkhardt, 1977, pp. 10–13). For example, Jean-Jacques Rousseau's encouragement of 'herborising' and botanical study is illustrated in Rousseau, 1782, 1785. Daubenton, Buffon's assistant, noted that 'In the present century the science of natural history is more cultivated than it ever has been; not only do the majority of men of letters make it an object of study or relaxation, but there is in addition a greater taste for the science spread throughout the public, and each day it becomes stronger and more general'; quoted in Burkhardt, 1977, p. 13. **Page 29**: Science professionalised much earlier in France than England, partly through lobbying by Jardin des Plantes' *savants* and revolutionary ideology (see Crosland, 1992, 1995). Roger, 1997, also refers to payments for Academicians. **Page 30**: '*Le style est l'homme même*', Buffon's own words, 1931 (1753), were thrown back at him as criticism. Buffon's controversial approach is from Roger, 1997. **Page 31**: From the seventeenth century onwards people changed dramatically the way they thought about the nature of life. The notion of some essential quality underlying all life was Aristotelean in origin, but pervaded folklore and common beliefs, such as barnacle geese growing out of old trees where they sheltered in winter or that Tartary lambs could be a moving plant with wool like a sheep. Eighteenth-century classification systems maintained that plants, animals and minerals were distinct, allowing a concept of species to develop. French classification systems were very thorough and precise, while Carolus Linnaeus (later also known as Carl von Linné) developed a simple system which proved extremely popular among both amateurs and English botanists (Fara, 2003). Buffon was opposed to Linnaeus (see Roger, 1997, p. 32) and Linnaeus for his part was not keen on loose French manners. Buffon felt that Linnaean taxonomy was ill-suited to animals—the specific examples in the text are those highlighted in 'La mangouste' (1765) from Buffon (1749–1804), vol. 13, p. 154. Ultimately taxonomy incorporated in both Linnaean and 'natural' French classifications systems (see Stevens, 1994); however, Linnaeus is immortalised in Linnaean societies set up to promote his system and for his binomial system of nomenclature, which attached his own authority to the bulk of previously known species. **Page 32**: '*form a general . . . Vegetable or Mineral*', Buffon quoted in Roger, 1997. **Page 32**: Buffon's death is described in Roger, 1997, p. 433. Cuvier's response to Buffon's death is from a letter from Cuvier to Pfaff, June 1788, in Cuvier, 1858, p. 49. **Page 33**: Linnaeus's statue was requested for the Jardin on 20 July 1790 by ninety-two scientific signatories. The plaster bust was unveiled on

23 August 1790 in front of a large crowd (Gillispie, 2004, pp. 170–1). Labillardière scrupulously references Buffon's work in his own writings with occasional references to Linnaeus also. However, his membership of the Société de Linné suggests he was sympathetic to Linnaeus's system. Some of Buffon's colleagues (such as Lamarck and Daubenton) were also happy to use or recommend Linnaean systematics when it suited them. **Page 33**: '*We have ... regenerated itself*', Labillardière to James Edward Smith, 29 July 1791, Smith papers, Linnean Society of London, folio 185, quoted in Duyker, 2003, p. 63. **Page 34**: For details of Lamarck's career, see Burkhardt, 1977, and Corsi, 1997. Labillardière's admiration for Lamarck from a letter to James Edward Smith, 4 August 1785, Smith papers, Linnean Society of London, vol. 6, folio 183, quoted in Duyker, 2003, p. 31. **Pages 35–6**: Political lobbying at the Jardin des Plantes during the Revolution (when other intellectual societies were disbanded) is evidenced in André Thouin, 1790: '*Note manuscrite proposant le nom de Musaeum—à la place de Jardin des Plantes*', 1790, Paris, Archives Nationales, J 15/502, quoted in Young Lee, 1997. **Pages 36–8**: '*Gentlemen, We call ... Jacob Forster et autres*', Lermina et autres, 22 Janvier 1791, Pétition de la société d,histoire naturelle de Paris. **Page 39**: Labillardière, 1800, describes his sailing experiences on pp. xi, 20.

ANTOINE-RAYMOND-JOSEPH BRUNI D'ENTRECASTEAUX

Page 41: Most commanders are named in officers' journals but d'Entrecasteaux is often described as 'the general' (also noted by Plomley & Piard-Bernier, 1993, p. vi). For a discussion of d'Entrecasteaux's appointment see Duyker & Duyker, 2001, pp. xvii–xxvi. His previous appointments as Assistant Director for Ports and Arsenals, and as Governor of Île de France (Mauritius) suggest he was a capable and skilled administrator. **Page 42:** For more biographical information on d'Entrecasteaux, see Plomley & Piard-Bernier, 1993. **Page 43**: The sighting of the *Espérance* is based on d'Auribeau's account of events: 'At 5.40 a.m. we sighted the *Espérance* again, having lost sight of her for nearly two hours.' D'Auribeau, 20 March 1792, cited in Plomley & Piard-Bernier, 1993, p. 58 (Plomley heads this 21 April 1792). The violent storm that injured d'Entrecasteaux is described by Plomley & Piard-Bernier, 1993, p. 56, and also in Ventenat's 1792 journal, quoted in Plomley & Piard-Bernier, 1993, p. 346. The description of the passage to Van Diemen's Land, particularly the storm and phosphorus and fire on Amsterdam Island, is described in Duyker & Duyker, 2001, pp. 24–6. **Page 44**: Biographical information on Kermadec and d'Auribeau from Plomley & Piard-Bernier, 1993, pp. 12–14. **Page 46**: This scene is adapted from La Motte du Portail's thirteenth letter to Zélie (1 April 1792) in relation to the sighting of St Paul. 'Everyone being concerned to show their keenness, had made sketches of the island as well as any land that came in sight and they would rush up to the deck, brandishing pencil and paper, and somehow or other start scribbling so as to make some sort of a presentation of the piece of land in sight', quoted in Plomley & Piard-Bernier, 1993, p. 327. **Page 47**: The approach to Tasmania and d'Entrecasteaux's decision to moor in Recherche Bay are documented in d'Auribeau's journal (quoted in Plomley & Piard-Bernier, 1993, p. 58) and Ventenat's journal (Plomley & Piard-Bernier, 1993, pp. 346–8). Ventenat says the general was confined to his cabin on the approach to Tasmania; however, a decision about where they were and where to moor could only have been made with direct observation of the coast. **Pages 48–49**: '*it will be difficult . . . old, and always new*', quoted in Duyker & Duyker, 2001, p. 32. **Page 49**: D'Entrecasteaux was scrupulous about shipboard hygiene (Plomley & Piard-Bernier, 1993, pp. 11, 39). The day's activities are derived from d'Auribeau's journal, 3 May 1792: 'The caulkers completed the starboard side of the frigate in its entirety', quoted in Plomley & Piard-Bernier, 1993, p. 70. **Page 51**: Non-noble officers (such as Lapérouse and d'Entrecasteaux) often suffered during peacetime from a lack of employment. The decision to abolish the *officiers bleu* and *rouge* distinction was in part influenced by Kerguelen's trial. Dunmore, 1969, vol. 1. **Page 52**: '*each one . . . human knowledge*' and '*leave no one . . . your orders*',

Fleurieu to d'Entrecasteaux (13 September 1791), quoted in Duyker & Duyker, 2001, pp. 296–7. **Page 53**: The debate between the surgeon Joannet and naturalists is in Duyker, 2003, pp. 90–1. D'Entrecasteaux's encouragement of all scientific endeavours is noted in Plomley & Piard-Bernier, 1993, p. 10, and Duyker, 2003, p. 91, who quotes d'Entrecasteaux as stating that science was like the 'air one breathes, belonging to everyone'. **Page 53**: Ventenat complains in his journal that they had 'no servant for ourselves, although the order had been given that we should have one' (quoted in Plomley & Piard-Bernier, 1993, p. 352). D'Entrecasteaux's unwillingness to grant them a boat was understandable—the naturalists had already been lost or late several times. **Page 54**: Neither Labillardière nor d'Entrecasteaux detail this incident; however, Ventenat describes it at length (quoted in Plomley & Piard-Bernier, 1993, p. 352). **Page 55**: The description of the naturalists is based on one of M. Riche of the *Espérance* in La Motte du Portail's fourteenth letter to Zélie (24 April 1792), quoted in Plomley & Piard-Bernier, 1993, p. 331. **Page 56**: Descriptions of the forests, native habitation, and species are from d'Entrecasteaux and Labillardière in Duyker & Duyker, 2001, ch. 4, and Duyker, 2003, ch. 8. **Page 57**: The 'hybrid' nature of Australia's fauna was noted by John Hunter on his voyage to New South Wales in 1786 (Hunter, 1793, p. 68). Hunter noted that the example cited for fish also applied to birds and quadrupeds and might be caused by 'promiscuous intercourse' between species, an idea taken up by Erasmus Darwin (Gruber, 1991, p. 53). Cross-species hybridisation must also have occurred to Hunter when he sent the first amphibious mole-like creature (platypus) to England in 1798. **Page 58**: '*On that melancholy . . . affected me*', Lapérouse to Fleurieu, Minister for Marine, Monterey, 19 September 1786 (quoted in Milet-Mureau, 1799, p. 444). **Page 58**: D'Entrecasteaux offered to resign from the navy after his nephew murdered his wife (see La Motte du Portail's fifteenth letter to Zélie, 6 May 1792, quoted in Plomley & Piard-Bernier, 1993, p. 333). Clearly d'Entrecasteaux felt responsible, a view not shared by his superiors given subsequent appointments (see Duyker, 2003, p. 277, n. 3. **Page 59**: For further information on Pacific sailing routes, see Cornell, 1987.

Elisabeth-Paul-Edouard de Rossel

Page 61: In the Foreword to Dumont d'Urville's expedition account (1830–35, pp. xcii–xciii) in which the remains of the Lapérouse expedition are located on Vanikoro, Rossel identifies Vanikoro as the same island they named Recherche Island during the d'Entrecasteaux expedition (see ch. 16). I have thus used Rossel's recollections as the basis for this reconstruction. The d'Entrecasteaux expedition also sailed past this island in July of the previous year. Duyker & Duyker, 2001, state that although the d'Entrecasteaux expedition 'reached the latitude of Pitt Island on the night of 7 July [1792], it was not sighted' and that 'we now know that Pitt Island is Vanikoro Island' (p. xxvii). It seems that both Pitt Island (named by Captain Edwards of the *Pandora*) and Recherche Island (named by d'Entrecasteaux) were Vanikoro Island. **Page 61**: Pacific canoes utilised a lateen rig, set characteristically for particular regions. In the Solomon Islands (known to the French as the Santa Cruz Islands), the two spars on the triangular sail were set almost vertically, positioning the luff of the sail at the top (rather than to the stern), giving them a horn-like appearance. The descriptions of the Santa Cruz and Admiralty islands and islanders are from d'Entrecasteaux's journal, edited by Rossel, translated and quoted in Duyker & Duyker, 2001, pp. 220–7 and 84–5. At the time of the d'Entrecasteaux expedition, a number of commanders had died in the Pacific at the hands of natives, often unexpectedly through transgressions of local laws (e.g. Cook in Hawaii, de Langle from the Lapérouse expedition in Samoa and Marion du Fresne in New Zealand). **Page 62:** For more biographical information on Rossel, see Plomley & Piard-Bernier, 1993. **Pages 63–5**: Observations of Tasmanian Aborigines were recorded by many crew members (summarised in Plomely, 1966, and Plomley & Piard-Bernier, 1993, particularly ch. 11 on ethnographic research in Tasmania, pp. 261–311).

Page 65: Eighteenth-century sailors were unusual for doing 'women's work' such as laundry, cooking and sewing. The contrast must have been even greater for indigenous cultures with a strict gender division of labour (Carol Harrison, pers. comm.). Masefield, 1937, describes fashion among sailors in the late eighteenth century and notes that the pigtail or braided queue originated from France and that it took sailors an hour to 'dress and be dressed'—shaving daily and braiding each other's hair (p. 141). **Page 65**: The steward was Louise Girardin, a widow, who disguised herself as a man to escape family disgrace, through a friend connected to Kermadec. Both d'Entrecasteaux and Kermadec must have known her true identity, and many of the officers and crew suspected, although it was not publicly acknowledged until after her death at sea (Plomley & Piard-Bernier, 1993, pp. 34–5). **Page 66**: Rossel's journals reveal him to be a meticulous and thorough mathematician and also detail the dispute over publications. Manuscrits de M. de Rossel, Archives Nationales 2. JJ 2–3 and 11–14, reproduced on microform reels 1–9 of the Papers of the d'Entrecasteaux expedition, National Library of Australia. **Page 67**: The state of the expedition and its health are described in Plomley & Piard-Bernier, 1993. The importance of d'Entrecasteaux's leadership and the affection with which he was held are evidenced by the responses generated by his death (see Plomley & Piard-Bernier, 1993). Pierre-Guillaume Destouches wrote: 'We all loved him. He had for us more of the qualities of a father than of a captain.' Journal de Gicquel, Archives Nationales, Marine 5 JJ 14, quoted in Duyker & Duyker, 2001, p. 263.

UNKNOWN SAILOR

Pages 69–72: According to Dumont d'Urville, Vanikoro had a reputation among other islanders as being a fever island, plagued by malaria. It is possible that survivors from the Lapérouse expedition were present on Vanikoro when the d'Entrecasteaux expedition sailed past. For details of the probable last days of the Lapérouse expedition see Shelton, 1987, and also Dumont d'Urville's account, translated and quoted in Rosenman, 1987, vol. 1, ch. 18. Horner,

1995, pp. 259–65, also summarises the discovery of the fate of the Lapérouse expedition. **Page 72:** '*Alone, alone . . . so did I*', Coleridge, 1798.

Joseph Banks

Page 74: For more biographical information on Banks, see Lyte, 1980 and O'Brian, 1989. **Page 75**: The French Academy was abolished in 1793 and the Institut National created to take its place (see Crosland, 1992). Staff at the Jardin des Plantes successfully negotiated for the creation of the Muséum d'Histoire Naturelle, effectively cementing their own positions within the new regime (see Gillispie, 2004). **Pages 75–6**: '*I have spoken . . . cultivate Science*', letter from Banks to Labillardière, 9 June 1796, quoted in Chambers, 2000, p. 171. **Page 77**: Banks's Soho Square office and residence is described in Lyte, 1980, while Banks's working practices in his supremely efficient (and transportable) office at his Revesby estate are described by Arthur Young, quoted on p. 181. **Pages 78–80**: British responses to the French Revolution range from Edmund Burke, 1790, to Banks's own letters (see Chambers, 2000). The phrases and beliefs in this section are those expressed by Banks in letters discussing events in France. Banks believed that the general prosperity in England would prevent the lower classes from revolting. In fact, he was wrong. A few years later Banks would defend his Soho home against mob invasion during the Corn Riots (see Lyte, 1980). **Pages 80–1**: Banks's belief in the French respect for science never abated (see De Beer, 1960, which also documents Banks's role in returning Labillardière's specimens). **Page 83**: Banks's sexual adventures in the Pacific, particularly Tahiti, were widely publicised on his return to England (see Fara, 2003). The coco-de-mer from the Seychelles bears a striking resemblance to a woman's pelvis. The naturalist Philibert Commerson from Louis de Bougainville's expedition named the species *Lodoicea*. Emboden, 1974, states the name is derived from Laodice, King Priam's most beautiful daughter (p. 112); however, Duyker, 2003, argues that it is latinised Louis XV. Labillardière formalised Commerson's name *Lodoicea sechellarum*

(Labillardière, 1801), later changed to *Lodoicea maldivicum*. Banks alludes to his admiration for Labillardière's collection in a letter to Labillardière, 15 July 1797, quoted in Chambers, 2000, p. 194. Banks's long-planned work on Australian flora, his *Florilegium*, was never completed in his lifetime, finally being published in 1983. **Pages 84–6**: Banks's meeting with Lord Grenville on 4 August 1796 is documented in the Kew Archives at the Royal Botanic Gardens, Banks Correspondence, vol. 2, folio 146. See also De Beer, 1960, p. 61. The quotes used by Banks in this section—'*Monseiur de la Billardière ... immeasurable esteem*', '*He will ... is refused*' and '*I fear... indulgence to science*'—are from a letter to Lord Grenville, 20 July 1796, quoted in Chambers, 2000, pp. 173–4. '*I would ... of Curiosities*' is drawn from a letter to Major William Price, 4 August 1796, quoted in Chambers, 2000, p. 175.

JOSÉPHINE BONAPARTE

Page 92: For a detailed exploration of Joséphine Bonaparte's life and career, see Gulland, 2000. **Page 93**: In the early days of the Consulate, Malmaison hosted regular festivities when Napoléon returned on the tenth day of each décade (Constant, 1907, vol. 1, ch. 3). 31 March was the first *jour du décadi* after the approval of Baudin's expedition. Napoléon was present at Malmaison at the end of March 1800 (Constant, 1907, vol. 1, ch. 3). Descriptions of Malmaison are from Hamilton, 1999, pp. 118–21. **Page 93**: Buffon estimated the Earth's age (at least 75 000 years old) from the rate at which iron spheres cooled (Buffon, 1778). Buffon thought New Holland was young because it lacked rivers and mountains and its people were simple and primitive (Buffon, 1749–1804, vol. 1, p. 155). Buffon interpreted liberally the 'days' of Genesis and religion generally (as did many *savants*); see Barthélemy-Madaule, 1982, p. 10. **Page 94**: Napoléon's relations with *savants* were documented by Joséphine's daughter, Hortense (Napoléon, 1820). Napoléon's love for working outdoors was noted by Talleyrand, quoted in Hamilton, 1999, p. 118. **Pages 94–5**: Thouin's involvement in the Italian campaign, including the quote '*a grand and sublime truth*' is documented in Blumer (1934).

Details of Labillardière's involvement in Italy, and that of the other Jardin *savants*, can be found in Duyker, 2003, pp. 212–22. '*True conquests . . . human knowledge*' is from Napoléon to Camus, president of the Sciences and Arts class of the Institut National, to which Napoléon was elected in 1797, quoted in Bourrienne, 1891, vol. 1, ch. 10. **Page 95**: '*rich in madrepores . . . and quadruped animals*', Jussieu to the Directorate, 8 Mess. IV (26 June 1796) Mar BB4 995 (4), quoted in Horner, 1987, p. 29. **Page 96:** '*Never before . . . completely fill*', Jussieu to the Directorate, 8 Mess. IV (26 June 1796) Mar BB4 995 (4), quoted in Horner, 1987, p. 29. **Page 96**: The chemist Lavoisier had identified the role of oxygen in plant respiration in 1789. **Page 97**: Hortense described how the First Consul took Joséphine and herself to visit the very elderly Daubenton (Napoléon, 1820). This must have been between 1799 (when Napoléon seized power) and 1800 (Daubenton's death). Baudin's collection was located at the Muséum d'Histoire Naturelle from 1798, so it seems likely that Joséphine would have visited it. For an example of Joséphine's correspondence, see Institut de France (1795–1835), vol. 3, p. 77. *Boronia pinnata* (illustrated in Ventenat, 1803) was one of many Australian plants probably already in Joséphine's garden in 1800. Many of the plants, including this boronia, were cultivated in England prior to 1800 (see Cavanagh, 1990). **Pages 97–8**: Based on and including quotes from Rousseau, 1782, Seventh Promenade. **Page 99**: '*Here all the . . . further new discoveries.*' Baudin to the Institut National, reproduced on Reel 1, Papers of the Baudin Expedition, National Library of Australia. **Page 100**: Napoléon's interest in the New Holland expedition is found in the minute signed by Farfait, 8 Flor. VIII (28 April 1800) Mar BB4 995(1), quoted in Horner, 1987, p. 42. Napoléon's fellow student, Alexandre-Jean des Mazis, recalled that Napoléon had applied to join Lapérouse's expedition as a midshipman (Dunmore, 1985, pp. 203–4) but doubt has been cast on the authenticity of these memoirs: see Duyker, 2003, p. 310n. Napoléon's regret at not having become a scientist is drawn from Geoffroy Saint-Hilaire's recollection of a conversation in Egypt (see ch. 9) from Geoffroy, 1835,

'*Etudes progressives d'un naturaliste pendant les années 1834 et 1835*', appendix to the 42-volume *Mémoires et annales du Muséum d'Histoire Naturelle* quoted in Le Guyader, 2004, p. 256n. Napoléon's interest in and support for science is well recognised (see Gillispie, 2004, p. 310, and Fox, 1992). Charles Blagden recorded Napoléon's interest in obtaining a platypus in a letter to Banks quoted in Hamilton, 1999, p. 9. Banks reportedly sent Napoléon a platypus specimen in 1802 (Moyal, 2000, p. 42). The first known specimen had arrived in England in 1797, and was described there in 1799, but the species became more widely known on the continent when described by Johann Blumenbach in 1800 (see Dugan, 1980). **Pages 100–1:** Baudin's private instructions from the Minister of Marine, from Jouanin, 2004. **Page 101:** Joséphine had an impressive array of Australian plants at Malmaison prior to the Baudin expedition's return in 1804 (see Ventenat, 1803) and quite probably before his departure in 1800. Many came from England. Australian plants that may have been in the Malmaison garden prior to Baudin's departure include those listed in both Ventenat, 1803, and Cavanagh, 1990, such as *Boronia pinnata* from Port Jackson, many paperbarks (or honey-myrtles) including *Melaleuca ericifolia, M. hypericifolia, M. nodosa, M. styphelioides, M. thymifolia* and *M. armillaris* as well as numerous wattles (known then as mimosas): *Acacia decurrens, A. longifolia, A. pubescens* and *A. verticillata.* Joséphine may also have had the readily cultivated climber happy wanderer, *Hardenbergia violacea* (then known as *Kennedia monophylla)* at this time.

NICOLAS BAUDIN

Page 103: Baudin's observations on the *Cumberland* and conditions are documented in Baudin, 2004, 10 December 1802, p. 443, and 13 December 1802, p. 445. **Page 104:** For more biographical information on Baudin, see Cornell, 1965; Horner, 1987; and Toft, 2002. **Page 105:** Memo from Baudin to Hamelin (1802): '*Moyens qui pourront contribuer à la conservation des Quadrupèdes, oiseaux et plantes vivantes embarqués à bord du* Naturaliste', from Reel 1 of the Baudin Papers, Microfilm at the National Library of Australia copied from the Archives Nationales, Marine BB4 995. **Page 106**: For Baudin's thoughts on Hamelin and his officers, see Baudin, 2004, p. 441. **Pages 106–7**: '*Sir, You will . . . Governor King*'. Letter from King to Baudin, 23 November 1802 (Bladen, 1896), vol. 4, p. 1007. **Page 108**: Baudin's opinion of Governor King is expressed in a letter to the Administrators-General of Île de France (also known as Mauritius) and Réunion (also known as Bonaparte or Bourbon), 2 November 1802, quoted in Bladen, 1896, vol. 4, p. 969. Some of Baudin's difficulties with his officers and civilian scientists arose from their sheer number. Baudin had asked for seven *savants* and no midshipmen. He departed with twenty-two *savants* and fifteen midshipmen (Tiley, 2002, p. 112). Midshipmen were trainee officers with no practical experience, but who were often from wealthy and influential families, such as Hyacinthe de Bougainville. The various disputes at Port Jackson, which occupied a considerable quantity of official correspondence for the Governor, include a dispute between Lieutenant Milius and Baudin (Milius to King and King to Milius, 9 July 1802, quoted in Bladen, 1896, vol. 4, pp. 949–53), where flags were flown on the French ship (see letters between Baudin, his officers and King and his officers (23–25 September 1802) quoted in Bladen, 1896, vol. 4, pp. 956–66) and a dispute about French officers (Henri de Freycinet was accused) selling sly grog in the colony. **Pages 108–9**: For differing accounts of the meeting between Flinders and Baudin, see Baudin, 2004, p. 380, and Flinders, 1814. For a comparison see Toft, 2002, pp. 139–46, and Brown, 2000. Baudin and Flinders had very different outlooks and interests in their expeditions. While Baudin's career had been forged as a collector, particularly of live specimens, Flinders had little or no interest in natural history (as documented in a letter by his botanist Brown and quoted in Toft, 2002, p. 173). **Page 109**: King was a lieutenant on the First Fleet and was one of the last people to dine with Lapérouse before his disappearance (Tiley, 2002, p. 138). Flinders headed north after leaving Port Jackson with the explicit intention of finding remains of Lapérouse's expedition on the Queensland coast. 'After passing Cape Capricorn, my first object on landing was to examine the refuse thrown up by the sea . . . but there were no marks of shipwreck.' Flinders quoted in Toft, 2002, p. 186. **Pages 109–10**: Henri de Freycinet's comment to Flinders, '*Captain, if we . . . South Coast before us*' was described in Flinders, 1814, vol. 1, ch. 8. **Page 110**: Baudin described Henri de Freycinet as being 'much too young for that rank' (Baudin, 2004, p. 28). Further concerns over Freycinet's violent temper are in Baudin, 2004, p. 36. Baudin's concerns over Louis de Freycinet's conduct are exemplified in Baudin, 2004, pp. 490–1. Throughout his journal, Baudin emerges more as a sailor than an officer, willing to undertake the work necessary to run the ship, while his officers will not undertake work they regard as beneath their station. This may reflect differences between the Merchant Navy in which Baudin trained and the French Navy, which was still dominated by aristocratic officers. Baudin was well aware of his officers' lack of respect for his command, e.g. Baudin, 2004, p. 409. **Page 111**: Baudin's complains of Bougainville's conduct in Baudin, 2004, pp. 217, 394, 408. **Page 111**: Baudin left the name of the commanding officer and ship blank so that King could fill the spaces in as required. '*Governor King had given . . . recommend particularly to you, Mr. —, Commander of HMS—*', quoted in Bladen, 1896, vol. 4, pp. 968–9. **Page 112**: Baudin had been detained at the Île de France (Mauritius) in 1801 on his way to New Holland, where the Governor refused to provision the expedition and rumours of the expedition's failure prompted many deserters. Baudin saved the expedition by threatening to keep thirty of the island's slaves in place of the deserters. Similar difficulties were encountered by the expedition on their return to France when General Decaen threatened to prevent their departure in order to use their ships for naval purposes. They were able to leave only after a concerted campaign by senior officers. Péron may have played a part in this, perhaps persuading Decaen that he had useful military information about Port Jackson and the English to pass on to the French government. Péron's comments may have fanned Decaen's suspicions about Flinders' expedition, which was forced to put in at Île de France. Flinders had not taken Baudin's letter with him and his passport was for the *Investigator*, which he had left in Port Jackson to sail the *Cumberland* back to England. He was detained on the Île de France for seven years. **Page 113**: Baudin's contempt for Péron (sometimes amused, sometimes annoyed), can be seen from various entries in his journal (e.g. Baudin, 2004, pp. 46, 215, 490). Baudin clearly felt that the scientists he had selected were more useful than the *savants* sent by the Muséum: see comments from Baudin, 2004, pp. 442, 490. Examples of Péron's tendency to get lost and Baudin's concerns can be found in Baudin, 2004, pp. 181, 208, 215, 509. **Page 114**: Even hagiographic biographies such as Wallace, 1984, pp. 6–7, mention the speed with which Péron abandoned his family to sign up with the Volunteer Battalion at the beginning of the Revolution. Péron seems to have regretted his hasty decision but his request for leave was denied. The term *girouette* was used during the Revolution for someone whose political opinions changed with the political climate. **Page 114**: '*I am dying . . . made for you.*' 21 February 1802, Baudin, 2004, p. 340. **Page 115**: Baudin wrote of Mary Beckwith: 'I had known her during my stay at Port Jackson . . . I had promised to interest myself in her case and indeed spoke of it to the Governor . . . he told me that if she wanted to leave, no inquiry would be made about her. She was, therefore, taken aboard the *Naturaliste* on the day before departure', 17 November 1802, Baudin, 2004, p. 425. The artist Lesueur wrote in his private journal 'Our commandant . . . secretly embarked a young woman at Port Jackson . . . During the voyage she had affairs with several members of the crew, and she also caused the commandant's health to worsen again', Lesueur, May–June 1803, Collection Lesueur, Muséum d'Histoire Naturelle, Le Havre, no. 17076-1, p. 62, quoted in Brown, 1998, p. 28. Henri de Freycinet wrote, 'The Citizen Commandant embarks a prostitute for his personal service' from the Helois manuscripts, Mitchell Library, quoted in Toft, 2002, p. 193. For a history of Mary Beckwith see Brown, 1998. **Pages 116–17**: The details of the British flag-raising ceremony are described in Baudin's journal for 14 December 1802 (Baudin, 2004, p. 446). Péron also described the events, 18 November–27 December 1802, Péron

and de Freycinet, 1824, republished 2003, vol. 2, p. 7. It was also
Péron who observed that England had taken 'to herself the possession of this vast expanse of earth and sea', p. 4, and that while the
flag-raising ceremony 'could appear trivial to people who know
little of English politics ... By means of the public and repeated dec-
larations, England seems every day to strengthen her claims, establish her rights more firmly and so contrive pretexts for repelling,
even by force of arms, any nation which might wish to found set-
tlements in these countries', Péron and de Freycinet, 1824, republished 2003, vol. 2, pp. 4, 7. **Pages 118–20**: '*The arrival of ... secret
from you*', Baudin to King, 23 December 1802, quoted in Bladen,
1896, vol. 4, p. 1009. '*I now write ... were unknown*', Baudin to
King, 23 December 1802, quoted in Bladen, 1897, vol. 5, pp. 830–1.
Page 120: '*I have never made so painful a voyage ... my sufferings
will soon be forgotten.*' Baudin to Jussieu from King Island, quoted
in Scott, 1910, p. 239.

ETIENNE GEOFFROY SAINT-HILAIRE

Page 123: Tattooing became popular among sailors after the Cook
expedition to the Pacific, whereby veterans identified themselves
with the islanders they had visited. Although Louis de Freycinet
notes that the officers on the Baudin expedition felt strangely down
when they returned home, it is unlikely that the crew felt the same
way. Milius mentioned the cold and drenching rain off the French
coast causing the loss of animals, in a letter to the Minister of Marine,
quoted in Horner, 1987, p. 324. **Page 124:** For more biographical
information on Geoffrey Saint-Hilaire, see Le Guyader, 2004 (esp.
p. 19). His mumbling, uncertain style of speech was often contrasted
with Cuvier's authoritative and persuasive lectures. Despite what
Cuvier (and others) saw as a lack of logic and rigour in his arguments,
Geoffroy remained adamantly committed to the opinions he held
(albeit with emotion stronger than reason, e.g. see Dugan's 1980 discussion of Geoffroy's debate with Owen over the platypus; Geoffroy
lost the argument at the time, but turned out to be partly right).

Page 125: Hamelin's report on his detention is detailed from Le Havre (7 June 1803) Mar BB4 995 (5): Fivre, *Le Contre amiral Hamelin*, pp. 52–3, while his letter from Le Havre to the Maritime Prefect regarding Banks's intervention (June 1803) is documented in Mar BB4 995 (5), both cited in Horner, 1987, p. 316. **Page 125**: '*That I may once ... the same persons*', Baudin quoted in Horner, 1987, p. 80, from *Magasin Encyclopédique*, 1800, vol. 3, pp. 259–62. **Pages 125–6**: For the circumstances and consequences of the difficulties experienced by the Baudin expedition at Île de France (Mauritius) and the departure of several *savants*, officers and crew, see Horner, 1987, pp. 119–36. Complaints by these men contributed to darkening Baudin's and the expedition's reputation long before the expedition returned to France. **Page 126**: Péron travelled to Paris two days after their arrival to gain permission to unload the collections, leaving Lesueur in charge of them. Letters from the Prefect of the Fourth Maritime Arrondissement to the Minister of Marine, 'Entrée et désarmement de la flûte le *Géographe*, capitaine Milieu, a L'Orient', 23 Mars–5 Septembre 1804, Archives Nationales Marine BB 4 996 (3), reproduced on Reel 2 of the papers of the Baudin expedition, National Library of Australia. **Page 126**: Flinders was forced to put in at Île de France (Mauritius) as Baudin had feared. His reception may have been coloured by Péron's account to General Decaen of the strategic, rather than scientific, nature of Flinders' expedition. General Decaen had an irascible temperament and Flinders was no diplomat. As a result, Flinders remained imprisoned for seven years on Île de France (see Toft, 2002, and Brown, 2000, for further details). Horner, 1987, pp. 338–40, discusses Napoléon's alleged '*Baudin did well to die ...*' comment. **Pages 126–7**: Geoffroy founded the menagerie at the Jardin des Plantes. He had a long-standing complaint with Cuvier over the 'creaming off' of collections. The *Géographe* arrived in Lorient on 25 March 1804. Joséphine's bird-handler (the *oiseleur*) Lefevre arrived on 6 April, with Geoffroy arriving two days later (see Préfet du 4e arrondissement maritime to the Ministre de la Marine, Entrée et désarmement

de la flûte le *Géographe*, capitaine Milieu, à L'Orient, 23 Mars–5
Septembre 1804 [AN Marine BB 4 996 (3)] reproduced on Reel 2 of
the papers of the Baudin expedition, National Library of Australia).
Hamilton, 1999, pp. 181–5, quotes various letters from government
ministers to the director of the Muséum d'Histoire Naturelle after
the arrival of both the *Naturaliste* and the *Géographe*, clarifying the
importance of providing the Empress with the specimens she
requested and ensuring that specimens were fairly 'shared' between
the Jardin and Malmaison. **Page 127**: For details on the transformation of the Jardin des Plantes to the Muséum d'Histoire Naturelle
see Gillispie, 2004, pp. 173–83. **Page 128**: Milbert's jackal escaped
during the journey to Paris, causing consternation among residents.
It was coolly recaptured by Lesueur, cited in Horner, 1987, p. 328.
Page 129: There are multiple versions of the lists of live animals disembarked from the *Géographe* which vary slightly in number and
names. I have used Péron's zoological list of seventy-nine animals in
total: Tableau général de tous les Animaux Vivans se trouvant à bord
du Géographe le 1st Germinal An XII de la République Française,
reproduced on Reel 2 of the Papers of the Baudin Expedition,
National Library of Australia. The description of the carriages is
from the *Annales du Muséum d'Histoire Naturalle*, Paris, 1804, vol.
1, p. 171, cited in Horner, 1987, p. 328. The live animals landed by
Hamelin are listed in Horner, 1987, p. 358n. **Page 130**: '*The profession of arms . . . a Newton*', '*It seems you don't . . . world to discover*',
'*There is nothing . . . sickens my soul*', all from Geoffroy (1835),
Etudes progressives d'un naturaliste pendant les années 1834 et 1835,
Appendix to the *Mémoires et annales du Muséum d'Histoire
Naturelle*, quoted in Le Guyader, 2004, p. 256n. **Page 131**: The official expedition narrative was usually completed by the commander
or, on his death, by a senior naval officer. Neither Milius nor
Hamelin, the surviving senior officers, undertook the task, perhaps
because neither was present for the entire expedition and both were
engaged in active military duties at the time. It was unusual for a
savant such as Péron to be given the task (with naval assistance from

Louis de Freycinet) and it had to have been facilitated by pressure from the Muséum. **Pages 131–2**: '*Apart from ... absolutely new*', Péron, quoted in Frost, 1988, p. 226. **Pages 132–3**: For the debates over the platypus up to this time see Dugan, 1980, pp. 191–201. **Page 134**: Cook's observation of kangaroos is from James Cook, 24 June 1770, *Endeavour* log, quoted in Parkin, 1997, p. 337. For information on the development of Geoffroy's thoughts on unity of plan, see Appel, 1987, and le Guyader, 2004. **Page 135**: '*Science should be ... in spite of systems!*', from Le Guyader, 2004. Goethe wrote that Cuvier worked 'as an anatomist, constantly occupied in separating and sorting, hesitates to unify anything ... to him is given the gift of observing unlimited particularities ... Geoffroy approaches more closely to the great abstract unity with which Buffon had had only a presentiment. It does not frighten him, and when he grasps it, he knows how to use its consequences to his advantage', JW Goethe, quoted in Le Guyader, 2004, p. 267.

FRANÇOIS PÉRON

Page 138: After Péron's death, a number of eulogistic biographies were written about him, while Baudin's reputation remained tarnished until work on manuscript sources in the 1970s. Wallace, 1984, is a recent example of an entirely uncritical appraisal of Péron's life and works. While it is not recommended as an adequate historical resource, I have drawn on it for this chapter (in particular pp. 147–64) as perhaps providing a sense of how Péron would like to be remembered, if not an accurate view of his actual contributions. **Page 139**: Joséphine argued that the garden was at its best at the end of April. Many Australian plants, however, flower in late winter and could be expected to be in bloom in the hothouses in March, in particular the *Kennedia monophylla* (now known as *Hardenbergia violacea*), *Diosma serratifolia* (now known as *Barosma serratifolia*) and the early-flowering acacias such as *Mimosa decurrens* (*Acacia decurrens* or early black wattle), *M. longifolia* (*A. longifolia* or sallow wattle) and *M. verticillata* (*A. verticillata* or prickly moses) (from

Ventenat, 1803). Hamilton, 1999, noted that Joséphine's ladies-in-waiting complained· of being bored by her lectures on plants. Joséphine's relationship with Péron is derived from Wallace, 1984. **Page 142**: The description of the coronation procession is from Wallace, 1984, p. 145. **Page 143**: Péron's lack of amusement at Baudin's sense of humour is noted in Baudin, 2004, p. 277. Péron's anger at Baudin's comments about his efforts is apparent from notes written by Péron on Baudin's manuscript (e.g. see Baudin, 2004, p. 478). **Pages 144–5:** 'increased zeal . . . of leadership', 9 June 1806, quoted in Wallace, 1984, p. 150; '*All that . . . at his own expense.*' Cuvier, Report to Government, 1816, quoted in Wallace, 1984, pp. 150–1. **Page 147**: All plant descriptions are derived from Ventenat, 1803. Tea-trees at Malmaison included *Leptospermum triloculare* (now *L. arachnoides*) and *L. juniperinum*. Golden paper daisies (*Xeranthemum bracteatum,* now known as *Bracteantha bracteatum)* were among the earliest Australian plants grown at Malmaison in 1800 (Hamilton, 1999, p. 165) and they flower in late spring. The handsome flat pea (*Platylobium formosum*) originated from Botany Bay and is described in Ventenat (1803) as flowering at the end of spring although it is often one of the early spring flowerers in its native habitat. The red flame pea (*Chorizema ilicofolium*) flowers spectacularly in late winter–early spring as does the wonga wonga vine (*Bignonia pandorana,* now *Pandorea pandorana). Honey myr-tles or the paperbark *Melaleucas* documented in Ventenat (1803) include *M. ericaefolia* (now *M. ericifolia), M. gnidiaefolia* (now *M. thymifolia), M. hypericifolia, M. nodosa* and *M. myrtifolia* (now *M. squarrosa). The false sarsaparilla (*Kennedea monophylla,* now known as *Hardenbergia violacea)* also flowers profusely in late winter–early spring. Plants in the Malmaison garden which Ventenat (1803) lists as having come from New Holland via Capt. Hamelin (on the *Naturaliste*) include *Josephinia imperatricis* (also known as *Josephinia grandiflora), Apium prostratum* (or sea parsley) and *Hibiscus heterophyllus*. Ventenat (1803) also lists the following plants as having come from New Holland from Capt. Baudin: *Conchium dactyloides (*now *Hakea dactyloides), C. aciculare* (now

Hakea aciculare) and *Callistachys lanceolata* (now *Chorizema lanceolata).* It is worth noting that although many other sources collectively regard all these specimens as having come from Péron, or at least the specimens from the *Géographe,* the contemporaneous Ventenat accurately sourced the plants to the captains of each vessel, even though Baudin did not return with his specimens. The early-flowering *Mimosa decurrens (Acacia decurrens* or early black wattle) and *M. longifolia (A. longifolia* or sallow wattle) have long supple branches with profuse and heavily scented flowers. **Page 148**: This description of Baudin on his death bed comes from an account by Milius at Île de France (Mauritius), quoted in Baldwin, 1964, p. 57.

JEAN-BAPTISTE LAMARCK

Page 150: For more biographical information on Lamarck, see Barthélemy-Madaule, 1982 and Burkhardt, 1977. **Page 151**: Lamarck was blind from 1818. It is not recorded how or why his vision declined but I have imagined him suffering from degenerative myopia, which sometimes results in an improved ability to see very fine details close up. The description of Lamarck's room and study habits are based on those of many museum curators and researchers and a comment by one of Lamarck's colleagues after his death: 'But then it is quite difficult to know precisely where he lived—he took up so little room among us', 26 November 1832, quoted in Barthélemy-Madaule, 1982, p. 13. **Pages 152–3**: The trigonia descriptions are derived from Lamarck, 1804, pp. 553–4. Jean Guillaume Bruguière (1749–98) was a French zoologist working primarily in molluscs and invertebrates, who travelled with Kerguelen on his first voyage. Bruguière's *Tableau encyclopédique et méthodique des trois Règnes de la Nature: vers, coquilles, mollusques et polypes divers* was published posthumously by Lamarck in 1827. Fossilised trigonia are renowned for discrepant sculpture (see Darragh, 1986). **Page 153**: Péron died on 14 December 1810, of tuberculosis. The martyrology of *savants* is mentioned by Burkhardt, 1977, p. 12. It is unclear whether Péron recognised the value of the trigonia when he first found it. He later wrote about the

first find on Maria Island 'trigonia (*Trigonia Antarctica*, N.) a kind
of shell never till now known to be a living subject; and which in our
climate forms such long banks of petrifications', Péron, 1809, pp.
187–8. However, this was written five years after Lamarck had
named the species and highlighted its significance. It is not clear why
Péron attached a new scientific name to a species already described
and named by Lamarck as *Trigonia margaritacae*. **Page 154**: See
ch. 7, note p. 274 for Buffon's approach to the age of the Earth and
religion. Buffon's research into the history of the Earth is documented in *The Epochs of Nature* (1778) in *Natural History: General
and Particular*. The French naturalists Jean-Etienne Guettard and
Nicolas Desmarest provided evidence of extensive volcanic activity across basalt masses from 1752 onwards, promoting the development of Cuvier's ideas regarding the 'cataclysmic' history of the
Earth. Cuvier's ideas were first discussed in *Discours préliminaire* in
1812, later republished as *Discours sur les révolutions de la surface
du globe . . .* (1825). Similarly, his magnum opus on extinction, the
four-volume *Researches into the Fossil Bones of Quadrupeds*, was
published in 1825. However, Cuvier began his research into extinction in 1796 with his study of the giant sloth *Megatherium*, and
continued through his research on the comparative anatomy of
living and fossil elephants. The more biblical overtones of Cuvier's
Discours were accentuated in early English translations (for a brief
history see Young, 1992, pp. 65–79). **Page 155**: Lamarck's theory of
transformation first appeared in the introduction to *Système des animaux sans vertèbres* (1801). He further developed the notion of
adaptations through local circumstances in *Zoological Philosophy*
(1809). The full account of his theory appears in *Histoire naturelle
des animaux sans vertèbres* (1815) (see Young, 1992, pp. 79–84).

ROSE DE FREYCINET

Page 160: For more biographical information on Rose de Freycinet,
see Bassett, 1962 and Rivière, 1996. **Page 161**: Rose's observations
on sailing under full rig and the pacificity of the Pacific on 1 October

1819, quoted in Bassett, 1962, p. 174. Her mild irritation with this deviation in the cause of science is documented in Bassett, 1962, p. 173. **Page 162**: Rose de Freycinet commented on her lack of children in a letter to her mother, translated and quoted in Bassett, 1962, p. 5. 'I am agitated by a thousand fears. The thought of that sea frightens me.' Rose de Freycinet to her mother, translated and quoted in Bassett, 1962, p. 5. Rose's presence on board was reported in the French press just a few weeks after she had left France. The king was unperturbed, reportedly stating that it did not call for punishment since such devotion was unlikely to infect many wives (Bassett, 1962, p. 14). The Minister of Marine was less impressed but was unable to do anything about it until the ship's return. Although Louis faced a court martial for the wreck of his ship on his return (from which he was honourably acquitted), Rose's presence was not mentioned at the tribunal. By this time her story was well known and she was widely regarded as a heroine (Bassett, 1962, p. 249). **Pages 162–3**: The description of Rose is by Jacques Arago, artist of the expedition, cited in Bassett, 1962, p. 149. On their return Arago wrote a racy account of the voyage, barely alluding to Rose's presence, but also provided comments on Rose published later. The events in Île de France (Mauritius) are described from February 1818, translated and quoted in Rivière, 1996, p. 35. Rose's account of her country retreat fantasy is from 1 October 1819, translated and quoted in Rivière, 1996, p. 109. **Pages 163–4**: Rose's comments about food are from 31 October 1817, translated and quoted in Bassett, 1962, p. 175. Details of her daily activity were described on 14 October 1817, from Bassett, 1962, p. 16. The comment about Louis's appreciation for his own voice is quoted in Bassett, 1962, p. 83. **Page 164**: Rose refers to her journal as 'quiet chats' with Caroline on 13 April 1819, translated and quoted in Rivière, 1996, p. 81. The journal was given to Rose's friend Caroline de Nanteuil on her return to France in 1820. It remained in the archives of the Nanteuil family until 1910 when Caroline's grand daughter passed it on to Henri de Freycinet, Rose's great-nephew. In 1923 Charles

Duplomb sought permission to publish it, which was granted in 1926 with some modification by the then Baron de Freycinet and his uncle. The journal does not cover the period from Timor to Port Jackson and material for this time is from letters to Rose's mother, Mme Pinon. **Pages 164–5**: Rose's description of Shark Bay is drawn from a letter to Caroline translated and quoted in Bassett, 1962, p. 92. The indescribable objects were white cotton drawers. Rose's admiration for Shark Bay oysters is documented in Bassett, 1962, p. 89. **Pages 165–6**: M. Quoy left on 12 September 1818 and returned on the 14th. Rose's encounter with the natives was on the 15th, when she ate oysters for lunch. However, some of the other descriptions of her time ashore (turtles and shell-collecting) are from a visit on 18–21 September, when she camped ashore with Louis for several days (see Rivière, 1996, pp. 49–53). See also Bassett, 1962, p. 92. **Pages 166–7**: On Louis de Freycinet's first visit to Shark Bay with the Baudin expedition, Hamelin ordered that the plaque be left and complemented with an additional plaque documenting the *Naturaliste*'s visit. De Freycinet felt the plate was too historic to leave exposed. He deposited the plate in the Académie Royale des Inscriptions et Belles-Lettres, where it was promptly lost and not found for more than a century, despite repeated requests from Australia. In 1940 François Renié found the plate in a box in the basement of the Académie's library and the plate was subsequently gifted to the Western Australian Maritime Museum. The original Dirk Hartog plate (returned to Holland by William Vlamingh) remains in the Netherlands (Playford, 1998, pp. 57–8). **Page 167**: M. Gaimard's escapade is described in Bassett, 1962, p. 92. **Page 168**: '*the water became shallow . . . on the rocks*', quoted in Rivière, 1996, p. 53. **Page 169**: '*It would . . . this part of the world*', Louis de Freycinet, 2001, p. 197. Louis de Freycinet commented that homesickness was not restricted to the Provençaux, but could afflict any Frenchman. **Page 170**: Rose did not write about either Matthew or Ann Flinders. However, given the difficulties Louis faced with accusations of plagiarism over Flinders she would have known about them, and perhaps been struck by the parallels between Ann's fate and her own. Rose also left no comments on Péron, but she was scathing about some of Louis's other naturalist acquaintances and it is unlikely that Rose would have favoured Péron, given the difficulties Louis subsequently faced. **Pages 170–1**: '*The English . . . their decision*', Matthew Flinders, 1814, vol. 1, ch. 8. **Page 171**: '*Happy will it . . . esteem and regrets*', quoted in Wallace, 1984. **Page 172**: For an account of Flinders' death, see Toft, 2002, p. 323. **Pages 173–4**: '*Ah! what a . . . pleasure to me.*' 19 November 1817, quoted in Bassett, 1962, p. 176. **Pages 174–5**: '*The coast that . . . colony has existed?*' Jacques Arago, 1823, vol. 2, p. 265; '*I cannot . . . leagues from Europe*', Jacques Arago, 1823, vol. 2, p. 163.

RENÉ LESSON

Page 177: The descriptions of Fish River and surrounding areas are all from Lesson's journey across the Blue Mountains, originally published in Duperrey, 1826–30, translated in Mackaness, 1950, pp. 143–65. **Page 179**: Details on gum arabic and *Acacia decurrens* are from Cribb & Cribb, 1981, p. 53. **Page 180**: Lesson described being woken the next morning by 'the call of myriads of small red-headed parrots the size of a sparrow', quoted and translated in Mackaness, 1950, p. 159. These were probably Little Lorikeets (*Glossopsitta pusilla*). **Page 181**: '*medicine and surgery . . . salutory results*', Procès-verbaux des délibérations du Collège de Pharmacie de Paris: adresse présentée à l'Assemblée Nationale, quoted in Cowen, 1984, p. 460. **Page 182**: 'Mr. d'Urville . . . when on board, was too frequently brusque (to use a polite term) for this not to be inherent in his character', Lesson, 1838, vol. 1, pp. 301–3, quoted in Dunmore, 1969, vol. 2, p. 128. **Page 182**: Dunmore, 1969, vol. 2, p. 110, notes that Duperrey had drawn up his plans 'jointly with our colleague Mr. d'Urville', quoting Duperrey, 1826–30, vol. 1, p. 5. **Page 183**: Details of Dumont d'Urville's and Duperrey's early careers are taken from Dunmore, 1969, pp. 110–15, and Rosenman, 1987, pp. xliv– xlviii. For further details on the story of the *Vénus de Milo*, see Curtis, 2003. **Page 183**: Lesson's observations on Dumont d'Urville are drawn from Lesson, 1846, translated and quoted in Rosenman, 1987, pp. xlvi–xlvii. **Page 184**: Dumont d'Urville was 'indisposed' on 5–6 February, quoted in Mackaness, 1950, pp. 160, 163. **Page 184**: 'At Mount Yorck may be found in the rainy weather that much sought and curious animal called Echidna and known in the country by the name of hedgehog. Some time before our departure M. Siebert, a German had obtained two live specimens and M. Carnot attempted to take one to France'; Lesson, quoted in Mackaness, 1950, p. 155. The turtle was the Macquarie Turtle, *Emydura macquarii*, first collected by Lesson but described by Gray (1830). The pretty golden frog was probably the green and golden bell frog (*Litoria aurea*), one of the few diurnal frog species, which Lesson described and named as *Rana aurea* in 1829. The Mackaness text quotes Lesson as collecting two 'river scallops'; however, it is more likely the shells Lesson found floating on the river were small freshwater snails, *Glyptophysa* spp., described from this locality as *Physa novaehollandiae* in Lesson, 1831, ch. 11, pp. 239–471. Some specimens were acquired at Bathurst, after the Fish River stop. **Pages 184–5**: Birds recorded in Mackaness, 1950, as having been seen and/or collected by Lesson during his Blue Mountains excursion include 'large white yellow-crested cockatoos, crows and the Blue Mountains' parrot', p. 151 (Sulphur-crested Cockatoo, *Cacatua galerita*; *Corvus* spp.; and the Rainbow Lorikeet, *Trichoglossus haematodus*, which seems to have been called the Blue Mountain Parrot in the early 1800s despite the fact that it is not particularly common in the Blue Mountains). Lesson (p. 157) describes the area as being full of 'the speckled philedon', which is a species of honeyeater. The 'monk (Marops [sic] manachus, *Latham*) whose head is covered with a black skin bereft of feathers, and whose song is sweet and melodious' is not a bee-eater (Merops) as suggested in Mackaness, but also a honeyeater—the Noisy Friarbird (*Philemon corniculatus*) and while it certainly has a characteristically bald head, its voice is far from being sweet and melodious. Lesson's 'flock of Banck's cockatoos' (p. 157) are Red-tailed Black-Cockatoos (*Calyptorhynchus banksii*) while the 'great many beautiful blue parrots' (p. 163) are probably Turquoise Parrots (*Neophema pulchella*). He also hoped to see 'the lyre (*Menura superba*)' (p. 150) now *Menura novaehollandiae*. The 'great kingfisher (*Alcedo fulvus*) whose cry is extraordinarily loud', p. 163, is the Kookaburra (*Dacelo novaeguineae*). (Species identification and taxonomic history facilitated by the online Australian Faunal Directory coordinated by the Australian Biological Resources Study of the Department of Environment and Heritage.)

Georges Cuvier

Page 187: The description of Cuvier in his Academician's uniform comes from le Guyader, 2004, p. 12. For details of Cuvier's childhood and personality, see Negrin, 1977. **Pages 187 and 189**: '*The Baudin . . . precious compilations have gone . . .*', Cuvier & Latreille, report on Duperrey expedition, 18 July 1825, quoted in Horner, 1987, p. 359. Péron left his papers to Lesueur (they were only returned to the Le Havre Museum in 1874–84). **Page 188:** For more biographical information on Cuvier, see Negrin, 1977; Outram, 1984; Appel, 1987; and Rudwick, 1997. **Page 189**: '*It would . . . national property*', from Labillardière to Thouin, 4 April 1796, Additional manuscript 8099, folio 75, to letter from Labillardière to Banks, 5 March 1800, British Library, quoted in Duyker, 2003, p. 207. **Page 190**: Details of Labillardière's publications and their success from Duyker, 2003, p. 226. The comment on Labillardière's *Novae Hollandiae plantarum specimen* that he '*neglected everything that was not involved in the composition of fascicules*' was made by Labillardière to Aylmer Bourke Lambert, 13 February 1805, British Library, Additional manuscript 28 545, folio 28 recto and verso, quoted in Duyker, 2003, p. 230. **Page 191**: Labillardière was also criticised by others for the brevity of his descriptions: Duyker, 2003, p. 234. Details relating to Labillardière's later life can also be found in Duyker, 2003, with the quote on his 'sullen misanthropy' coming from p. 240 (see also letter from Baudin to Labillardière (29 Fructidor 8) about returning books from the d'Entrecasteaux expedition, Reel 2, Papers of the Baudin Expedition, National Library of Australia). **Page 192**: See Burkhardt, 2001, for details of the school for naturalists. **Pages 193–4**: '*It is a great . . . in the laboratory.*' Cuvier quoted in Burkhardt, 2001, p. 337. **Page 194**: Great confusion arose (perhaps cultivated by Cuvier) over Lamarck's notion that transformation could be driven by an animal's need, which many interpreted as meaning an animal's individual will. Under modern evolutionary theory of natural selection, Lamarck's concept of need driving change seems quite reasonable. **Page 195**: 'the ornithorhynchus . . . whose feet resemble those of a seal and the mouth that of a duck', Cuvier, 1828, p. 274, translated and quoted in Gruber, 1991, p. 61. Despite its publication date, this report was presented in 1808. For the debate over the platypus, see Dugan, 1980, Dugan, 1987, and Gruber, 1991. The debate over whether monotremes belonged within or alongside mammals raged bitterly among protagonists. This debate had more to do with ideological positions for or against the proliferation of groupings within a taxonomy than to quantifiable levels of difference between species. Classification remains strongly influenced by tradition and convenience today. For example, the class Aves (birds) clearly belongs at a lower level to (and possibly within) the class Reptilia, yet it remains on an equal footing for historical rather than scientific reasons. **Page 196**: '*These animals are . . . a special class*', Lamarck, 1809. It would be many years before platypus reproduction was understood. Both sides were misled by their belief that lactation and live birth must be linked. Geoffroy eventually conceded that the platypus did feed its young milk and therefore must have live young—suggesting that eggs hatched internally as with some reptiles. It wasn't until 1884 (forty years after Geoffroy died) that British zoologist W.H. Caldwell telegraphed the news 'Monotremes oviparous, ovum meroblastic'. At the same time, W. Haacke displayed an echidna eggshell at the Royal Society of South Australia. Owen, after a lifetime of arguing the contrary, had to concede that monotremes did lay eggs and that lactation and egg-laying were not mutually exclusive characteristics. **Page 197**: Cuvier was famous for his weekly salons. This guest list is derived from a contemporary woodcut featuring the author Stendhal (Henri Beyle) to one side, the poet Alfred de Vigny with influential diplomat Charles Maurice de Talleyrand in the background, as is novelist Prosper Mérimée. Alexander von Humboldt is sitting while General Etienne Maurice Gérard stands in the centre of the image. The foreground, however, is dominated by the seated and detailed figure of Cuvier.

HYACINTHE DE BOUGAINVILLE

Page 200: For more biographical information on Bougainville, see Rivière, 1999 and Dunmore, 2005. **Page 201**: This description is adapted directly from Bougainville's official account of Sydney, translated and quoted in Rivière, 1999, p. 178 and the slightly less flattering account from his journal, Rivière, 1999, notebook 1, p. 49. **Page 203**: Bougainville's account of his visit with Baudin is from Rivière, 1999, pp. 235–40. Bougainville's service record for the period is reproduced on Reel 30 of the papers of the Baudin Expedition, National Library of Australia, with even the more generous Hamelin describing him as imperious and rude to his captain. There is no indication in Bougainville's own writings that he had any sympathy for Baudin as commander at the time or subsequently; however, a fellow midshipman on the voyage, Charles Baudin (no relation), later commented on their youth and the lack of early discipline as a problem. Charles Baudin stood out as the only midshipman to obey Baudin's commands, even when the tasks requested were regarded by his fellow officers as being beneath their station. (See Memoirs of Admiral Charles Baudin AN Marine GG 2 11, pp. 54–56 reproduced on Reel 25 of the papers of the Baudin Expedition, National Library of Australia.) **Page 204**: '*Never forget that ... for a father*', anonymous private letter to Hyacinthe de Bougainville, 1799, quoted in Rivière, 1999, p. 3. **Page 205**: Bougainville describes how he sent out hunters to collect birds and paid them a shilling each, quoted in Rivière, 1999, pp. 113–14. **Page 206**: Bougainville does not mention the Duperrey expedition, except in reference to their earlier visit to Lapérouse's camp at Botany Bay. He must, however, have been aware of the political circumstances surrounding his own and Duperrey's expeditions and would have been aware of Dumont d'Urville's career to that point. Information on the Duperrey expedition is drawn from Dunmore, 1969, vol. 2, pp. 109–55. **Page 206**: The description of the site of Lapérouse's camp is from Rivière, 1999, pp. 111–12. '*Near this tree . . . March 1824*' is quoted on p. 112. **Page 207**: Details of the construction of the monument are from Rivière, 1999, pp. 244–50. **Page 208**: Bougainville's departure from Sydney and his feelings on that occasion are adapted from the account in his notebook quoted in Rivière, 1999, pp. 132–3. **Page 209**: '*Sic voluere fata!*' or 'Thus fate turns' is from Bougainville's published account quoted in Rivière, 1999, p. 161.

JULES DUMONT D'URVILLE

Page 214: For more biographical information on Dumont d'Urville, see Rosenman, 1987, vol. 1. **Pages 215–16**: The description of the expedition at Vanikoro and Dumont d'Urville's concerns are from 15 March 1828, and 17 March 1828, from Rosenman, 1988, vol. 1, p. 233; 'a sacred duty was calling me to this place', Dumont d'Urville, 15 February 1828, from Rosenman, 1987, vol. 1, p. 206; '*explore some of the . . . which resulted from [that] voyage*', from Dumont d'Urville's official instructions, in Rosenman, 1988, vol. 1, pp. 5–6; '*interest will accrue . . . companions in misfortune*', from Dumont d'Urville's official instructions, translated and quoted by Rosenman, 1987, vol. 1, p. 7. **Page 217**: 'I could see myself on the scene of that great calamity, and summoned to give to the shades of our luckless compatriots the final testimony of the sorrow felt by the whole of France.' 24 December 1828, from Rosenman, 1987, vol. 1, p. 174. Dumont d'Urville's description of the trip from Hobart and the health of his crew is from 21 February 1828, from Rosenman, 1988, vol. 1, p. 209. **Page 219**: '*At this . . . our efforts*', Dumont d'Urville, 12 February 1828, from Rosenman, 1987, vol. 1, p. 203.

Page 220: Dumont d'Urville's description of the plants and animals of Vanikoro is from 22 Februrary 1828, from Rosenman, 1987, vol. 1, p. 210. **Pages 220–1**: D'Urville's frustration at lack of information from the natives from Rosenman, 1987, vol. 1, p. 237; their success locating the wreck is from Rosenman, 1987, vol. 1, p. 217. **Page 221**: 'Would it be possible for us to do more than pay our sorrowful tribute to the memory of our unfortunate compatriots? Such were the sad thoughts that left us deep in mournful introspection.' Dumont d'Urville, 12 February 1828, in Rosenman, 1987, vol. 1, p. 203. **Pages 223–4**: Scene derived from 13 March 1828, Rosenman, 1988, vol. 1, pp. 231–2. **Page 225**: 'Just the sight of a pistol can put twenty savages to flight, whereas they would equally be capable of hurling themselves like wild animals at a whole detachment firing at them.' Dumont d'Urville, 17 March 1828, in Rosenman, 1987, vol. 1, p. 234.

ELISABETH-PAUL-EDOUARD DE ROSSEL

Pages 230–1: '*May I be allowed . . . on the island*', Rossel in the foreword to Dumont d'Urville, 1830–5, pp. xcii–xciii, quoted by Dunmore, 1985, p. 264. **Page 232**: Rossel died unexpectedly in 1829, presumably shortly after writing the report on the Dumont d'Urville expedition that was used as a foreword for the account of the voyage. Given Rossel's age, stout build and the sudden, unexpected nature of his death, it is possible that he may have died of a heart attack; however, I have no evidence to confirm this. His assistance and support for Dumont d'Urville and his death are drawn from the epilogue (vol. 5) of Dumont d'Urville, 1830–5, translated in Rosenman, 1987, pp. 271–8. Details of Dumont d'Urville's personality and reception in Paris are drawn from the biographical note in Rosenman, 1987, pp. xli–liii.

CHARLES DARWIN

Pages 235 and 237: '*Here, in . . . towns in England*', Darwin, 12 January 1836, in Darwin, 1845, p. 408. **Pages 235 and 237:** The scenes described are drawn from Darwin, 1845, pp. 408–18. **Page 239**: '*You care*

for nothing ... your family', Robert Darwin to Charles quoted in
Olby, 1967, p. 8. Uncle Josiah was Josiah Wedgwood, friend and
cousin to Darwin's grandfather Erasmus (see Olby, 1967, pp. 11–12,
re Charles's decision to join the *Beagle*); '*a finished naturalist*', '*amply
qualified ... Natural History*', in Moyal, 2000, p. 104. **Page 240**:
Darwin's reputation as a scientist was founded on the success of his
theory of coral reefs. It secured him the friendship and respect of the
geologist Charles Lyell (among others), whose own work and support were hugely influential for Darwin's theory of natural selection.
Darwin had been preoccupied by coral reefs for much of the time he
had spent in South America, where geological subsidence and
upheaval are particularly obvious. By the time he observed the coral
reefs off Tahiti (described in his diary on 17 November 1835), he had
fully formulated his theory, which he probably wrote in manuscript
form some time between 3 and 21 December 1835. His theory is also
documented in his diary of 12 April 1836 and was eventually published both in his popular *Journal of Researches ...* , and *The
Structure and Distribution of Coral Reefs*, 1842 (see Stoddart, 1962).
Darwin refers to Quoy and Gaimard's work on coral polyps from
their voyage with de Freycinet in his 1835 manuscript (Stoddart,
1962). It is probable that the ship would have carried a copy of Louis
de Freycinet's account; however, Darwin would also have been
aware of their work from the summary in Beche, 1831. In later years,
Darwin also used Quoy and Gaimard's work from the Dumont
d'Urville expedition (Darwin, 1842), particularly reproducing and
discussing their material from Vanikoro. However, at the time of his
voyage on the *Beagle*, Darwin would not have had access to this
publication, which only came out in 1834. Darwin's surprise at
Quoy and Gaimard only discussing fringing reefs is derived from
Darwin, 1842, p. 131. **Page 244**: Darwin's observations on his own
attempts to explain the origin and diversity of species, and the
comfort he drew from Lamarck's efforts, are from a letter to
J.D. Hooker, 10 September 1845, quoted in Burkhardt, 1998, pp.
89–90. Lamarck termed 'biology' the study of all organisms and

their common features, rather than particular kingdoms such as botany and zoology; see Young, 1992, p. 82. **Page 245**: 'I consider it a great feat, to be in at the death of so wonderful an animal', Darwin to Philip King, 23 January 1836, quoted in Moyal, 2000, p. 105. Darwin's musings on the platypus and natural selection of its mammary glands are from letters to Lyell, quoted in Moyal, 2000, p. 109.

Jules Dumont d'Urville

Pages 248–61: Details of 20 and 21 January 1840 are from Dumont d'Urville's published account, in Rosenman, 1987, vol. 2, pp. 470–8 (including accounts by other officers). **Page 249**: Adèle-Dorothée Pépin married Jules Sébastien César Dumont d'Urville in 1816. She was a well-educated and well-read daughter of a watch-maker from Toulon and had no fortune or connections. She was reported to be 'lively, generous and gay'. Dumont d'Urville's domineering mother opposed the marriage and refused to receive her daughter-in-law or grandchildren. Adèle and Jules had four children, a son (1817–1822/24?), Jules (1826–42), Sophie (1833–35) and Emile (1836–37). Their surviving child, Jules, was a child prodigy. A biographical summary of Dumont d'Urville and his family is in Rosenman, 1987, vol. 1 , pp. xli–lii. Adèle's support for her husband's work is evidenced in her careful transcription of his New Zealand novel, recently translated by Carol Legge: see Dumont d'Urville, 1992. **Pages 249–51**: '*D'Urville, husband . . . God has cursed me*', letter from Adèle Dumont d'Urville to her husband, 10 September 1837, quoted in Rosenman, 1987, vol. 2, pp. 566–7. **Page 251**: Dunmoulin, the hydrographer on the expedition, wrote 'For anyone who could have seen, as we did, the tears running down his cheeks, his face contorted, when at Valparaiso on our arrival there were letters telling him of the death of his younger son and the mother's despair, it will be easy to understand how sad it was for him to leave his family'. Quoted in Rosenman, 1987, vol. 1, p. li. **Page 252**: '*Why have you . . . gone to pieces*', letter from Jules Dumont d'Urville to his father, 20 September 1837, quoted in Rosenman, 1987, vol. 2, p. 567. **Page 252**: Dumont d'Urville wrote about his dreams of the South Pole and Cook's three voyages in the introduction to his expedition (see Rosenman, 1987, vol. 2, p. 323), where he also expressed his gratitude for his wife's support. **Page 253**: '*What does glory . . . a long separation?*' Letter from Adèle Dumont d'Urville to her husband, 2 September 1839, quoted in Rosenman, 1987, vol. 2, p. 568. **Page 253**: 'Doctor, you must not take fright over nothing; you'll see plenty more; it's your job to see men die on board.' Quote attributed to Dumont d'Urville by M. Leguillou, who reported on the dysentery epidemic on his return to France. Dumont d'Urville was undoubtedly a hard task-master (see also the will of Dumont d'Urville dated 1 November 1839, from Archives Nationales (Marine), Carton GG 2 30, Sundry Dumont d'Urville papers), trans. and quoted in Rosenman, 1987, vol. 2, pp. 574–5). For accounts of the lives of MM. Quoy and Gaimard, see Rosenman, 1987, vol. 2, p. 282. While M. Quoy tended to Adèle in Toulon, M. Gaimard pursued his own medical interests in the northern ice with the *Recherche* expedition. **Page 254**: '*The discovery . . . still be discovered*', quote from Buffon, 1781, 'On geography', 1749–1804, vol. 1, pp. 140–1. These musings on Antarctica and the formation of ice in southern latitudes are from Buffon, 1781, vol. 1, 1749–1804, p. 143. **Pages 257–8**: '*Listen, Stranger . . . of a swound!*' Coleridge, 1798. **Pages 260–61 and 261**: '*Never was Bordeaux wine . . . a bottle emptied more appropriately*', M. Dubouzet's diary, Rosenman, 1987, vol. 2, p. 474.

Bibliography

UNPUBLISHED SOURCES

Dugan, K.G., Marsupials and Monotremes in Pre-Darwinian Australia, PhD, University of Kansas, 1980.

Lermina et autres (1791) Pétition de la société d'histoire naturelle de Paris lue dans la Séance du 22 Janvier 1791, Procés-verbal Assemblée Nationale, No. 539, Chez Baudouin, Paris, BNF document électronique.

Negrin, H.E., Georges Cuvier: Administrator and educator, PhD, New York University, 1977.

Papers of Jacques-Julien Houtou de Labillardière, 1791, 3 leaves, NLA MS 7394.

Papers relating to the voyage of d'Entrecasteaux, 1791–93, Archives Nationales Service Photographique: Paris, 15 microfilm reels, NLA Mfm G 24786-24800.

Papers on the Baudin expedition, 1800–04, Archives Nationales, Société Française du Microfilm: Paris, 33 microfilm reels, NLA Mfm G 2155–2188.

PUBLISHED SOURCES

Appel, T.A., *The Cuvier–Geoffroy Debate: French biology in the decades before Darwin*, Oxford University Press, New York, 1987.

Arago, J., *Narrative of a Voyage Around the World in the* Uranie *and* Physicienne *Corvettes*, Treuttel & Würtz, London, 1823, republished 1971.

Atran, S., *Cognitive Foundations of Natural History*, Cambridge University Press, Cambridge, 1990.

Baldwin, B.S., 'Flinders and the French', *Proceedings of the Royal Geographic Society of Australasia*, SA Branch, vol. 65, 1964.

Barthélemy-Madaule, M., *Lamarck: The mythical precursor,* trans. M.H. Shank, MIT Press, Cambridge, Mass., 1982.

Bassett, M., *The Governor's Lady: Mrs Philip Gidley King*, Oxford University Press, London, 1940.

——*Realms and Islands: The world voyage of Rose de Freycinet in the corvette* Uranie, *1817–1820*, Oxford University Press, London, 1962.

Baudin, N., *The Journal of Post Captain Nicolas Baudin*, trans. Christine Cornell, Friends of the State Library of South Australia, Adelaide, 2004.

Beche, H.T. de la, *A Geological Manual,* Treuttel & Würtz, London, 1831.

Bladen, F.M. (ed.), *Historical Records of New South Wales, Vol. IV—Hunter and King 1800, 1801, 1802*, Charles Potter, Sydney, 1896.

——*Historical Records of New South Wales, Vol. V—King 1803, 1804, 1805,* William Applegate Gullick, Sydney, 1897.

Blainville, H.D. de, 'Sur les mamelles de l'Ornithorhyinque femelle, et sur l'ergot du male', *Société Philomathique de Paris, Nouveau Bulletin,* 1826, pp. 138–40.

Blumer, M.-L., 'La commission pour la recherche des objets de sciences et arts en Italie (1796–1797)', *La Révolution Française*, no. 87, 1934, pp. 237–8.

Blunt, W., *Linnaeus: The compleat naturalist*, Princeton University Press, Princeton, 2001.

Bougainville, H.Y.P.P. de, *Journal de la navigation autour du globe: de la frégate* La Thétis *et de la corvette* L'Esperance *pendant les années 1824, 1825 et 1826*, Arthus Bertrand, Paris, 1837.

Bourrienne, L.A.F. de, *Memoirs of Napoleon Bonaparte*, ed. R.W. Phipps, Charles Scribner's Sons, New York, 1891.

Brosses, C. de, *Histoire des navigations aux terres Australes. Contenant ce que l'on scait des moeurs & des productions des contreés découvertes jusqu'à ce jour; & où il est traité de l'utilité d'y faire de plus amples découvertes, & des moyens d'y former un établissement*, Chez Durand, Paris, 1756.

Brown, A., 'The Captain and the Convict Maid: A Chapter in the life of Nicolas Baudin', *South Australian Geographical Journal*, no. 97, 1998, pp. 20–32.

——*Ill-starred Captains: Flinders and Baudin*, Crawford House, Adelaide, 2000.

Buffon, G.L., *Natural History: General and particular* (1749–1804), 44 volumes., trans. W. Smellie, T. Cadell & W. Davies, London, 1812.

——*Les Epoques de la nature*, Editions du Muséum, Paris, 1778, republished 1962.

——*Discours sur le style*, Hachette, Paris, 1931 [1753].

Burke, E., *Reflections on the Revolution in France*, 1790, republished Penguin Books, London, 1983.

Burkhardt, R.W., *The Spirit of System: Lamarck and evolutionary biology*, Harvard University Press, Cambridge, Mass. 1977.

Burkhardt, F., *Charles Darwin's Letters: A selection 1825–1859*, Cambridge University Press, Cambridge, 1998.

——, 'Naturalists' practices and Nature's Empire: Paris and the platypus: 1815–1833', *Pacific Science*, vol. 55, no. 4, 2001, pp. 327–41.

Callander, J., *Voyages to Terra Australis*, Hawes, Clark & Collins, Edinburgh, 1766 (English translation of Brosses, 1756).

Cannon, M., *The Exploration of Australia*, Reader's Digest, Sydney, 1987.

Carr, D.J. & Carr, S.G.M., *People and Plants in Australia*, Academic Press, Sydney, 1981.

Caullery, M.J.G.C., *A History of Biology*, Walker, New York, 1966.

Cavanagh, T., 'Australian plants cultivated in England, 1771–1800', in P.S. Short, (ed.), *History of Systematic Botany in Australasia*, Australian Systematic Botany Society, Melbourne, 1990.

Chambers, N., *The Letters of Sir Joseph Banks, A Selection 1768–1820*, Imperial College Press, London, 2000.

Coleman, W., *Georges Cuvier, Zoologist: A study in the history of evolution theory*, Harvard University Press, Cambridge, Mass., 1964.

Coleridge, S.T., *The Rime of the Ancyent Marinere*, 1798, republished Bedford, Boston, 1999.

Constant, L. (Wairy), *Memoirs of Constant* (also known as the *Private Life of Napoleon*), trans. E.G. Martin, The Century Company, New York, 1907.

Cornell, C., *Questions Relating to Nicolas Baudin's Australian Expedition, 1800–1804*, Libraries Board of South Australia, Adelaide, 1965.

Cornell, J., *World Cruising Routes*, International Marine Publishing Co., Camden, Maine, 1987.

Corsi, P., 'Celebrating Lamarck', in G. Laurent (ed.), *Jean-Baptiste Lamarck*, Edition to CTHS, Paris, 1997, pp. 51–61.

Cowen, D.L., 'Pharmacy and freedom', *American Journal of Hospital Pharmacy*, no. 41, 1984, pp. 459–67.

Cribb, A.B. & Cribb, J.W., *Wild Medicine in Australia,* Collins, Sydney, 1981.

Crosland, M., *The Society of Arcueil: A vision of French science at the time of Napoleon*, Heinemann, London, 1967.

——, '"Nature" and measurement in eighteenth century France', *Studies on Voltaire and the Eighteenth Century*, no. 87, 1972, pp. 277–309, reprinted in *Studies in the Culture of Science in France and Britain since the Enlightenment*, Variorum, Aldershot, Hampshire, 1995.

——, 'The image of science as a threat: Burke vs Priestly and the "Philosophic Revolution"', *British Journal for the History of Science*, no. 20, 1987, pp. 277–307.

——, *Science Under Control: The French Academy of Sciences 1795–1914*, Cambridge University Press, Cambridge, 1992.

——, 'Anglo-continental scientific relations, c. 1780–1820, with special reference to the correspondence of Sir Joseph Banks', in R.E.R. Banks, B. Elliott, J.G. Harkers et al. (eds), *Sir Joseph*

Banks: A global perspective, Royal Botanic Gardens, Kew, 1994, pp. 13–22.

——, *Studies in the Culture of Science in France and Britain since the Enlightenment*, Variorum, Aldershot, Hampshire, 1995.

Crosland, M. & Bugge, T., *Science in France in the Revolutionary Era*, Society for the History of Technology, Cambridge, Mass., 1969.

Curtis, G., *Disarmed: The story of the Venus de Milo*, Knopf, New York, 2003.

Cuvier, G., 'Mémoire sur le cloportes terrestres', *Journal d'Histoire Naturelle*, no. 2, 1792, pp. 18–31.

——, *Leçons d'anatomie comparée*, Crochard, Fantin, Paris, 1805.

——, *Rapport historique sur les progrès des sciences naturelles depuis 1789 et sur leur état actuel, présenté au government, le 6 février 1808 . . .* Académie des Sciences, Paris, 1810.

——, *Essay on the Theory of the Earth*, trans. R. Kerr, T. Cadell, London, 1822.

——, *Discours sur les révolutions de la surface du globe, et sur les changemens qu'elles ont produits dans le règne animal*, G. Dufour et E. d'Ocagne, Paris, 1825.

——, *Researches into the Fossil Bones of Quadrupeds*, G. Dufour et E. d'Ocagne, Paris, 1825.

——, 'Elegy of Lamarck', *Edinburgh New Philosophical Journal*, vol. 20, 1836, pp. 1–22.

——, *Lettres à C.M. Pfaff 1788–92*, Masson, Paris, 1858.

Darragh, T.A., 'The Cainozoic Trigoniidae of Australia', *Alcheringa*, no. 10, 1986, pp. 1–34.

Darwin, C., *The Structure and Distribution of Coral Reefs*, Smith, Elder & Co., London, 1842.

——, *Journal of Researches into the Natural History and Geology of the Countries Visited During the Voyage of HMS* Beagle *Round the World*, Ward, Lock & Co., London, 1845.

Dawson, J., 'New Zealand science: the French connection', in J. Dunmore (ed.), *New Zealand and the French: Two centuries of contact*, Heritage Press, Waikanae, 1997, pp. 165–70.

De Beer, G., *The Sciences Were Never at War*, Thomas Nelson & Son, London, 1960.

Dening, G., 'Empowering imaginations', *Readings/Writings*, Melbourne University Press, Melbourne, 1998.

Denison, C.D., *French master drawing*, Pierpont Morgan Library, New York, 1993.

Desmond, A., *The Politics of Evolution: Morphology, medicine, and reform in radical London*, University of Chicago Press, Chicago, 1989.

Dobzhansky, T., 'Nothing in biology makes sense except in the light of evolution', *American Biology Teacher*, no. 35, 1973, pp. 125–9.

Dugan, K.G., 'The zoological exploration of the Australian region and its impact on biological theory', in N. Reingold & M. Rothenberg (eds), *Scientific Colonialism: A cross-cultural comparison*, Smithsonian Institution Press: Washington, DC, 1987.

Dumont d'Urville, J.S.-C., *The New Zealanders: A story of Austral lands*, trans. C. Legge, Victoria University Press, Wellington, NZ, 1992.

——, *Voyage de la corvette* l'Astrolabe, *exécuté par ordre du Roi pendant les années 1826, 1827, 1828, 1829, sous le commandement de M. Jules S.-C. Dumont d'Urville*, vols 1–13, Tastu et Cie, Paris, 1830–5.

——, *Voyage au Pôle Sud et dans l'Océanie, sur les corvettes* l'Astrolabe *et la Zélée exécuté par ordre du Roi pendant les années 1837, 1838, 1839, 1840 sous le commandement de M. Jules Dumont d'Urville, Capitaine de vaisseau*, vols 1–23, Gide et Cie, Paris, 1841–54.

Dunmore, J., *French Explorers in the Pacific* (2 vols), Clarendon Press, Oxford, 1969.

——, *Pacific Explorer: The life of Jean-François de la Pérouse, 1741–1788*, Dunmore Press, Palmerston North, NZ, 1985.

——, 'French navigators in New Zealand 1769–1840', in J. Dunmore (ed.), *New Zealand and the French: Two centuries of contact*, Heritage Press, Waikanae, 1997, pp. 9–19.

——, 'New Zealand and early French literature', in J. Dunmore (ed.), *New Zealand and the French: Two centuries of contact*, Heritage Press, Waikanae, 1997, pp. 48–53.

——, *Storms and Dreams: Louis de Bougainville, soldier, explorer, statesman*, ABC Books, Sydney, 2005.

Dunmore, J. & Brossard, M. (eds), *Le voyage de La Pérouse: 1785–1788, récits et documents originaux présentés*, Impr. nationale, Paris, 1985.

Duperrey, I.L., *Voyage autour du monde, exécuté par ordre du Roi, sur la Corvette de sa Majesté, La Coquille, pendant les Années 1822–5* (9 vols), Arthus Bertrand, Paris, 1826–30.

Duyker, E., *An Officer of the Blue: Marc-Joseph Marion du Fresne, south sea explorer 1724–1772*, Melbourne University Press, Melbourne, 1994.

——, *Citizen Labillardière: A naturalist's life in revolution and exploration (1755–1834)*, Melbourne University Press, Melbourne, 2003.

Duyker, E. & Duyker, M. (eds & trans), *Bruny d'Entrecastaux, Voyage to Australia and the Pacific 1791–1793*, Melbourne University Press, Melbourne, 2001.

Ehrman, J., *The Younger Pitt*, Constable, London, 1983.

Emboden, W.A., *Bizarre Plants: Magical, monstrous and mythical*, Studio Vista, London, 1974.

Erickson, L.O., *Metafact: Essayistic science in eighteenth century France*, North Carolina Studies in the Romance Languages and Literatures, Chapel Hill, North Carolina, 2004.

Fara, P., *Sex, Botany and Empire: The story of Carl Linnaeus and Joseph Banks*, Icon, Cambridge, 2003.

Findlen, P. , 'Courting nature', in N. Jardine, J.A. Secord & E.C. Spary (eds), *Cultures of Natural History*, Cambridge University Press, Cambridge, 1996.

Flinders, M., *Voyage to Terra Australis*, G. & W. Nicol, London, 1814.

Fornasiero, J., Monteath, P. & West-Sooby, J., *Encountering Terra Australis*, Wakefield Press, Adelaide, 2004.

Fox, R., 'Scientific enterprise and the patronage of research in France 1800–1870', in R. Fox (ed.), *The Culture of Science in France 1700–1900*, Variorum, Aldershot, Hampshire, 1992.

Freycinet, L. de, *Voyage autour du monde: entrepris par ordre du roi ... exécuté sur les corvettes de* S.M. l'Uranie *et* la Physicienne, *pendant les années 1817, 1818, 1819 et 1820*, Chez Pillet Aîné, Paris, 1824.

——, *Reflections on New South Wales*, trans. from *Voyage autour du monde* (Paris, 1824–44) by T. Cullity, Hordern House Rare Books, Sydney, 2001.

Frost, A., 'Australia: The emergence of a continent', in G. Williams & A. Frost (eds), *Terra Australis to Australia*, Oxford University Press, Melbourne, 1988, pp. 209–38.

Gascoigne, J., *Joseph Banks and the English Enlightenment: Useful knowledge and polite culture*, Cambridge University Press, Cambridge, 1994.

Geoffroy Saint-Hilaire, E., 'Sur un appareil glanduleux récemment découvert en Allemagne dans l'Ornithorhynque situé sur les flancs de la région abdominale et faussement considéré comme une glande mammaire', *Annales des Sciences Naturelles,* no. 9, 1826, pp. 458–60.

Gillispie, C.C., *Science and Polity in France: The revolutionary and Napoleonic years*, Princeton University Press, New York, 2004.

Gray, J.E., 'A synopsis of the species of the class Reptilia', in E. Griffith, *The Animal Kingdom Arranged in Conformity with its Organization by the Baron Cuvier*, Whittaker, Treacher & Co., London, 1830, pp. 1–110.

Gruber, J.W., 'Does the platypus lay eggs? The history of an event in science', *Archives of Natural History*, vol. 18, no. 1, 1991, pp. 51–123.

Gulland, S., *The Josephine Bonaparte Collection*, vols 1–3, Headline Book Publishing, London, 2000.

Le Guyader, H., *Etienne Geoffroy Saint-Hilaire 1772–1844: A visionary naturalist,* University of Chicago Press, Chicago, 2004.

Hall, J.H., *A Documentary Survey of the French Revolution*, Macmillan, New York, 1951, pp. 392–3.

Hamilton, J., *Napoleon, the Empress and the Artist*, Kangaroo Press, Sydney, 1999.

Hanet-Cléry, J.B.C., *The Royal Family in the Temple Prison (journal of the imprisonment) with a supplementary chapter on the Last Hours of Louis XVI by his confessor l'Abbé Edgeworth de Firmont*, trans. E.J. Méras, London, 1910.

Hardman, J., *Louis XVI*, Yale University Press, New Haven, 1993.

Harvey, A.D., *Lord Grenville 1759–1834: A bibliography*, Meckler, London, 1989.

Horner, F.B., *The French Reconnaissance: Baudin in Australia 1801–1803*, Melbourne University Press, Melbourne, 1987.

——, *Looking for La Pérouse: d'Entrecasteaux in Australia and the South Pacific, 1792–1793*, Melbourne University Press, Melbourne, 1995.

Hubert, G., *Malmaison*, Editions de la Réunion des Musées Nationaux, Paris, 1980.

Hunter, J., *An Historical Journal of the Transactions at Port Jackson and Norfolk Island . . .*, John Stockdale, London, 1793.

Institut de France (1795–1835), *Procés-Verbaux de l'Académie des Sciences*, Imprimerie Nationale, Paris, republished 1979.

Jouanin, C., 'Nicolas Baudin chargé de réunir une collection pour la future Impératrice Joséphine', *Australian Journal of French Studies*, vol. 41, no. 2, 2004, pp. 43–53.

Kimborough, M., *Louis-Antoine de Bougainville 1729–1811: A study in French naval history and politics*, Edwin Mellen Press, New York, 1990.

King, J. & King, J., *Philip Gidley King: A biography of the third governor of New South Wales*, Methuen, Sydney, 1981.

Labillardière, J.J., *Icones plantarum Syriae rariorum* (5 vols), Paris, 1791–1812, republished J. Cramer Lehre, Germany, 1968.

——, *Voyage in search of La Pérouse*, trans. J. Stockdale, 1800, reprinted N. Israel, Amsterdam, 1971.

——, 'Sur le cocotier des Maldives', *Annales du muséum national d'histoire naturelle*, no. 6, 1807, pp. 451–6.

Lamarck, J.B., *La flore française*, Imprimerie Royale, Paris, 1778.

——, *Système des animaux sans vertèbres*, Déterville, Paris, 1801.

——, 'Sur une nouvelle espèce de Trigonie, et sur une nouvelle espèce d'Huître, découvertes dans le voyage du capitaine Baudin', *Annales d'histoire naturelle,* Paris, vol. 4, 1804, pp. 351–9.

——, *Zoological Philosophy*, 1809, trans. H. Elliot, Macmillan, London, 1914.

——, *Histoire naturelle des animaux sans vertèbres,* 7 vols, Déterville, Paris, 1815–22.

La Pérouse, J.-F. de G., *The Journal of Jean-François de Galaup de la Pérouse, 1785–1788*, 2 vols, trans. & ed. J. Dunmore, Hakluyt Society, London, 1994–95.

Larson, J.L., *Interpreting Nature: The science of living from Linnaeus to Kant*, John Hopkins University Press, Baltimore, 1994.

Legge, C., 'Dumont d'Urville and the Maori: 1824', in J. Dunmore (ed.), *New Zealand and the French: Two centuries of contact*, Heritage Press, Waikanae, 1997, pp. 54–61.

Lesson, R.P., *Voyage autour du monde exécuté par ordre du Roi, sur la corvette de sa Majesté*, La Coquille, *pendant les années 1822, 1823, 1824 et 1825*, Zoologie, 2 vols., Bertrand, Paris, 1831.

——, *Voyage autour de monde entrepris par ordre du gouvernement sur la corvette* La Coquille, 2 vols, P. Pourrat frères, Paris, 1838.

——, *Notice historique sur l'Amiral Dumont d'Urville,* Imprimerie de Henry Loustau, Rochefort, 1846.

Lyte, C., *Sir Joseph Banks: 18th century explorer, botanist and entrepreneur*, David & Charles, London, 1980.

Mackaness, G., *Fourteen Journeys over the Blue Mountains of New South Wales, 1813-1841*, Ford, Sydney, 1950.

MacLeod, R., *Nature and Empire: Science and the colonial enterprise*, University of Chicago Press, Chicago, 2001.

Marchant, L.R., *France Australe*, Artlook Books, Perth, 1982.

Masefield, J., *Sea Life in Nelson's Time*, Methuen, London, 1937.

Meckel, J.F., 'Die Säugerthiernatur des Ornithorynchus', *Notizen aus dem Gebiet der Natur- und Heilkunde*, vol. 6, 1824, p. 144.

——, *Ornithorynchi paradoxi descriptio anatomica*, Gerard Fleischer, Leipzig, 1826.

Milet-Mureau, L.A., *A Voyage Around the World Performed in the Years 1785, 1786, and 1788 by the* Boussole *and* Astrolabe *under the Command of J.F.G. de la Pérouse*, English trans., vols 1–3, A. Hamilton, London, 1799.

Moyal, A., *A Bright and Savage Land: Scientists in colonial Australia*, Collins, Sydney, 1986.

——, *Platypus*, Allen & Unwin, Sydney, 2000.

Napoléon, Prince (ed.), *Memoirs of Queen Hortense*, 1820, trans. A.K. Griggs & F.M. Robinson, Thornton Butterworth, London, 1928.

O'Brian, P., *Joseph Banks*, Collins Harvill, London, 1989.

Olby, R.C., *Charles Darwin*, Oxford University Press, Oxford, 1967.

Osborne, M.A., *Nature, the Exotic and the Science of French Colonialism*, Indiana University Press, Bloomington, 1994.

Outram, D., *Georges Cuvier: Vocation, science and authority in post-revolutionary France*, Manchester University Press, Manchester, 1984.

Packard, A.S., *Lamarck, the Founder of Evolution: His life and work with translations of his writings on organic evolution*, Arno Press, New York, 1980.

Palmer, A., *The Life and Times of George IV*, Weidenfeld & Nicolson, London, 1972.

Parkin, R., *HM Bark* Endeavour: *Her place in Australian history*, Melbourne University Press, Melbourne, 1997.

Péron, F., *Voyage de découvertes aux terres australes, exécuté par ordre de sa Majesté, l'Empereur et Roi, sur les corvettes* le Géographe, le Naturaliste *et* la Goëlette le Casuarina, *pendant les années 1800, 1801, 1802, 1803 et 1804*, vol. 1–3, De L'Imprimerie Impériale, Paris, 1807–17.

——, *Voyage of Discovery to the Southern Hemisphere*, vol. 1 (English trans.), Richard Phillips, London, 1809.

Péron, F. & de Freycinet, L. *Voyage of Discovery to the Southern Lands*, 1824, book IV, comprising chs 12–34, trans. C. Cornell, republished Friends of the State Library of South Australia, Adelaide, 2003.

Playford, P., *Voyage of Discovery to Terra Australis, by William de Vlamingh 1696–97*, Western Australian Museum, Perth, 1998.

Plomley, N.J.B., *French Manuscripts Referring to the Tasmanian Aborigines: A preliminary report*, Launceston Museum Committee, Launceston, 1966.

Plomley, B. & Piard-Bernier, J., *The General: The visits of the expedition led by Bruny d'Entrecastaux to Tasmanian waters in 1792 and 1793*, Queen Victoria Museum, Launceston, 1993.

Riskin, J., *Science in the Age of Sensibility: The sentimental empiricists of the French enlightenment*, Chicago University Press, Chicago, 2002.

Rivière, M.S., *A Woman of Courage*, National Library of Australia, Canberra, 1996.

——, (trans. & ed.), *The Governor's Noble Guest: Hyacinthe de Bougainville's account of Port Jackson, 1825*, Melbourne University Press, Melbourne, 1999.

Rivière, M.S. & Einam, T.H. (eds), *Any Port in a Storm: From Provence to Australia: Rolland's journal of the voyage of* La Coquille *(1822–1825)*, James Cook University, Townsville, 1993.

Roche, D., 'Natural history in the academies', in N. Jardine, J.A. Secord & E.C. Spary (eds), *Cultures of Natural History*, Cambridge University Press, Cambridge, 1996, pp. 127–44.

Roger, J., *Buffon: A Life in Natural History*, Cornell University Press, New York, 1997.

——, *The Life Sciences in Eighteenth Century French Thought*, Stanford University Press, Stanford, 1997.

Rosenman, H. (trans. & ed.), *An Account in Two Volumes of Two Voyages to the South Seas by Jules Dumont d'Urville*, Melbourne University Press, Melbourne, 1987.

Rousseau, J.J., *Les rêveries du promeneur solitaire*, 1782, *The Reveries of the Solitary Walker*, trans. C.E. Butterworth, New York University Press, New York, 1979.

——, *Lettres élémentaires sur la botanique*, 1771–73, *Letters on the Elements of Botany, Addressed to a Lady*, trans. T. Martyn, B. White, London, 1785.

Rudwick, M.J.S., *Georges Cuvier, Fossil Bones and Geological Catastrophes: New translations and interpretations of the primary texts*, Chicago University Press, Chicago, 1997.

Schiebinger, L., 'Jeanne Baret: the first woman to circumnavigate the globe', *Endeavour*, vol. 27, no. 1, 2003, pp. 22–5.

Scott, E., *Terre Napoléon: A history of French explorations and projects in Australia*, Methuen & Co., London, 1910.

——, *Lapérouse*, Angus & Robertson, Sydney, 1912.

Shelton, R.C., *From Hudson Bay to Botany Bay: The lost frigates of Lapérouse*, NC Press, Toronto, 1987.

Slaughter, M.M., *Universal Language and Scientific Taxonomy in the Seventeenth Century*, Cambridge University Press, Cambridge, 1982.

Sobel, D., *Longitude: The true story of a lone genius who solved the greatest scientific problem of his time*, Walker, New York, 1995.

Stafleau, F.A., *Linnaeus and the Linnaeans: The spreading of their ideas in systematic botany, 1735–1789*, Oosthoek, Utrecht, 1971.

Stevens, P.F., *The Development of Biological Systematics: Antoine-Laurent de Jussieu, nature, and the natural system*, Columbia University Press, New York, 1994.

Stewart, J.H., *A Documentary Survey of the French Revolution*, Macmillan, New York, 1951.

Stoddart, D.R., 'Coral Islands by Charles Darwin with introduction, maps and remarks', *Atoll Research Bulletin*, no. 88, 1962, pp. 1–20.

Thompson, J.M. (ed.), *English Witnesses of the French Revolution*, Basil Blackwell, Oxford, 1938.

Tiley, R., *Australian Navigators: Picking up shells and catching butterflies in an age of revolution*, Kangaroo Press, Sydney, 2002.

Toft, K., *The Navigators*, Duffy & Snellgrove, Sydney, 2002.

Triebel, L.A. & Batt, J.C., *The French Exploration of Australia*, L.G. Shea, Hobart, 1957.

Van-Praet, M., *Stroller's Guide to the Jardin des Plantes*, National Museum of Natural History, Paris, 1991.

Ventenat, E.P., *Jardin de la Malmaison*, Imprimerie de Crapelet, Paris, 1803.

Walker, J.B., 'The French in Van Diemen's Land and the early settlement of the Derwent River', in *Early Tasmania: Papers read before the Royal Society of Tasmania during the years 1888–1899*, M.C. Reed, Tasmania (facsimile edition), 1989.

Wallace, C., *The Lost Australia of François Péron*, Nottingham Court Press, London, 1984.

Wallis, H., 'Java la Grande: The enigma of the Dieppe Maps', in G. Williams & A. Frost (eds), *Terra Australis to Australia*, Oxford University Press, Melbourne, 1988, pp. 39–81.

Williams, G., 'New Holland to New South Wales: The English approaches', in G. Williams & A. Frost (eds), *Terra Australis to Australia*, Oxford University Press, Melbourne, 1988, pp. 117–59.

——, *Captain Cook: Explorations and reassessments*, Boydell Press, Woodbridge, UK, 2004.

Williams, G. & Frost, A., 'Terra Australis: Theory and speculation', in G. Williams & A. Frost (eds), *Terra Australis to Australia*, Oxford University Press, Melbourne, 1988, pp. 1–37.

——, 'New South Wales: Expectations and reality', in G. Williams & A. Frost (eds), *Terra Australis to Australia*, Oxford University Press, Melbourne, 1988, pp. 161–207.

Young, D., *The Discovery of Evolution*, Cambridge University Press, London, 1992.

Young Lee, P., 'The Museum of Alexandria and the formation of the "Museum" in eighteenth-century France', *Art Bulletin*, September 1997.

Picture Sources

The images throughout this book are from the State Library of Victoria, unless otherwise credited. Where possible, original sources have been provided; however, if this information was not available, secondary sources have been listed.

LOOKING FOR LAPÉROUSE, PP. XXIV–87

pp. xxiv–1: D'Entrecasteaux's ship, the Espérance, off Western Australia, Musee de l'Homme, Paris, in Plomley & Piard-Bernier, 1993; **pp. 3 and 4:** Mondain, *Louis XVI*, engraving, nla.pic-an9633621, National Library of Australia; **pp. 23 and 24:** Labillardière lithograph by Langlumé after a portrait by Alexis Nicolas Noël, Mitchell Library, State Library of New South Wales, in Duyker, 2003; **pp. 40 and 42:** D'Entrecasteaux engraving (c. 1791) by Edme Quenedey, in Duyker, 2003; **pp. 60, 62 and 227:** Rossel in Duyker & Duyker, 2001; **pp. 68 and 70:** 'Unknown sailor', *Head of a young man in red chalk* by Jean-Baptiste Greuze, Pierpont Morgan Library, in Denison, 1993; **pp. 73 and 74:** Banks engraving (1789) by Joseph Collyer from a pastel sketch by John Russell, National Library of Australia, in Duyker, 2003.

PICKING UP SHELLS AND CATCHING BUTTERFLIES, PP. 88–155

pp. 88–9: A view of Malmaison by Charles Lesueur, in Péron, 1807. Background image, detail Victor Pillement, *Nouvelle-Hollande, Nelle. Galles du Sud, vue d'une partie de la ville de Sydney, capitale des colonies anglaises aux terres australes, et de l'entree du Port Jackson dans lequel cette ville est situee*, nla.pic–an7568617, National Library of Australia; **pp. 91 and 92:** Detail from *Josephine Tasher de la Pagerie, Empress of France* (1808) by Antoine-Jean Gros, Musée Masséna, Nice, in Hamilton, 1999; **pp. 102 and 104:** Baudin engraving by Andre Joseph Mecou from a drawing by Joseph Jauffret, Bibliotheque National, in Baudin, 2004; **pp. 122 and 124:** Geoffroy Saint-Hilaire (c. 1842), Wellcome Institute Library, London, in Desmond, 1989; **pp. 137 and 138:** Péron engraving by Choubard from a drawing by Charles Lesueur, Muséum d'Histoire naturelle, Le Havre, in Péron, 1807–17; **pp. 149 and 150:** Lamarck in 1821, Wellcome Institute Library, London, in Desmond, 1989.

IN THE FOOTSTEPS OF OTHERS, PP. 156–209
pp. 156–7: from Pillement, *Nouvelle-Hollande, Nelle. Galles du Sud* ..., nla.pic–an7568617, National Library of Australia; **pp. 159 and 160:** Rose de Freycinet in Riviére, 1996; **pp. 176 and 178:** Lesson engraving from the frontispiece of Lesson, 1838; **pp. 186 and 188:** Cuvier engraving by J. Thompson, Society for the Diffusion of Useful Knowledge; **pp. 199 and 200:** Bougainville, Bougainville, 1837, in Riviére, 1999.

THE LAST GREAT CONTINENT, PP. 210–61
pp 210–11: *Leon Jean Baptiste Sabatier, Decouverte de la Terre Adelie le 19 janvier 1840, parages Antarctiques*, nla.pic-an20826782, National Library of Australia; **pp. 213, 214 and 247:** Dumont d'Urville lithograph (1833) by Antoine Maurin, in Dumont d'Urville, 1830–35, Atlas Historique; **pp. 234 and 236:** Darwin lithograph (1849) by T.H. Maguire, Wellcome Institute for the History of Medicine, in Olby, 1967.

COLOUR PLATES
Between pp. 54 & 55
Paperbark by Redoubte in Ventenat, 1803, plate 47; Quoll by Prévost in Freycinet, 1824, *Atlas Historique naturelle: Zoologie*, plate 4; Skink by Prévost in Freycinet, 1824, *Atlas Historique naturelle: Zoologie*, plate 41; Mother and Child by Petit in Péron, 1807–17, *Atlas*, plate xii.
Between pp. 70 & 71
Austral Indigo by Redoubte in Ventenat, 1803, plate 45; Potoroo by Prévost from Freycinet, 1824, *Atlas Historique naturelle: Zoologie*, plate 4; Whiting by Bévalet from Dumont d'Urville, 1830–35, *Atlas Zoologie, Poissons, vol. 19*, plate 1; Pirogue by de Sainson in Dumont d'Urville, 1830–35, *Atlas Historique, vol. 18*, plate 241.

Between pp. 102 & 103

Butterflies by Vauthier in Lesson, 1831, *Insectes*, plate 14; Paper Daisy by Redoute from Ventenat, 1803, plate 2; Jellyfish by Lesueur in Péron, 1807–17, *Atlas*, plate 29; Helmet Shell by Pretre in Dumont d'Urville, 1830–35, *Atlas Zoologie, vol. 19, Mollusques*, plate 43.

Between pp. 118 & 119

Gang-gang by Bessa in Bougainville, 1837, *Atlas*, plate 39; Wombat by Lesueur in Péron, 1807–17, *Atlas*, plate 28; Emu by Lesueur in Péron, 1807–17, *Atlas*, plate 36; Happy Wanderer by Redoute from Ventenat, 1803, plate 106.

Between pp. 182 & 183

Hare-wallaby by Lesueur in Péron, 1807–17, *Atlas*, plate 27; Fish by Bévalet from Dumont d'Urville, 1830–35, *Atlas Zoologie, vol. 19, Poissons*, plate 4; Platypus by Lesueur in Péron, 1807–17, *Atlas*, plate 24; Squid by Vauthier in Lesson, 1831, *Mollusques*, plate 2.

Between pp. 198 & 199

Kookaburra by Prévost in Dumont d'Urville, 1841–54, *Atlas Histoire Naturelle: Zoologie, Oiseaux*, plate 23; Red-capped Parrot by Prévost from Dumont d'Urville, 1830–35, *Atlas Zoologie, vol. 19, Oiseaux*, plate 22; Wattle by Redoute from Ventenat, 1803, plate 162; Running Postman by Redoute from Ventenat, 1803, plate 104.

Between pp. 230 & 231

Vanikoran by de Sainson in Dumont d'Urville, 1830–35, *Atlas Historique, vol. 18*, plate 176; Butterflies by Vauthier in Lesson, 1831, *Insectes*, plate 14; Fish by Coutant in Freycinet, 1824, *Atlas Historique naturelle: Zoologie*, plate 4; Red-winged Parrot by Bévalet in Freycinet, 1824, *Atlas Historique naturelle: Zoologie*, plate 4.

Between pp. 246 & 247

Possum by Werner in Dumont d'Urville, 1841–54, *Atlas Histoire Naturelle: Zoologie, Mammiferes*, plate 14; Hermit Crabs by Bévalet in Freycinet, 1824, *Atlas Historique naturelle: Zoologie*, plate 4; Native Rosella by Redoute from Ventenat, 1803, plate 103; Penguins by Oudart in Dumont d'Urville, 1841–54, *Atlas Histoire Naturelle: Zoologie, Oiseaux*, plate 23.